TensorFlow for Deep Learning
From Linear Regression to Reinforcement Learning

Bharath Ramsundar and Reza Bosagh Zadeh

Beijing · Boston · Farnham · Sebastopol · Tokyo

TensorFlow for Deep Learning

by Bharath Ramsundar and Reza Bosagh Zadeh

Published by O'Reilly Media, Inc., 1005 Gravenstein Highway North, Sebastopol, CA 95472.

O'Reilly books may be purchased for educational, business, or sales promotional use. Online editions are also available for most titles (*http://oreilly.com/safari*). For more information, contact our corporate/institutional sales department: 800-998-9938 or *corporate@oreilly.com*.

Editors: Rachel Roumeliotis and Alicia Young
Production Editor: Kristen Brown
Copyeditor: Kim Cofer
Proofreader: James Fraleigh

Indexer: Judy McConville
Interior Designer: David Futato
Cover Designer: Karen Montgomery
Illustrator: Rebecca Demarest

March 2018:   First Edition

Revision History for the First Edition
2018-03-01:   First Release
2018-05-25:   Second Release

See *http://oreilly.com/catalog/errata.csp?isbn=9781491980453* for release details.

978-1-491-98045-3

[LSI]

Table of Contents

Preface

This book will introduce you to the fundamentals of machine learning through TensorFlow. TensorFlow is Google's new software library for deep learning that makes it straightforward for engineers to design and deploy sophisticated deep learning architectures. You will learn how to use TensorFlow to build systems capable of detecting objects in images, understanding human text, and predicting the properties of potential medicines. Furthermore, you will gain an intuitive understanding of TensorFlow's potential as a system for performing tensor calculus and will learn how to use Tensor-Flow for tasks outside the traditional purview of machine learning.

Importantly, *TensorFlow for Deep Learning* is one of the first deep learning books written for practitioners. It teaches fundamental concepts through practical examples and builds understanding of machine learning foundations from the ground up. The target audience for this book is practicing developers, who are comfortable with designing software systems, but not necessarily with creating learning systems. At times we use some basic linear algebra and calculus, but we will review all necessary fundamentals. We also anticipate that our book will prove useful for scientists and other professionals who are comfortable with scripting, but not necessarily with designing learning algorithms.

Conventions Used in This Book

The following typographical conventions are used in this book:

Italic
> Indicates new terms, URLs, email addresses, filenames, and file extensions.

`Constant width`
> Used for program listings, as well as within paragraphs to refer to program elements such as variable or function names, databases, data types, environment variables, statements, and keywords.

Constant width bold
> Shows commands or other text that should be typed literally by the user.

Constant width italic
> Shows text that should be replaced with user-supplied values or by values determined by context.

 This element signifies a tip or suggestion.

 This element signifies a general note.

 This element indicates a warning or caution.

Using Code Examples

Supplemental material (code examples, exercises, etc.) is available for download at *https://github.com/matroid/dlwithtf*.

This book is here to help you get your job done. In general, if example code is offered with this book, you may use it in your programs and documentation. You do not need to contact us for permission unless you're reproducing a significant portion of the code. For example, writing a program that uses several chunks of code from this book does not require permission. Selling or distributing a CD-ROM of examples from O'Reilly books does require permission. Answering a question by citing this book and quoting example code does not require permission. Incorporating a significant amount of example code from this book into your product's documentation does require permission.

We appreciate, but do not require, attribution. An attribution usually includes the title, author, publisher, and ISBN. For example: *"TensorFlow for Deep Learning* by Bharath Ramsundar and Reza Bosagh Zadeh (O'Reilly). Copyright 2018 Reza Zadeh, Bharath Ramsundar, 978-1-491-98045-3."

If you feel your use of code examples falls outside fair use or the permission given above, feel free to contact us at *permissions@oreilly.com*.

O'Reilly Safari

 *Safari* (formerly Safari Books Online) is a membership-based training and reference platform for enterprise, government, educators, and individuals.

Members have access to thousands of books, training videos, Learning Paths, interactive tutorials, and curated playlists from over 250 publishers, including O'Reilly Media, Harvard Business Review, Prentice Hall Professional, Addison-Wesley Professional, Microsoft Press, Sams, Que, Peachpit Press, Adobe, Focal Press, Cisco Press, John Wiley & Sons, Syngress, Morgan Kaufmann, IBM Redbooks, Packt, Adobe Press, FT Press, Apress, Manning, New Riders, McGraw-Hill, Jones & Bartlett, and Course Technology, among others.

For more information, please visit *http://oreilly.com/safari*.

How to Contact Us

Please address comments and questions concerning this book to the publisher:

O'Reilly Media, Inc.
1005 Gravenstein Highway North
Sebastopol, CA 95472
800-998-9938 (in the United States or Canada)
707-829-0515 (international or local)
707-829-0104 (fax)

We have a web page for this book, where we list errata, examples, and any additional information. You can access this page at *http://bit.ly/tensorflowForDeepLearning*.

To comment or ask technical questions about this book, send email to *bookquestions@oreilly.com*.

For more information about our books, courses, conferences, and news, see our website at *http://www.oreilly.com*.

Find us on Facebook: *http://facebook.com/oreilly*

Follow us on Twitter: *http://twitter.com/oreillymedia*

Watch us on YouTube: *http://www.youtube.com/oreillymedia*

Acknowledgments

Bharath is thankful to his PhD advisor for letting him work on this book during his nights and weekends, and especially thankful to his family for their unstinting support during the entire process.

Reza is thankful to the open source communities on which much of software and computer science is based. Open source software is one of the largest concentrations of human knowledge ever created, and this book would have been impossible without the entire community behind it.

## CHAPTER 1

Introduction to Deep Learning

Deep learning has revolutionized the technology industry. Modern machine translation, search engines, and computer assistants are all powered by deep learning. This trend will only continue as deep learning expands its reach into robotics, pharmaceuticals, energy, and all other fields of contemporary technology. It is rapidly becoming essential for the modern software professional to develop a working knowledge of the principles of deep learning.

In this chapter, we will introduce you to the history of deep learning, and to the broader impact deep learning has had on the research and commercial communities. We will next cover some of the most famous applications of deep learning. This will include both prominent machine learning architectures and fundamental deep learning primitives. We will end by giving a brief perspective of where deep learning is heading over the next few years before we dive into TensorFlow in the next few chapters.

Machine Learning Eats Computer Science

Until recently, software engineers went to school to learn a number of basic algorithms (graph search, sorting, database queries, and so on). After school, these engineers would go out into the real world to apply these algorithms to systems. Most of today's digital economy is built on intricate chains of basic algorithms laboriously glued together by generations of engineers. Most of these systems are not capable of adapting. All configurations and reconfigurations have to be performed by highly trained engineers, rendering systems brittle.

Machine learning promises to change the field of software development by enabling systems to adapt dynamically. Deployed machine learning systems are capable of learning desired behaviors from databases of examples. Furthermore, such systems can be regularly retrained as new data comes in. Very sophisticated software systems, powered by machine learning, are capable of dramatically changing their behavior without major changes to their code (just to their training data). This trend is only likely to accelerate as machine learning tools and deployment become easier and easier.

As the behavior of software-engineered systems changes, the roles of software engineers will change as well. In some ways, this transformation will be analogous to the transformation following the development of programming languages. The first computers were painstakingly programmed. Networks of wires were connected and interconnected. Then punchcards were set up to enable the creation of new programs without hardware changes to computers. Following the punchcard era, the first assembly languages were created. Then higher-level languages like Fortran or Lisp. Succeeding layers of development have created very high-level languages like Python, with intricate ecosystems of precoded algorithms. Much modern computer science even relies on autogenerated code. Modern app developers use tools like Android Studio to autogenerate much of the code they'd like to make. Each successive wave of simplification has broadened the scope of computer science by lowering barriers to entry.

Machine learning promises to lower barriers even further; programmers will soon be able to change the behavior of systems by altering training data, possibly without writing a single line of code. On the user side, systems built on spoken language and natural language understanding such as Alexa and Siri will allow nonprogrammers to perform complex computations. Furthermore, ML powered systems are likely to become more *robust* against errors. The capacity to retrain models will mean that codebases can shrink and that maintainability will increase. In short, machine learning is likely to completely upend the role of software engineers. Today's programmers will need to understand how machine learning systems learn, and will need to understand the classes of errors that arise in common machine learning systems. Furthermore, they will need to understand the design patterns that underlie machine learning systems (very different in style and form from classical software design patterns). And, they will need to know enough tensor calculus to understand why a sophisticated deep architecture may be misbehaving during learning. It's not an understatement to say that understanding machine learning (theory and practice) will become a fundamental skill that every computer scientist and software engineer will need to understand for the coming decade.

In the remainder of this chapter, we will provide a whirlwind tour of the basics of modern deep learning. The remainder of this book will go into much greater depth on all the topics we touch on here.

Deep Learning Primitives

Most deep architectures are built by combining and recombining a limited set of architectural primitives. Such primitives, typically called neural network layers, are the foundational building blocks of deep networks. In the rest of this book, we will provide in-depth introductions to such layers. However, in this section, we will provide a brief overview of the common modules that are found in many deep networks. This section is not meant to provide a thorough introduction to these modules. Rather, we aim to provide a rapid overview of the building blocks of sophisticated deep architectures to whet your appetite. The art of deep learning consists of combining and recombining such modules and we want to show you the alphabet of the language to start you on the path to deep learning expertise.

Fully Connected Layer

A fully connected network transforms a list of inputs into a list of outputs. The transformation is called fully connected since any input value can affect any output value. These layers will have many learnable parameters, even for relatively small inputs, but they have the large advantage of assuming no structure in the inputs. This concept is illustrated in Figure 1-1.

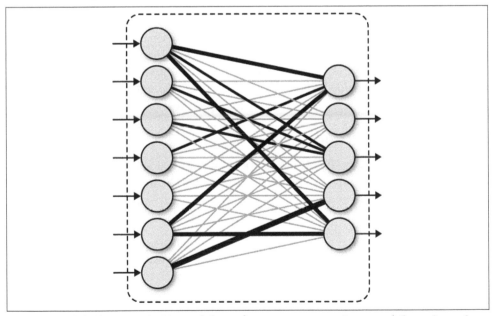

Figure 1-1. A fully connected layer. Inbound arrows represent inputs, while outbound arrows represent outputs. The thickness of interconnecting lines represents the magnitude of learned weights. The fully connected layer transforms inputs into outputs via the learned rule.

Convolutional Layer

A convolutional network assumes special spatial structure in its input. In particular, it assumes that inputs that are close to each other spatially are semantically related. This assumption makes most sense for images, since pixels close to one another are likely semantically linked. As a result, convolutional layers have found wide use in deep architectures for image processing. This concept is illustrated in Figure 1-2.

Just like fully connected layers transform lists to lists, convolutional layers transform images into images. As a result, convolutional layers can be used to perform complex image transformations, such as applying artistic filters to images in photo apps.

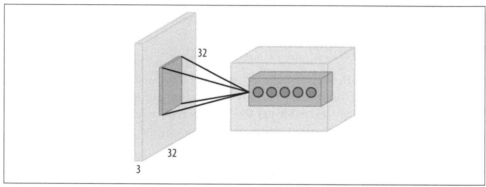

Figure 1-2. A convolutional layer. The red shape on the left represents the input data, while the blue shape on the right represents the output. In this particular case, the input is of shape (32, 32, 3). That is, the input is a 32-pixel-by-32-pixel image with three RGB color channels. The highlighted region in the red input is a "local receptive field," a group of inputs that are processed together to create the highlighted region in the blue output.

Recurrent Neural Network Layers

Recurrent neural network (RNN) layers are primitives that allow neural networks to learn from sequences of inputs. This layer assumes that the input evolves from step to step following a defined update rule that can be learned from data. This update rule presents a prediction of the next state in the sequence given all the states that have come previously. An RNN is illustrated in Figure 1-3.

An RNN layer can learn this update rule from data. As a result, RNNs are very useful for tasks such as language modeling, where engineers seek to build systems that can predict the next word users will type from history.

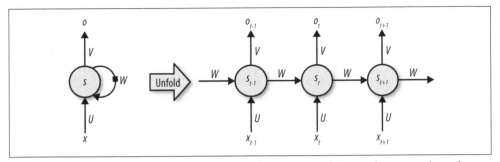

Figure 1-3. A recurrent neural network (RNN). Inputs are fed into the network at the bottom, and outputs extracted at the top. W represents the learned transformation (shared at all timesteps). The network is represented conceptually on the left and is unrolled on the right to demonstrate how inputs from different timesteps are processed.

Long Short-Term Memory Cells

The RNN layers presented in the previous section are capable of learning arbitrary sequence-update rules in theory. In practice, however, such layers are incapable of learning influences from the distant past. Such distant influences are crucial for performing solid language modeling since the meaning of a complex sentence can depend on the relationship between far-away words. The long short-term memory (LSTM) cell is a modification to the RNN layer that allows for signals from deeper in the past to make their way to the present. An LSTM cell is illustrated in Figure 1-4.

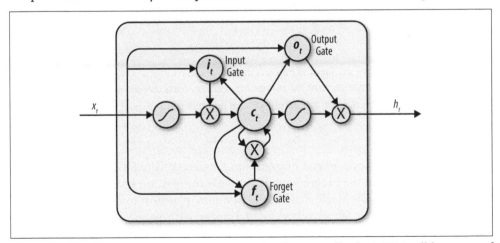

Figure 1-4. A long short-term memory (LSTM) cell. Internally, the LSTM cell has a set of specially designed operations that attain much of the learning power of the vanilla RNN while preserving influences from the past. Note that the illustration depicts one LSTM variant of many.

Deep Learning Architectures

There have been hundreds of different deep learning models that combine the deep learning primitives presented in the previous section. Some of these architectures have been historically important. Others were the first presentations of novel designs that influenced perceptions of what deep learning could do.

In this section, we present a selection of different deep learning architectures that have proven influential for the research community. We want to emphasize that this is an episodic history that makes no attempt to be exhaustive. There are certainly important models in the literature that have not been presented here.

LeNet

The LeNet architecture is arguably the first prominent "deep" convolutional architecture. Introduced in 1988, it was used to perform optical character recoginition (OCR) for documents. Although it performed its task admirably, the computational cost of the LeNet was extreme for the computer hardware available at the time, so the design languished in (relative) obscurity for a few decades after its creation. This architecture is illustrated in Figure 1-5.

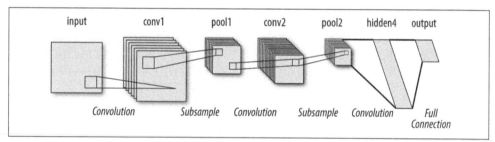

Figure 1-5. The LeNet architecture for image processing. Introduced in 1988, it was arguably the first deep convolutional model for image processing.

AlexNet

The ImageNet Large Scale Visual Recognition Challenge (ILSVRC) was first organized in 2010 as a test of the progress made in visual recognition systems. The organizers made use of Amazon Mechanical Turk, an online platform to connect workers to requesters, to catalog a large collection of images with associated lists of objects present in the image. The use of Mechanical Turk permitted the curation of a collection of data significantly larger than those gathered previously.

The first two years the challenge ran, more traditional machine-learned systems that relied on systems like HOG and SIFT features (hand-tuned visual feature extraction methods) triumphed. In 2012, the AlexNet architecture, based on a modification of LeNet run on powerful graphics processing units (GPUs), entered and dominated the challenge with error rates half that of the nearest competitors. This victory dramatically galvanized the (already nascent) trend toward deep learning architectures in computer vision. The AlexNet architecture is illustrated in Figure 1-6.

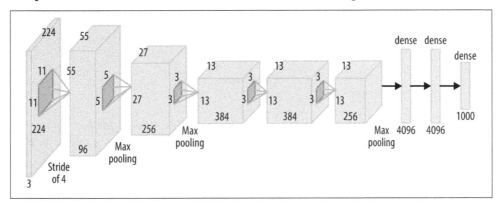

Figure 1-6. The AlexNet architecture for image processing. This architecture was the winning entry in the ILSVRC 2012 challenge and galvanized a resurgence of interest in convolutional architectures.

ResNet

Since 2012, convolutional architectures consistently won the ILSVRC challenge (along with many other computer vision challenges). Each year the contest was held, the winning architecture increased in depth and complexity. The ResNet architecture, winner of the ILSVRC 2015 challenge, was particularly notable; ResNet architectures extended up to 130 layers deep, in contrast to the 8-layer AlexNet architecture.

Very deep networks historically were challenging to learn; when networks grow this deep, they run into the vanishing gradients problem. Signals are attenuated as they progress through the network, leading to diminished learning. This attenuation can be explained mathematically, but the effect is that each additional layer multiplicatively reduces the strength of the signal, leading to caps on the effective depth of networks.

The ResNet introduced an innovation that controlled this attenuation: the bypass connection. These connections allow part of the signal from deeper layers to pass through undiminished, enabling significantly deeper networks to be trained effectively. The ResNet bypass connection is illustrated in Figure 1-7.

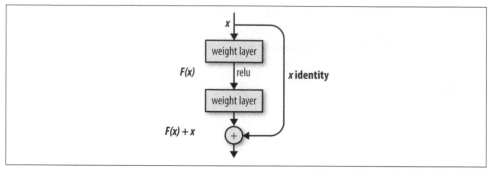

Figure 1-7. The ResNet cell. The identity connection on the righthand side permits an unmodified version of the input to pass through the cell. This modification allows for the effective training of very deep convolutional architectures.

Neural Captioning Model

As practitioners became more comfortable with the use of deep learning primitives, they experimented with mixing and matching primitive modules to create higher-order systems that could perform more complex tasks than basic object detection. Neural captioning systems automatically generate captions for the contents of images. They do so by combining a convolutional network, which extracts information from images, with an LSTM layer that generates a descriptive sentence for the image. The entire system is trained *end-to-end*. That is, the convolutional network and the LSTM network are trained together to achieve the desired goal of generating descriptive sentences for provided images.

This end-to-end training is one of the key innovations powering modern deep learning systems since it lessens the need for complicated preprocessing of inputs. Image captioning models that don't use deep learning would have to use complicated image featurization methods such as SIFT, which can't be trained alongside the caption generator.

A neural captioning model is illustrated in Figure 1-8.

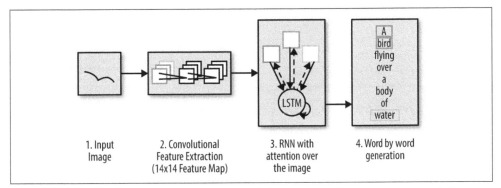

Figure 1-8. A neural captioning architecture. Relevant input features are extracted from the input image using a convolutional network. Then a recurrent network is used to generate a descriptive sentence.

Google Neural Machine Translation

Google's neural machine translation (Google-NMT) system uses the paradigm of end-to-end training to build a production translation system, which takes sentences from the source language directly to the target language. The Google-NMT system depends on the fundamental building block of the LSTM, which it stacks over a dozen times and trains on an extremely large dataset of translated sentences. The final architecture provided for a breakthrough advance in machine-translation by cutting the gap between human and machine translations by up to 60%. The Google-NMT architecture is illustrated in Figure 1-9.

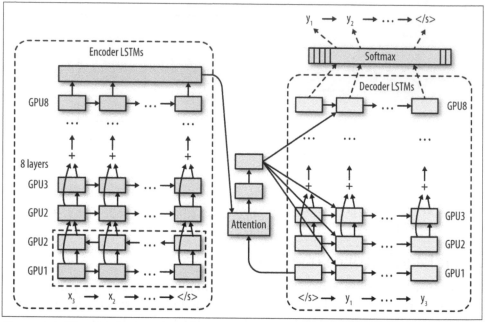

Figure 1-9. The Google neural machine translation system uses a deep recurrent architecture to process the input sentence and a second deep recurrent architecture to generate the translated output sentence.

One-Shot Models

One-shot learning is perhaps the most interesting new idea in machine/deep learning. Most deep learning techniques typically require very large amounts of data to learn meaningful behavior. The AlexNet architecture, for example, made use of the large ILSVRC dataset to learn a visual object detector. However, much work in cognitive science has indicated that humans can learn complex concepts from just a few examples. Take the example of baby learning about giraffes for the first time. A baby shown a single giraffe at the zoo might be capable of learning to recognize all giraffes she sees from then on.

Recent progress in deep learning has started to invent architectures capable of similar learning feats. Given only a few examples of a concept (but given ample sources of side information), such systems can learn to make meaningful predictions with very few datapoints. One recent paper (by an author of this book) used this idea to demonstrate that one-shot architectures can learn even in contexts babies can't, such as in medical drug discovery. A one-shot architecture for drug discovery is illustrated in Figure 1-10.

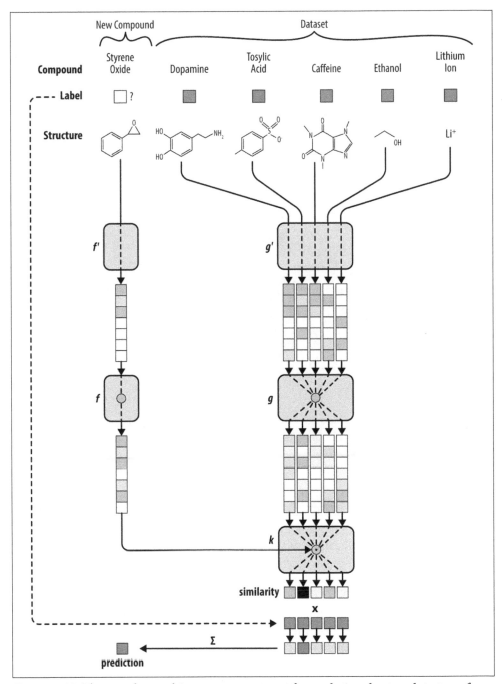

Figure 1-10. The one-shot architecture uses a type of convolutional network to transform each molecule into a vector. The vector for styrene oxide is compared with vectors from the experimental dataset. The label for the most similar datapoint (tosylic acid) is imputed for the query.

AlphaGo

Go is an ancient board game, widely influential in Asia. Computer Go has been a major challenge for computer science since the late 1960s. Techniques that enabled the computer chess system Deep Blue to beat chess grandmaster Garry Kasparov in 1997 don't scale to Go. Part of the issue is that Go has a much bigger board than chess; Go boards are of size 19 × 19 as opposed to 8 × 8 for chess. Since far more moves are possible per step, the game tree of possible Go moves expands much more quickly, rendering brute force search with contemporary computer hardware insufficient for adequate Go gameplay. Figure 1-11 illustrates a Go board.

Figure 1-11. An illustration of a Go board. Players alternately place white and black pieces on a 19 × 19 grid.

Master level computer Go was finally achieved by AlphaGo from Google DeepMind. AlphaGo proved capable of defeating one of the world's strongest Go champions, Lee Sedol, in a five-game match. Some of the key ideas from AlphaGo include the use of a deep value network and deep policy network. The value network provides an estimate of the value of a board position. Unlike chess, it's very difficult to guess whether white or black is winning in Go from the board state. The value network solves this problem by learning to make this prediction from game outcomes. The policy network, on the other hand, helps estimate the best move to take given a current board state. The combination of these two techniques with Monte Carlo Tree search (a classical search method) helped overcome the large branching factor in Go games. The basic AlphaGo architecture is illustrated in Figure 1-12.

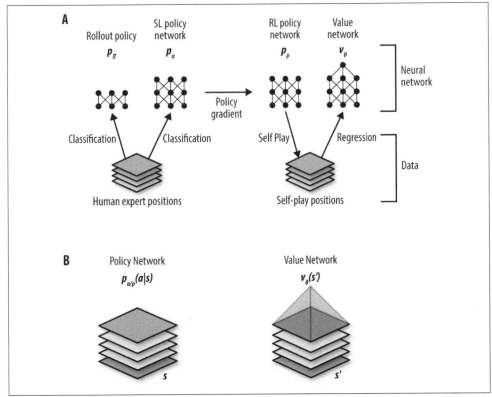

Figure 1-12. A) Depiction of AlphaGo's architecture. Initially a policy network to select moves is trained on a dataset of expert games. This policy is then refined by self-play. "RL" indicates reinforcement learning and "SL" indicates supervised learning. B) Both the policy and value networks operate on representations of the game board.

Generative Adversarial Networks

Generative adversarial networks (GANs) are a new type of deep network that uses two competing neural networks, the generator and the adversary (also called the discriminator), which duel against each other. The generator tries to draw samples from a training distribution (for example, tries to generate realistic images of birds). The discriminator works on differentiating samples drawn from the generator from true data samples. (Is a particular bird a real image or generator-created?) This "adversarial" training for GANs seems capable of generating image samples of considerably higher fidelity than other techniques and may be useful for training effective discriminators with limited data. A GAN architecture is illustrated in Figure 1-13.

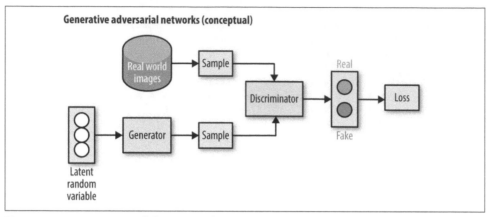

Figure 1-13. A conceptual depiction of a generative adversarial network (GAN).

GANs have proven capable of generating very realistic images, and will likely power the next generation of computer graphics tools. Samples from such systems are now approaching photorealism. However, many theoretical and practical caveats still remain to be worked out with these systems and much research is still needed.

Neural Turing Machines

Most of the deep learning systems presented so far have learned complex functions with limited domains of applicability; for example, object detection, image captioning, machine translation, or Go game-play. But, could we perhaps have deep architectures that learn general algorithmic concepts such as sorting, addition, or multiplication?

The Neural Turing machine (NTM) is a first attempt at making a deep learning architecture capable of learning arbitrary algorithms. This architecture adds an external memory bank to an LSTM-like system, to allow the deep architecture to make use of scratch space to compute more sophisticated functions. At the moment, NTM-like architectures are still quite limited, and only capable of learning simple algorithms. Nevertheless, NTM methods remain an active area of research and future advances may transform these early demonstrations into practical learning tools. The NTM architecture is conceptually illustrated in Figure 1-14.

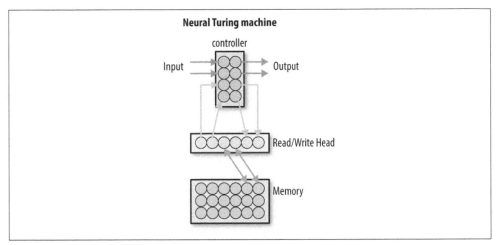

Figure 1-14. A conceptual depiction of a Neural Turing machine. It adds an external memory bank to which the deep architecture reads and writes.

Deep Learning Frameworks

Researchers have been implementing software packages to facilitate the construction of neural network (deep learning) architectures for decades. Until the last few years, these systems were mostly special purpose and only used within an academic group. This lack of standardized, industrial-strength software made it difficult for non-experts to use neural networks extensively.

This situation has changed dramatically over the last few years. Google implemented the DistBelief system in 2012 and made use of it to construct and deploy many simpler deep learning architectures. The advent of DistBelief, and similar packages such as Caffe, Theano, Torch, Keras, MxNet, and so on have widely spurred industry adoption.

TensorFlow draws upon this rich intellectual history, and builds upon some of these packages (Theano in particular) for design principles. TensorFlow (and Theano) in particular use the concept of tensors as the fundamental underlying primitive powering deep learning systems. This focus on tensors distinguishes these packages from systems such as DistBelief or Caffe, which don't allow the same flexibility for building sophisticated models.

While the rest of this book will focus on TensorFlow, understanding the underlying principles should enable you to take the lessons learned and apply them with little difficulty to alternative deep learning frameworks.

Limitations of TensorFlow

One of the major current weaknesses of TensorFlow is that constructing a new deep learning architecture is relatively slow (on the order of multiple seconds to initialize an architecture). As a result, it's not convenient in TensorFlow to construct some sophisticated deep architectures that change their structure dynamically. One such architecture is the TreeLSTM, which uses syntactic parse trees of English sentences to perform tasks that require understanding of natural language. Since each sentence has a different parse tree, each sentence requires a slightly different architecture. Figure 1-15 illustrates the TreeLSTM architecture.

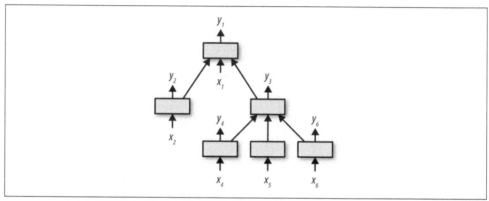

Figure 1-15. A conceptual depiction of a TreeLSTM architecture. The shape of the tree is different for each input datapoint, so a different computational graph must be constructed for each example.

While such models can be implemented in TensorFlow, doing so requires significant ingenuity due to the limitations of the current TensorFlow API. New frameworks such as Chainer, DyNet, and PyTorch promise to remove these barriers by making the construction of new architectures lightweight enough so that models like the TreeLSTM can be constructed easily. Luckily, TensorFlow developers are already working on extensions to the base TensorFlow API (such as TensorFlow Eager) that will enable easier construction of dynamic architectures.

One takeaway is that progress in deep learning frameworks is rapid, and today's novel system can be tomorrow's old news. However, the fundamental principles of the underlying tensor calculus date back centuries, and will stand readers in good stead regardless of future changes in programming models. This book will emphasize using TensorFlow as a vehicle for developing an intuitive knowledge of the underlying tensor calculus.

Review

In this chapter, we've explained why deep learning is a subject of critical importance for the modern software engineer and taken a whirlwind tour of a number of deep architectures. In the next chapter, we will start exploring TensorFlow, Google's framework for constructing and training deep architectures. In the chapters after that, we will dive deep into a number of practical examples of deep architectures.

Machine learning (and deep learning in particular), like much of computer science, is a very empirical discipline. It's only really possible to understand deep learning through significant practical experience. For that reason, we've included a number of in-depth case studies throughout the remainder of this book. We encourage you to delve into these examples and to get your hands dirty experimenting with your own ideas using TensorFlow. It's never enough to understand algorithms only theoretically!

## CHAPTER 2

Introduction to TensorFlow Primitives

This chapter will introduce you to fundamental aspects of TensorFlow. In particular, you will learn how to perform basic computation using TensorFlow. A large part of this chapter will be spent introducing the concept of tensors, and discussing how tensors are represented and manipulated within TensorFlow. This discussion will necessitate a brief overview of some of the mathematical concepts that underlie tensorial mathematics. In particular, we'll briefly review basic linear algebra and demonstrate how to perform basic linear algebraic operations with TensorFlow.

We'll follow this discussion of basic mathematics with a discussion of the differences between declarative and imperative programming styles. Unlike many programming languages, TensorFlow is largely declarative. Calling a TensorFlow operation adds a description of a computation to TensorFlow's "computation graph." In particular, TensorFlow code "describes" computations and doesn't actually perform them. In order to run TensorFlow code, users need to create `tf.Session` objects. We introduce the concept of sessions and describe how users perform computations with them in TensorFlow.

We end the chapter by discussing the notion of variables. Variables in TensorFlow hold tensors and allow for stateful computation that modifies variables to occur. We demonstrate how to create variables and update their values via TensorFlow.

Introducing Tensors

Tensors are fundamental mathematical constructs in fields such as physics and engineering. Historically, however, tensors have made fewer inroads in computer science, which has traditionally been more associated with discrete mathematics and logic. This state of affairs has started to change significantly with the advent of machine learning and its foundation on continuous, vectorial mathematics. Modern machine learning is founded upon the manipulation and calculus of tensors.

Scalars, Vectors, and Matrices

To start, we will give some simple examples of tensors that you might be familiar with. The simplest example of a tensor is a scalar, a single constant value drawn from the real numbers (recall that the real numbers are decimal numbers of arbitrary precision, with both positive and negative numbers permitted). Mathematically, we denote the real numbers by $\mathbb{R}$. More formally, we call a scalar a rank-0 tensor.

Aside on Fields

Mathematically sophisticated readers will protest that it's entirely meaningful to define tensors based on the complex numbers, or with binary numbers. More generally, it's sufficient that the numbers come from a *field*: a mathematical collection of numbers where 0, 1, addition, multiplication, subtraction, and division are defined. Common fields include the real numbers $\mathbb{R}$, the rational numbers $\mathbb{Q}$, the complex numbers $\mathbb{C}$, and finite fields such as $\mathbb{Z}_2$. For simplicity, in much of the discussion, we will assume real valued tensors, but substituting in values from other fields is entirely reasonable.

If scalars are rank-0 tensors, what constitutes a rank-1 tensor? Formally, speaking, a rank-1 tensor is a vector; a list of real numbers. Traditionally, vectors are written as either column vectors

$$\begin{pmatrix} a \\ b \end{pmatrix}$$

or as row vectors

$$(a \quad b)$$

Notationally, the collection of all column vectors of length 2 is denoted $\mathbb{R}^{2 \times 1}$ while the set of all row vectors of length 2 is $\mathbb{R}^{1 \times 2}$. More computationally, we might say that the shape of a column vector is (2, 1), while the shape of a row vector is (1, 2). If we don't wish to specify whether a vector is a row vector or column vector, we can say it comes from the set $\mathbb{R}^2$ and has shape (2). This notion of tensor shape is quite important for understanding TensorFlow computations, and we will return to it later on in this chapter.

One of the simplest uses of vectors is to represent coordinates in the real world. Suppose that we decide on an origin point (say the position where you're currently standing). Then any position in the world can be represented by three displacement values from your current position (left-right displacement, front-back displacement, up-down displacement). Thus, the set of vectors (vector space) $\mathbb{R}^3$ can represent any position in the world.

For a different example, let's suppose that a cat is described by its height, weight, and color. Then a video game cat can be represented as a vector

$$\begin{pmatrix} \text{height} \\ \text{weight} \\ \text{color} \end{pmatrix}$$

in the space $\mathbb{R}^3$. This type of representation is often called a *featurization*. That is, a featurization is a representation of a real-world entity as a vector (or more generally as a tensor). Nearly all machine learning algorithms operate on vectors or tensors. Thus the process of featurization is a critical part of any machine learning pipeline. Often, the featurization system can be the most sophisticated part of a machine learning system. Suppose we have a benzene molecule as illustrated in Figure 2-1.

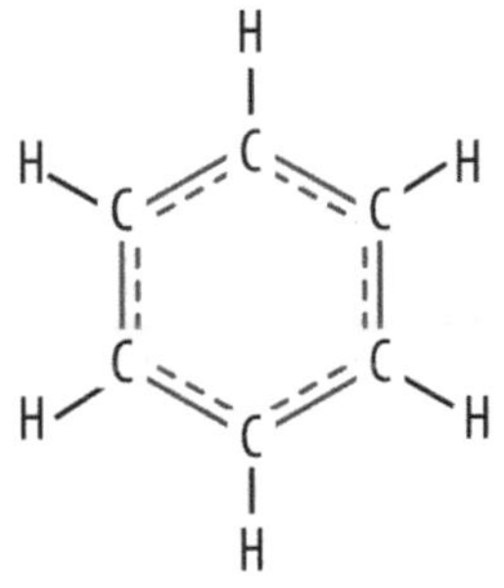

Figure 2-1. A representation of a benzene molecule.

How can we transform this molecule into a vector suitable for a query to a machine learning system? There are a number of potential solutions to this problem, most of which exploit the idea of marking the presence of subfragments of the molecule. The presence or absence of specific subfragments is marked by setting indices in a binary vector (in $\{0, 1\}^n$) to 1/0, respectively. This process is illustrated in Figure 2-2.

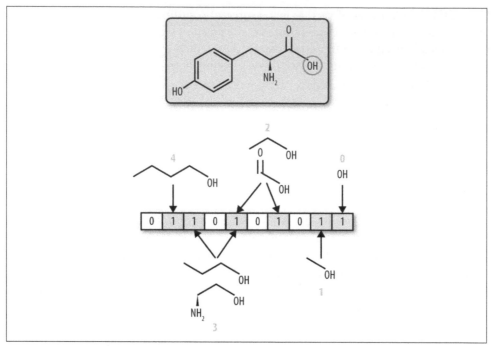

Figure 2-2. Subfragments of the molecule to be featurized are selected (those containing OH). These fragments are hashed into indices in a fixed-length vector. These positions are set to 1 and all other positions are set to 0.

Note that this process sounds (and is) fairly complex. In fact, one of the most challenging aspects of building a machine learning system is deciding how to transform the data in question into a tensorial format. For some types of data, this transformation is obvious. For others (such as molecules), the transformation required can be quite subtle. For the practitioner of machine learning, it isn't usually necessary to invent a new featurization method since the scholarly literature is extensive, but it will often be necessary to read research papers to understand best practices for transforming a new data stream.

Now that we have established that rank-0 tensors are scalars ($\mathbb{R}$) and that rank-1 tensors are vectors ($\mathbb{R}^n$), what is a rank-2 tensor? Traditionally, a rank-2 tensor is referred to as a matrix:

$$\begin{pmatrix} a & b \\ c & d \end{pmatrix}$$

This matrix has two rows and two columns. The set of all such matrices is referred to as $\mathbb{R}^{2 \times 2}$. Returning to our notion of tensor shape earlier, the shape of this matrix is

(2, 2). Matrices are traditionally used to represent transformations of vectors. For example, the action of rotating a vector in the plane by angle α can be performed by the matrix

$$R_\alpha = \begin{pmatrix} \cos(\alpha) & -\sin(\alpha) \\ \sin(\alpha) & \cos(\alpha) \end{pmatrix}$$

To see this, note that the x unit vector (1, 0) is transformed by matrix multiplication into the vector (cos (α), sin (α)). (We will cover the detailed definition of matrix multiplication later in the chapter, but will simply display the result for the moment).

$$\begin{pmatrix} \cos(\alpha) & -\sin(\alpha) \\ \sin(\alpha) & \cos(\alpha) \end{pmatrix} \cdot \begin{pmatrix} 1 \\ 0 \end{pmatrix} = \begin{pmatrix} \cos(\alpha) \\ \sin(\alpha) \end{pmatrix}$$

This transformation can be visualized graphically as well. Figure 2-3 demonstrates how the final vector corresponds to a rotation of the original unit vector.

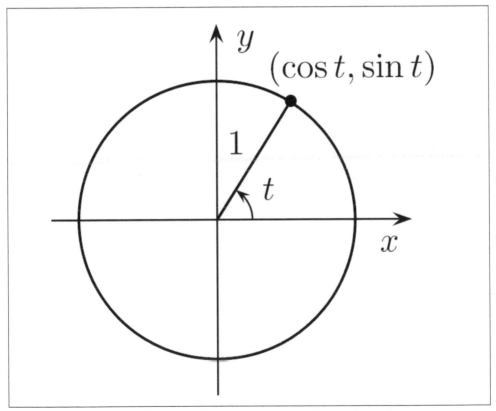

Figure 2-3. Positions on the unit circle are parameterized by cosine and sine.

Matrix Mathematics

There are a number of standard mathematical operations on matrices that machine learning programs use repeatedly. We will briefly review some of the most fundamental of these operations.

The matrix transpose is a convenient operation that flips a matrix around its diagonal. Mathematically, suppose A is a matrix; then the transpose matrix A^T is defined by equation $A_{ij}^T = A_{ji}$. For example, the transpose of the rotation matrix R_α is

$$R_\alpha^T = \begin{pmatrix} \cos{(\alpha)} & \sin{(\alpha)} \\ -\sin{(\alpha)} & \cos{(\alpha)} \end{pmatrix}$$

Addition of matrices is only defined for matrices of the same shape and is simply performed elementwise. For example:

$$\begin{pmatrix} 1 & 2 \\ 3 & 4 \end{pmatrix} + \begin{pmatrix} 1 & 1 \\ 1 & 1 \end{pmatrix} = \begin{pmatrix} 2 & 3 \\ 4 & 5 \end{pmatrix}$$

Similarly, matrices can be multiplied by scalars. In this case, each element of the matrix is simply multiplied elementwise by the scalar in question:

$$2 \cdot \begin{pmatrix} 1 & 2 \\ 3 & 4 \end{pmatrix} = \begin{pmatrix} 2 & 4 \\ 6 & 8 \end{pmatrix}$$

Furthermore, it is sometimes possible to multiply two matrices directly. This notion of matrix multiplication is probably the most important mathematical concept associated with matrices. Note specifically that matrix multiplication is not the same notion as elementwise multiplication of matrices! Rather, suppose we have a matrix A of shape (m, n) with m rows and n columns. Then, A can be multiplied on the right by any matrix B of shape (n, k) (where k is any positive integer) to form matrix AB of shape (m, k). For the actual mathematical description, suppose A is a matrix of shape (m, n) and B is a matrix of shape (n, k). Then AB is defined by

$$(AB)_{ij} = \sum_k A_{ik} B_{kj}$$

We displayed a matrix multiplication equation earlier in brief. Let's expand that example now that we have the formal definition:

$$\begin{pmatrix} \cos{(\alpha)} & -\sin{(\alpha)} \\ \sin{(\alpha)} & \cos{(\alpha)} \end{pmatrix} \cdot \begin{pmatrix} 1 \\ 0 \end{pmatrix} = \begin{pmatrix} \cos{(\alpha)} \cdot 1 - \sin{(\alpha)} \cdot 0 \\ \sin{(\alpha)} \cdot 1 - \cos{(\alpha)} \cdot 0 \end{pmatrix} = \begin{pmatrix} \cos{(\alpha)} \\ \sin{(\alpha)} \end{pmatrix}$$

The fundamental takeaway is that rows of one matrix are multiplied against columns of the other matrix.

This definition hides a number of subtleties. Note first that matrix multiplication is not commutative. That is, $AB \neq BA$ in general. In fact, AB can exist when BA is not meaningful. Suppose, for example, A is a matrix of shape (2, 3) and B is a matrix of shape (3, 4). Then AB is a matrix of shape (2, 4). However, BA is not defined since the respective dimensions (4 and 2) don't match. As another subtlety, note that, as in the rotation example, a matrix of shape (m, n) can be multiplied on the right by a matrix of shape $(n, 1)$. However, a matrix of shape $(n, 1)$ is simply a column vector. So, it is meaningful to multiply matrices by vectors. Matrix-vector multiplication is one of the fundamental building blocks of common machine learning systems.

One of the nicest properties of standard multiplication is that it is a linear operation. More precisely, a function f is called linear if $f(x + y) = f(x) + f(y)$ and $f(cx) = cf(x)$ where c is a scalar. To demonstrate that scalar multiplication is linear, suppose that a, b, c, d are all real numbers. Then we have

$$a \cdot (b \cdot c) = b \cdot (ac)$$

$$a \cdot (c + d) = ac + ad$$

We make use of the commutative and distributive properties of scalar multiplication here. Now suppose that instead, A, C, D are now matrices where C, D are of the same size and it is meaningful to multiply A on the right with either C or D (b remains a real number). Then matrix multiplication is a linear operator:

$$A(b \cdot C) = b \cdot (AC)$$

$$A(C + D) = AC + AD$$

Put another way, matrix multiplication is distributive and commutes with scalar multiplication. In fact, it can be shown that any linear transformation on vectors corresponds to a matrix multiplication. For a computer science analogy, think of linearity as a property demanded by an abstract method in a superclass. Then standard multiplication and matrix multiplication are concrete implementations of that abstract method for different subclasses (respectively real numbers and matrices).

Tensors

In the previous sections, we introduced the notion of scalars as rank-0 tensors, vectors as rank-1 tensors, and matrices as rank-2 tensors. What then is a rank-3 tensor? Before passing to a general definition, it can help to think about the commonalities between scalars, vectors, and matrices. Scalars are single numbers. Vectors are lists of numbers. To pick out any particular element of a vector requires knowing its index. Hence, we need one index element into the vector (thus a rank-1 tensor). Matrices are tables of numbers. To pick out any particular element of a matrix requires knowing its row and column. Hence, we need two index elements (thus a rank-2 tensor). It follows naturally that a rank-3 tensor is a set of numbers where there are three required indices. It can help to think of a rank-3 tensor as a rectangular prism of numbers, as illustrated in Figure 2-4.

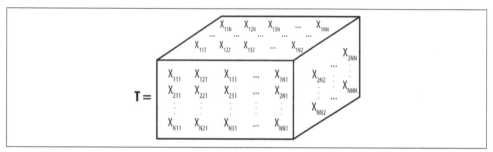

Figure 2-4. A rank-3 tensor can be visualized as a rectangular prism of numbers.

The rank-3 tensor T displayed in the figure is of shape (N, N, N). An arbitrary element of the tensor would then be selected by specifying (i, j, k) as indices.

There is a linkage between tensors and shapes. A rank-1 tensor has a shape of dimension 1, a rank-2 tensor a shape of dimension 2, and a rank-3 tensor of dimension 3. You might protest that this contradicts our earlier discussion of row and column vectors. By our definition, a column vector has shape $(n, 1)$. Wouldn't that make a column vector a rank-2 tensor (or a matrix)? This is exactly what has happened. Recall that a vector which is not specified to be a row vector or column vector has shape (n). When we specify that a vector is a row vector or a column vector, we in fact specify a method of transforming the underlying vector into a matrix. This type of dimension expansion is a common trick in tensor manipulation.

Note that another way of thinking about a rank-3 tensor is as a list of matrices all with the same shape. Suppose that W is a matrix with shape (n, n). Then the tensor $T_{ijk} = (W_1, \cdots, W_n)$ consists of n copies of the matrix W.

Note that a black-and-white image can be represented as a rank-2 tensor. Suppose we have a 224 × 224-pixel black and white image. Then, pixel (i, j) is 1/0 to encode a black/white pixel, respectively. It follows that a black and white image can be represented as a matrix of shape (224, 224). Now, consider a 224 × 224 color image. The color at a particular pixel is typically represented by three separate RGB channels. That is, pixel (i, j) is represented as a tuple of numbers (r, g, b) that encode the amount of red, green, and blue at the pixel, respectively. r, g, b are typically integers from 0 to 255. It follows now that the color image can be encoded as a rank-3 tensor of shape (224, 224, 3). Continuing the analogy, consider a color video. Suppose that each frame of the video is a 224 × 224 color image. Then a minute of video (at 60 fps) would be a rank-4 tensor of shape (224, 224, 3, 3600). Continuing even further, a collection of 10 such videos would then form a rank-5 tensor of shape (10, 224, 224, 3, 3600). In general, tensors provide for a convenient representation of numeric data. In practice, it's not common to see tensors of higher order than rank-5 tensors, but it's smart to design any tensor software to allow for arbitrary tensors since intelligent users will always come up with use cases designers don't consider.

Tensors in Physics

Tensors are used widely in physics to encode fundamental physical quantities. For example, the stress tensor is commonly used in material science to define the stress at a point within a material. Mathematically, the stress tensor is a rank-2 tensor of shape (3, 3):

$$\sigma = \begin{pmatrix} \sigma_{11} & \tau_{12} & \tau_{13} \\ \tau_{21} & \sigma_{22} & \tau_{23} \\ \tau_{31} & \tau_{32} & \sigma_{33} \end{pmatrix}$$

Then, suppose that n is a vector of shape (3) that encodes a direction. The stress T^n in direction n is specified by the vector $T^n = T \cdot n$ (note the matrix-vector multiplication). This relationship is depicted pictorially in Figure 2-5.

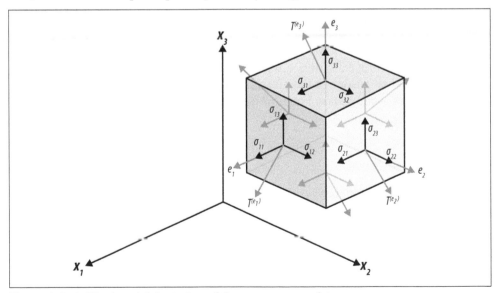

Figure 2-5. A 3D pictorial depiction of the components of stress.

As another physical example, Einstein's field equations of general relativity are commonly expressed in tensorial format:

$$R_{\mu\nu} - \frac{1}{2}Rg_{\mu\nu} + \Lambda g_{\mu\nu} = \frac{8\pi G}{c^4}T_{\mu\nu}$$

Here $R_{\mu\nu}$ is the Ricci curvature tensor, $g_{\mu\nu}$ is the metric tensor, $T_{\mu\nu}$ is the stress-energy tensor, and the remaining quantities are scalars. Note, however, that there's an important subtlety distinguishing these tensors and the other tensors we've discussed previously. Quantities like the metric tensor provide a separate tensor (in the sense of an array of numbers) for each point in space-time (mathematically, the metric tensor is a tensor field). The same holds for the stress tensor previously discussed, and for the other tensors in these equations. At a given point in space-time, each of these quantities becomes a symmetric rank-2 tensor of shape (4, 4) using our notation.

Part of the power of modern tensor calculus systems such as TensorFlow is that some of the mathematical machinery long used for classical physics can now be adapted to solve applied problems in image processing and language understanding. At the same time, today's tensor calculus systems are still limited compared with the mathematical machinery of physicists. For example, there's no simple way to talk about a quantity such as the metric tensor using TensorFlow yet. We hope that as tensor calculus becomes more fundamental to computer science, the situation will change and that systems like TensorFlow will serve as a bridge between the physical world and the computational world.

Mathematical Asides

The discussion so far in this chapter has introduced tensors informally via example and illustration. In our definition, a tensor is simply an array of numbers. It's often convenient to view a tensor as a function instead. The most common definition introduces a tensor as a multilinear function from a product of vector spaces to the real numbers:

$$T: V_1 \times V_2 \times \cdots V_n \to \mathbb{R}$$

This definition uses a number of terms you haven't seen. A vector space is simply a collection of vectors. You've seen a few examples of vector spaces such as $\mathbb{R}^3$ or generally $\mathbb{R}^n$. We won't lose any generality by holding that $V_i = \mathbb{R}^{d_i}$. As we defined previously, a function f is linear if $f(x + y) = f(x) + f(y)$ and $f(cx) = cf(x)$. A multilinear function is simply a function that is linear in each argument. This function can be viewed as assigning individual entries of a multidimensional array, when provided indices into the array as arguments.

We won't use this more mathematical definition much in this book, but it serves as a useful bridge to connect the deep learning concepts you will learn about with the centuries of mathematical research that have been undertaken on tensors by the physics and mathematics communities.

Covariance and Contravariance

Our definition here has swept many details under the rug that would need to be carefully attended to for a formal treatment. For example, we don't touch upon the notion of covariant and contravariant indices here. What we call a rank-n tensor is better described as a (p, q)-tensor where $n = p + q$ and p is the number of contravariant indices, and q the number of covariant indices. Matrices are $(1,1)$-tensors, for example. As a subtlety, there are rank-2 tensors that are not matrices! We won't dig into these topics carefully here since they don't crop up much in machine learning, but we encourage you to understand how covariance and contravariance affect the machine learning systems you construct.

Basic Computations in TensorFlow

We've spent the last sections covering the mathematical definitions of various tensors. It's now time to cover how to create and manipulate tensors using TensorFlow. For this section, we recommend you follow along using an interactive Python session (with IPython). Many of the basic TensorFlow concepts are easiest to understand after experimenting with them directly.

Installing TensorFlow and Getting Started

Before continuing this section, you will need to install TensorFlow on your machine. The details of installation will vary depending on your particular hardware, so we refer you to the official TensorFlow documentation (*https://www.tensorflow.org/api_docs/*) for more details.

Although there are frontends to TensorFlow in multiple programming languages, we will exclusively use the TensorFlow Python API in the remainder of this book. We recommend that you install Anaconda Python (*https://anaconda.org/anaconda/python*), which packages many useful numerical libraries along with the base Python executable.

Once you've installed TensorFlow, we recommend that you invoke it interactively while you're learning the basic API (see Example 2-1). When experimenting with

TensorFlow interactively, it's convenient to use `tf.InteractiveSession()`. Invoking this statement within IPython (an interactive Python shell) will make TensorFlow behave almost imperatively, allowing beginners to play with tensors much more easily. You will learn about imperative versus declarative style in greater depth later in this chapter.

Example 2-1. Initialize an interactive TensorFlow session

```
>>> import tensorflow as tf
>>> tf.InteractiveSession()
<tensorflow.python.client.session.InteractiveSession>
```

The rest of the code in this section will assume that an interactive session has been loaded.

Initializing Constant Tensors

Until now, we've discussed tensors as abstract mathematical entities. However, a system like TensorFlow must run on a real computer, so any tensors must live on computer memory in order to be useful to computer programmers. TensorFlow provides a number of functions that instantiate basic tensors in memory. The simplest of these are `tf.zeros()` and `tf.ones()`. `tf.zeros()` takes a tensor shape (represented as a Python tuple) and returns a tensor of that shape filled with zeros. Let's try invoking this command in the shell (Example 2-2).

Example 2-2. Create a zeros tensor

```
>>> tf.zeros(2)
<tf.Tensor 'zeros:0' shape=(2,) dtype=float32>
```

TensorFlow returns a reference to the desired tensor rather than the value of the tensor itself. To force the value of the tensor to be returned, we will use the method `tf.Tensor.eval()` of tensor objects (Example 2-3). Since we have initialized `tf.InteractiveSession()`, this method will return the value of the zeros tensor to us.

Example 2-3. Evaluate the value of a tensor

```
>>> a = tf.zeros(2)
>>> a.eval()
array([ 0.,  0.], dtype=float32)
```

Note that the evaluated value of the TensorFlow tensor is itself a Python object. In particular, `a.eval()` is a `numpy.ndarray` object. NumPy is a sophisticated numerical system for Python. We won't attempt an in-depth discussion of NumPy here beyond noting that TensorFlow is designed to be compatible with NumPy conventions to a large degree.

We can call `tf.zeros()` and `tf.ones()` to create and display tensors of various sizes (Example 2-4).

Example 2-4. Evaluate and display tensors

```
>>> a = tf.zeros((2, 3))
>>> a.eval()
array([[ 0.,  0.,  0.],
       [ 0.,  0.,  0.]], dtype=float32)
>>> b = tf.ones((2,2,2))
>>> b.eval()
array([[[ 1.,  1.],
        [ 1.,  1.]],

       [[ 1.,  1.],
        [ 1.,  1.]]], dtype=float32)
```

What if we'd like a tensor filled with some quantity besides 0/1? The `tf.fill()` method provides a nice shortcut for doing so (Example 2-5).

Example 2-5. Filling tensors with arbitrary values

```
>>> b = tf.fill((2, 2), value=5.)
>>> b.eval()
array([[ 5.,  5.],
       [ 5.,  5.]], dtype=float32)
```

`tf.constant` is another function, similar to `tf.fill`, which allows for construction of tensors that shouldn't change during the program execution (Example 2-6).

Example 2-6. Creating constant tensors

```
>>> a = tf.constant(3)
>>> a.eval()
3
```

Sampling Random Tensors

Although working with constant tensors is convenient for testing ideas, it's much more common to initialize tensors with random values. The most common way to do this is to sample each entry in the tensor from a random distribution. `tf.random_nor mal` allows for each entry in a tensor of specified shape to be sampled from a Normal distribution of specified mean and standard deviation (Example 2-7).

Symmetry Breaking

Many machine learning algorithms learn by performing updates to a set of tensors that hold weights. These update equations usually satisfy the property that weights initialized at the same value will continue to evolve together. Thus, if the initial set of tensors is initialized to a constant value, the model won't be capable of learning much. Fixing this situation requires *symmetry breaking*. The easiest way of breaking symmetry is to sample each entry in a tensor randomly.

Example 2-7. Sampling a tensor with random Normal entries

```
>>> a = tf.random_normal((2, 2), mean=0, stddev=1)
>>> a.eval()
array([[-0.73437649, -0.77678096],
       [ 0.51697761,  1.15063596]], dtype=float32)
```

One thing to note is that machine learning systems often make use of very large tensors that often have tens of millions of parameters. When we sample tens of millions of random values from the Normal distribution, it becomes almost certain that some sampled values will be far from the mean. Such large samples can lead to numerical instability, so it's common to sample using `tf.truncated_normal()` instead of `tf.random_normal()`. This function behaves the same as `tf.random_normal()` in terms of API, but drops and resamples all values more than two standard deviations from the mean.

`tf.random_uniform()` behaves like `tf.random_normal()` except for the fact that random values are sampled from the Uniform distribution over a specified range (Example 2-8).

Example 2-8. Sampling a tensor with uniformly random entries

```
>>> a = tf.random_uniform((2, 2), minval=-2, maxval=2)
>>> a.eval()
array([[-1.90391684,  1.4179163 ],
       [ 0.67762709,  1.07282352]], dtype=float32)
```

Tensor Addition and Scaling

TensorFlow makes use of Python's operator overloading to make basic tensor arithmetic straightforward with standard Python operators (Example 2-9).

Example 2-9. Adding tensors together

```
>>> c = tf.ones((2, 2))
>>> d = tf.ones((2, 2))
>>> e = c + d
>>> e.eval()
array([[ 2.,  2.],
       [ 2.,  2.]], dtype=float32)
>>> f = 2 * e
>>> f.eval()
array([[ 4.,  4.],
       [ 4.,  4.]], dtype=float32)
```

Tensors can also be multiplied this way. Note, however, when multiplying two tensors we get elementwise multiplication and not matrix multiplication, which can be seen in Example 2-10.

Example 2-10. Elementwise tensor multiplication

```
>>> c = tf.fill((2,2), 2.)
>>> d = tf.fill((2,2), 7.)
>>> e = c * d
>>> e.eval()
array([[ 14.,  14.],
       [ 14.,  14.]], dtype=float32)
```

Matrix Operations

TensorFlow provides a variety of amenities for working with matrices. (Matrices by far are the most common type of tensor used in practice.) In particular, TensorFlow provides shortcuts to make certain types of commonly used matrices. The most widely used of these is likely the identity matrix. Identity matrices are square matrices that are 0 everywhere except on the diagonal, where they are 1. tf.eye() allows for fast construction of identity matrices of desired size (Example 2-11).

Example 2-11. Creating an identity matrix

```
>>> a = tf.eye(4)
>>> a.eval()
array([[ 1.,  0.,  0.,  0.],
       [ 0.,  1.,  0.,  0.],
       [ 0.,  0.,  1.,  0.],
       [ 0.,  0.,  0.,  1.]], dtype=float32)
```

Diagonal matrices are another common type of matrix. Like identity matrices, diagonal matrices are only nonzero along the diagonal. Unlike identity matrices, they may take arbitrary values along the diagonal. Let's construct a diagonal matrix with ascending values along the diagonal (Example 2-12). To start, we'll need a method to construct a vector of ascending values in TensorFlow. The easiest way for doing this is invoking `tf.range(start, limit, delta)`. Note that `limit` is excluded from the range and `delta` is the step size for the traversal. The resulting vector can then be fed to `tf.diag(diagonal)`, which will construct a matrix with the specified diagonal.

Example 2-12. Creating diagonal matrices

```
>>> r = tf.range(1, 5, 1)
>>> r.eval()
array([1, 2, 3, 4], dtype=int32)
>>> d = tf.diag(r)
>>> d.eval()
array([[1, 0, 0, 0],
       [0, 2, 0, 0],
       [0, 0, 3, 0],
       [0, 0, 0, 4]], dtype=int32)
```

Now suppose that we have a specified matrix in TensorFlow. How do we compute the matrix transpose? `tf.matrix_transpose()` will do the trick nicely (Example 2-13).

Example 2-13. Taking a matrix transpose

```
>>> a = tf.ones((2, 3))
>>> a.eval()
array([[ 1.,  1.,  1.],
       [ 1.,  1.,  1.]], dtype=float32)
>>> at = tf.matrix_transpose(a)
>>> at.eval()
array([[ 1.,  1.],
       [ 1.,  1.],
       [ 1.,  1.]], dtype=float32)
```

Now, let's suppose we have a pair of matrices we'd like to multiply using matrix multiplication. The easiest way to do so is by invoking `tf.matmul()` (Example 2-14).

Example 2-14. Performing matrix multiplication

```
>>> a = tf.ones((2, 3))
>>> a.eval()
array([[ 1.,  1.,  1.],
       [ 1.,  1.,  1.]], dtype=float32)
>>> b = tf.ones((3, 4))
>>> b.eval()
array([[ 1.,  1.,  1.,  1.],
       [ 1.,  1.,  1.,  1.],
       [ 1.,  1.,  1.,  1.]], dtype=float32)
```

```
>>> c = tf.matmul(a, b)
>>> c.eval()
array([[ 3.,   3.,   3.,   3.],
       [ 3.,   3.,   3.,   3.]], dtype=float32)
```

You can check that this answer matches the mathematical definition of matrix multi-plication we provided earlier.

Tensor Types

You may have noticed the dtype notation in the preceding examples. Tensors in Ten-sorFlow come in a variety of types such as tf.float32, tf.float64, tf.int32, tf.int64. It's possible to to create tensors of specified types by setting dtype in tensor construction functions. Furthermore, given a tensor, it's possible to change its type using casting functions such as tf.to_double(), tf.to_float(), tf.to_int32(), tf.to_int64(), and others (Example 2-15).

Example 2-15. Creating tensors of different types

```
>>> a = tf.ones((2,2), dtype=tf.int32)
>>> a.eval()
array([[0, 0],
       [0, 0]], dtype=int32)
>>> b = tf.to_float(a)
>>> b.eval()
array([[ 0.,   0.],
       [ 0.,   0.]], dtype=float32)
```

Tensor Shape Manipulations

Within TensorFlow, tensors are just collections of numbers written in memory. The different shapes are views into the underlying set of numbers that provide different ways of interacting with the set of numbers. At different times, it can be useful to view the same set of numbers as forming tensors with different shapes. tf.reshape() allows tensors to be converted into tensors with different shapes (Example 2-16).

Example 2-16. Manipulating tensor shapes

```
>>> a = tf.ones(8)
>>> a.eval()
array([ 1.,   1.,   1.,   1.,   1.,   1.,   1.,   1.], dtype=float32)
>>> b = tf.reshape(a, (4, 2))
>>> b.eval()
array([[ 1.,   1.],
       [ 1.,   1.],
       [ 1.,   1.],
       [ 1.,   1.]], dtype=float32)
```

```
>>> c = tf.reshape(a, (2, 2, 2))
>>> c.eval()
array([[[ 1.,  1.],
        [ 1.,  1.]],

       [[ 1.,  1.],
        [ 1.,  1.]]], dtype=float32)
```

Notice how we can turn the original rank-1 tensor into a rank-2 tensor and then into a rank-3 tensor with `tf.reshape`. While all necessary shape manipulations can be performed with `tf.reshape()`, sometimes it can be convenient to perform simpler shape manipulations using functions such as `tf.expand_dims` or `tf.squeeze`. `tf.expand_dims` adds an extra dimension to a tensor of size 1. It's useful for increasing the rank of a tensor by one (for example, when converting a rank-1 vector into a rank-2 row vector or column vector). `tf.squeeze`, on the other hand, removes all dimensions of size 1 from a tensor. It's a useful way to convert a row or column vector into a flat vector.

This is also a convenient opportunity to introduce the `tf.Tensor.get_shape()` method (Example 2-17). This method lets users query the shape of a tensor.

Example 2-17. Getting the shape of a tensor

```
>>> a = tf.ones(2)
>>> a.get_shape()
TensorShape([Dimension(2)])
>>> a.eval()
array([ 1.,  1.], dtype=float32)
>>> b = tf.expand_dims(a, 0)
>>> b.get_shape()
TensorShape([Dimension(1), Dimension(2)])
>>> b.eval()
array([[ 1.,  1.]], dtype=float32)
>>> c = tf.expand_dims(a, 1)
>>> c.get_shape()
TensorShape([Dimension(2), Dimension(1)])
>>> c.eval()
array([[ 1.],
       [ 1.]], dtype=float32)
>>> d = tf.squeeze(b)
>>> d.get_shape()
TensorShape([Dimension(2)])
>>> d.eval()
array([ 1.,  1.], dtype=float32)
```

Introduction to Broadcasting

Broadcasting is a term (introduced by NumPy) for when a tensor system's matrices and vectors of different sizes can be added together. These rules allow for conveniences like adding a vector to every row of a matrix. Broadcasting rules can be quite complex, so we will not dive into a formal discussion of the rules. It's often easier to experiment and see how the broadcasting works (Example 2-18).

Example 2-18. Examples of broadcasting

```
>>> a = tf.ones((2, 2))
>>> a.eval()
array([[ 1.,  1.],
       [ 1.,  1.]], dtype=float32)
>>> b = tf.range(0, 2, 1, dtype=tf.float32)
>>> b.eval()
array([ 0.,  1.], dtype=float32)
>>> c = a + b
>>> c.eval()
array([[ 1.,  2.],
       [ 1.,  2.]], dtype=float32)
```

Notice that the vector b is added to every row of matrix a. Notice another subtlety; we explicitly set the dtype for b. If the dtype isn't set, TensorFlow will report a type error. Let's see what would have happened if we hadn't set the dtype (Example 2-19).

Example 2-19. TensorFlow doesn't perform implicit type casting

```
>>> b = tf.range(0, 2, 1)
>>> b.eval()
array([0, 1], dtype=int32)
>>> c = a + b
ValueError: Tensor conversion requested dtype float32 for Tensor with dtype int32:
'Tensor("range_2:0", shape=(2,), dtype=int32)
```

Unlike languages like C, TensorFlow doesn't perform implicit type casting under the hood. It's often necessary to perform explicit type casts when doing arithmetic operations.

Imperative and Declarative Programming

Most situations in computer science involve imperative programming. Consider a simple Python program (Example 2-20).

Example 2-20. Python program imperatively performing an addition

```
>>> a = 3
>>> b = 4
>>> c = a + b
>>> c
7
```

This program, when translated into machine code, instructs the machine to perform a primitive addition operation on two registers, one containing 3, and the other containing 4. The result is then 7. This style of programming is called *imperative* since the program tells the computer explicitly which actions to perform.

An alternative style of programming is *declarative*. In a declarative system, a computer program is a high-level description of the computation that is to be performed. It does not instruct the computer exactly how to perform the computation. Example 2-21 is the TensorFlow equivalent of Example 2-20.

Example 2-21. TensorFlow program declaratively performing an addition

```
>>> a = tf.constant(3)
>>> b = tf.constant(4)
>>> c = a + b
>>> c
<tf.Tensor 'add_1:0' shape=() dtype=int32>
>>> c.eval()
7
```

Note that the value of c isn't 7! Rather, it's a symbolic tensor. This code specifies the computation of adding two values together to create a new tensor. The actual computation isn't executed until we call c.eval(). In the sections before, we have been using the eval() method to simulate imperative style in TensorFlow since it can be challenging to understand declarative programming at first.

However, declarative programming is by no means an unknown concept to software engineering. Relational databases and SQL provide an example of a widely used declarative programming system. Commands like SELECT and JOIN may be implemented in an arbitrary fashion under the hood so long as their basic semantics are preserved. TensorFlow code is best thought of as analogous to a SQL program; the TensorFlow code specifies a computation to be performed, with details left up to TensorFlow. The TensorFlow developers exploit this lack of detail under the hood to tailor the execution style to the underlying hardware, be it CPU, GPU, or mobile device.

It's important to note that the grand weakness of declarative programming is that the abstraction is quite leaky. For example, without detailed understanding of the underlying implementation of the relational database, long SQL programs can become unbearably inefficient. Similarly, large TensorFlow programs implemented without understanding of the underlying learning algorithms are unlikely to work well. In the rest of this section, we will start paring back the abstraction, a process we will continue throughout the rest of the book.

TensorFlow Eager

The TensorFlow team recently added a new experimental module, TensorFlow Eager, that enables users to run TensorFlow calculations imperatively. In time, this module will likely become the preferred entry mode for new programmers learning TensorFlow. However, at the timing of writing, this module is still very new with many rough edges. As a result, we won't teach you about Eager mode, but encourage you to check it out for yourself.

It's important to emphasize that much of TensorFlow will remain declarative even after Eager matures, so it's worth learning declarative TensorFlow regardless.

TensorFlow Graphs

Any computation in TensorFlow is represented as an instance of a `tf.Graph` object. Such a graph consists of a set of instances of `tf.Tensor` objects and `tf.Operation` objects. We have covered `tf.Tensor` in some detail, but what are `tf.Operation` objects? You have already seen them over the course of this chapter. A call to an operation like `tf.matmul` creates a `tf.Operation` instance to mark the need to perform the matrix multiplication operation.

When a `tf.Graph` is not explicitly specified, TensorFlow adds tensors and operations to a hidden global `tf.Graph` instance. This instance can be fetched by `tf.get_default_graph()` (Example 2-22).

Example 2-22. Getting the default TensorFlow graph

```
>>> tf.get_default_graph()
<tensorflow.python.framework.ops.Graph>
```

It is possible to specify that TensorFlow operations should be performed in graphs other than the default. We will demonstrate examples of this in future chapters.

TensorFlow Sessions

In TensorFlow, a `tf.Session()` object stores the context under which a computation is performed. At the beginning of this chapter, we used `tf.InteractiveSession()` to set up an environment for all TensorFlow computations. This call created a hidden global context for all computations performed. We then used `tf.Tensor.eval()` to execute our declaratively specified computations. Underneath the hood, this call is evaluated in context of this hidden global `tf.Session`. It can be convenient (and often necessary) to use an explicit context for a computation instead of a hidden context (Example 2-23).

Example 2-23. Explicitly manipulating TensorFlow sessions

```
>>> sess = tf.Session()
>>> a = tf.ones((2, 2))
>>> b = tf.matmul(a, a)
>>> b.eval(session=sess)
array([[ 2.,   2.],
       [ 2.,   2.]], dtype=float32)
```

This code evaluates b in the context of `sess` instead of the hidden global session. In fact, we can make this more explicit with an alternate notation (Example 2-24).

Example 2-24. Running a computation within a session

```
>>> sess.run(b)
array([[ 2.,   2.],
       [ 2.,   2.]], dtype=float32)
```

In fact, calling `b.eval(session=sess)` is just syntactic sugar for calling `sess.run(b)`.

This entire discussion may smack a bit of sophistry. What does it matter which session is in play given that all the different methods seem to return the same answer? Explicit sessions don't really show their value until you start to perform computations that have state, a topic you will learn about in the following section.

TensorFlow Variables

All the example code in this section has used constant tensors. While we could combine and recombine these tensors in any way we chose, we could never change the value of tensors themselves (only create new tensors with new values). The style of programming so far has been *functional* and not *stateful*. While functional computations are very useful, machine learning often depends heavily on stateful computations. Learning algorithms are essentially rules for updating stored tensors to explain provided data. If it's not possible to update these stored tensors, it would be hard to learn.

The `tf.Variable()` class provides a wrapper around tensors that allows for stateful computations. The variable objects serve as holders for tensors. Creating a variable is easy enough (Example 2-25).

Example 2-25. Creating a TensorFlow variable

```
>>> a = tf.Variable(tf.ones((2, 2)))
>>> a
<tf.Variable 'Variable:0' shape=(2, 2) dtype=float32_ref>
```

What happens when we try to evaluate the variable a as though it were a tensor, as in Example 2-26?

Example 2-26. Evaluating an uninitialized variable fails

```
>>> a.eval()
FailedPreconditionError: Attempting to use uninitialized value Variable
```

The evaluation fails since variables have to be explicitly initialized. The easiest way to initialize all variables is to invoke tf.global_variables_initializer. Running this operation within a session will initialize all variables in the program (Example 2-27).

Example 2-27. Evaluating initialized variables

```
>>> sess = tf.Session()
>>> sess.run(tf.global_variables_initializer())
>>> a.eval(session=sess)
array([[ 1.,   1.],
       [ 1.,   1.]], dtype=float32)
```

After initialization, we are able to fetch the value stored within the variable as though it were a plain tensor. So far, there's not much more to variables than plain tensors. Variables only become interesting once we can assign to them. tf.assign() lets us do this. Using tf.assign() we can update the value of an existing variable (Example 2-28).

Example 2-28. Assigning values to variables

```
>>> sess.run(a.assign(tf.zeros((2,2))))
array([[ 0.,   0.],
       [ 0.,   0.]], dtype=float32)
>>> sess.run(a)
array([[ 0.,   0.],
       [ 0.,   0.]], dtype=float32)
```

What would happen if we tried to assign a value to variable a not of shape (2,2)? Let's find out in Example 2-29.

Example 2-29. Assignment fails when shapes aren't equal

```
>>> sess.run(a.assign(tf.zeros((3,3))))
ValueError: Dimension 0 in both shapes must be equal, but are 2 and 3 for 'Assign_3'
(op: 'Assign') with input shapes: [2,2], [3,3].
```

You can see that TensorFlow complains. The shape of the variable is fixed upon initialization and must be preserved with updates. As another interesting note, `tf.assign` is itself a part of the underlying global `tf.Graph` instance. This allows TensorFlow programs to update their internal state every time they are run. We will make heavy use of this feature in the chapters to come.

Review

In this chapter, we've introduced the mathematical concept of tensors, and briefly reviewed a number of mathematical concepts associated with tensors. We then demonstrated how to create tensors in TensorFlow and perform these same mathematical operations within TensorFlow. We also briefly introduced some underlying TensorFlow structures like the computational graph, sessions, and variables. If you haven't completely grasped the concepts discussed in this chapter, don't worry much about it. We will repeatedly use these same concepts over the remainder of the book, so there will be plenty of chances to let the ideas sink in.

In the next chapter, we will teach you how to build simple learning models for linear and logistic regression using TensorFlow. Subsequent chapters will build on these foundations to teach you how to train more sophisticated models.

## CHAPTER 3

Linear and Logistic Regression with TensorFlow

This chapter will show you how to build simple, but nontrivial, examples of learning systems in TensorFlow. The first part of this chapter reviews the mathematical foundations for building learning systems and in particular will cover functions, continuity, and differentiability. We introduce the idea of loss functions, then discuss how machine learning boils down to the ability to find the minimal points of complicated loss functions. We then cover the notion of gradient descent, and explain how it can be used to minimize loss functions. We end the first section by briefly discussing the algorithmic idea of automatic differentiation. The second section focuses on introducing the TensorFlow concepts underpinned by these mathematical ideas. These concepts include placeholders, scopes, optimizers, and TensorBoard, and enable the practical construction and analysis of learning systems. The final section provides case studies of how to train linear and logistic regression models in TensorFlow.

This chapter is long and introduces many new ideas. It's OK if you don't grasp all the subtleties of these ideas in a first reading. We recommend moving forward and coming back to refer to the concepts here as needed later. We will repeatedly use these fundamentals in the remainder of the book in order to let these ideas sink in gradually.

Mathematical Review

This first section reviews the mathematical tools needed to conceptually understand machine learning. We attempt to minimize the number of Greek symbols required, and focus instead on building conceptual understanding rather than technical manipulations.

Functions and Differentiability

This section will provide you with a brief overview of the concepts of functions and differentiability. A function *f* is a rule that takes an input to an output. There are functions in all computer programming languages, and the mathematical definition of a function isn't really much different. However, mathematical functions commonly used in physics and engineering have other important properties such as continuity and differentiability. A continuous function, loosely speaking, is one that can be drawn without lifting your pencil from the paper, as shown in Figure 3-1. (This is of course not the technical definition, but it captures the spirit of the continuity condition.)

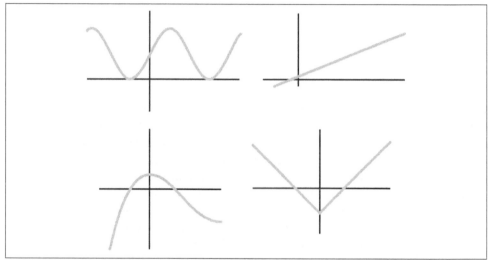

Figure 3-1. Some continuous functions.

Differentiability is a type of smoothness condition on functions. It says no sharp corners or turns are allowed in the function (Figure 3-2).

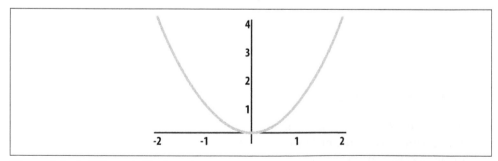

Figure 3-2. A differentiable function.

The key advantage of differentiable functions is that we can use the slope of the function at a particular point as a guide to find places where the function is higher or lower than our current position. This allows us to find the *minima* of the function. The *derivative* of differentiable function f, denoted f', is another function that provides the slope of the original function at all points. The conceptual idea is that the derivative of a function at a given point gives a signpost pointing to directions where the function is higher or lower than its current value. An optimization algorithm can follow this signpost to move closer to a minima of f. At the minima itself, the function will have derivative zero.

The power of derivative-driven optimization isn't apparent at first. Generations of calculus students have suffered through stultifying exercises minimizing tiny functions on paper. These exercises aren't useful since finding the minima of a function with only a small number of input parameters is a trivial exercise best done graphically. The power of derivative-driven optimization only becomes evident when there are hundreds, thousands, millions, or billions of variables. At these scales, understanding the function analytically is nigh impossible, and all visualizations are fraught exercises that may well miss the key attributes of the function. At these scales, the *gradient* of the function ∇f, a generalization of f' to multivariate functions, is likely the most powerful mathematical tool to understand the function and its behavior. We will dig into gradients in more depth later in this chapter. (Conceptually that is; we won't cover the technical details of gradients in this work.)

At a very high level, machine learning is simply the act of function minimization: learning algorithms are nothing more than minima finders for suitably defined functions. This definition has the advantage of mathematical simplicity. But, what are these special differentiable functions that encode useful solutions in their minima and how can we find them?

Loss Functions

In order to solve a given machine learning problem, a data scientist must find a way of constructing a function whose minima encode solutions to the real-world problem at hand. Luckily for our hapless data scientist, the machine learning literature has built up a rich history of *loss functions* that perform such encodings. Practical machine learning boils down to understanding the different types of loss functions available and knowing which loss function should be applied to which problems. Put another way, the loss function is the mechanism by which a data science project is transmuted into mathematics. All of machine learning, and much of artificial intelligence, boils down to the creation of the right loss function to solve the problem at hand. We will give you a whirlwind tour of some common families of loss functions.

We start by noting that a loss function $\mathcal{L}$ must satisfy some mathematical properties to be meaningful. First $\mathcal{L}$ must use both datapoints x and labels y. We denote this by writing the loss function as $\mathcal{L}(x, y)$. Using our language from the previous chapter, both x and y are tensors, and $\mathcal{L}$ is a function from pairs of tensors to scalars. What should the functional form of the loss function be? A common assumption that people use is to make loss functions *additive*. Suppose that (x_i, y_i) are the data available for example i and that there are N total examples. Then the loss function can be decomposed as

$$\mathcal{L}(x, y) = \sum_{i=1}^{N} \mathcal{L}_i(x_i, y_i)$$

(In practice $\mathcal{L}_i$ is the same for every datapoint.) This additive decomposition allows for many useful advantages. The first is that derivatives factor through addition, so computing the gradient of the total loss simplifies as follows:

$$\nabla \mathcal{L}(x, y) = \sum_{i=1}^{N} \nabla \mathcal{L}_i(x_i, y_i)$$

This mathematical trick means that so long as the smaller functions $\mathcal{L}_i$ are differentiable, so too will the total loss function be. It follows that the problem of designing loss functions resolves into the problem of designing smaller functions $\mathcal{L}_i(x_i, y_i)$. Before we dive into designing the $\mathcal{L}_i$, it will be convenient to take a small detour that explains the difference between classification and regression problems.

Classification and regression

Machine learning algorithms can be broadly categorized as supervised or unsupervised problems. Supervised problems are those for which both datapoints x and labels y are available, while unsupervised problems have only datapoints x without labels y. In general, unsupervised machine learning is much harder and less well-defined (what does it mean to "understand" datapoints x?). We won't delve into unsupervised loss functions at this point since, in practice, most unsupervised losses are cleverly repurposed supervised losses.

Supervised machine learning can be broken up into the two subproblems of classification and regression. A classification problem is one in which you seek to design a machine learning system that assigns a discrete label, say 0/1 (or more generally $0, \cdots, n$) to a given datapoint. Regression is the problem of designing a machine learning system that attaches a real valued label (in $\mathbb{R}$) to a given datapoint.

At a high level, these problems may appear rather different. Discrete objects and continuous objects are typically treated differently by mathematics and common sense. However, part of the trickery used in machine learning is to use continuous, differentiable loss functions to encode both classification and regression problems. As we've mentioned previously, much of machine learning is simply the art of turning complicated real-world systems into suitably simple differentiable functions.

In the following sections, we will introduce you to a pair of mathematical functions that will prove very useful for transforming classification and regression tasks into suitable loss functions.

L^2 Loss

The L^2 loss (pronounced *ell-two* loss) is commonly used for regression problems. The L^2 loss (or L^2-norm as it's commonly called elsewhere) provides for a measure of the magnitude of a vector:

$$\| a \|_2 = \sqrt{\sum_{i=1}^{N} a_i^2}$$

Here, a is assumed to be a vector of length N. The L^2 norm is commonly used to define the distance between two vectors:

$$\| a - b \|_2 = \sqrt{\sum_{i=1}^{N} (a_i - b_i)^2}$$

This idea of L^2 as a distance measurement is very useful for solving regression problems in supervised machine learning. Suppose that x is a collection of data and y the associated labels. Let f be some differentiable function that encodes our machine learning model. Then to encourage f to predict y, we create the L^2 loss function

$$\mathscr{L}(x, y) = \| f(x) - y \|_2$$

As a quick note, it's common in practice to not use the L^2 loss directly, but rather its square

$$\| a - b \|_2^2 = \sum_{i=1}^{N} (a_i - b_i)^2$$

in order to avoid dealing with terms of the form $1/\sqrt{(x)}$ in the gradient. We will use the squared L^2 loss repeatedly in the remainder of this chapter and book.

Failure Modes of L^2 Loss

The L^2 sharply penalizes large-scale deviances from true labels, but doesn't do a great job of rewarding exact matches for real-valued labels. We can understand this discrepancy mathematically, by studying the behavior of the functions x^2 and x near the origin (Figure 3-3).

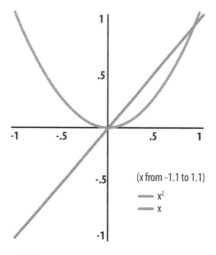

Figure 3-3. A comparison of the square and identity functions near the origin.

Notice how x^2 dwindles rapidly to 0 for small values of x. As a result, small deviations aren't penalized heavily by the L^2 loss. In low-dimensional regression, this isn't a major issue, but in high-dimensional regression, the L^2 becomes a poor loss function since there may be many small deviations that together make the regression output poor. For example, in image prediction, L^2 loss creates blurry images that are not visually appealing. Recent progress in machine learning has devised ways to learn loss functions. These learned loss functions, commonly styled Generative Adversarial Networks or GANs, are much more suitable for high-dimensional regression and are capable of generating nonblurry images.

Probability distributions

Before introducing loss functions for classification problems, it will be useful to take a quick aside to introduce probability distributions. To start, what is a probability distribution and why should we care about it for the purposes of machine learning? Probability is a deep subject, so we will only delve far enough into it for you to gain the required minimal understanding. At a high level, probability distributions provide a mathematical trick that allows you to relax a discrete set of choices into a continuum. Suppose, for example, you need to design a machine learning system that predicts whether a coin will fall heads up or heads down. It doesn't seem like heads up/down can be encoded as a continuous function, much less a differentiable one. How can you then use the machinery of calculus or TensorFlow to solve problems involving discrete choices?

Enter the probability distribution. Instead of hard choices, make the classifier predict the chance of getting heads up or heads down. For example, the classifier may learn to predict that heads has probability 0.75 and tails has probability 0.25. Note that probabilities vary continuously! Consequently by working with the probabilities of discrete events rather than with the events themselves, you can neatly sidestep the issue that calculus doesn't really work with discrete events.

A probability distribution p is simply a listing of the probabilities for the possible discrete events at hand. In this case, $p = (0.75, 0.25)$. Note, alternatively, you can view $p:\{0, 1\} \to \mathbb{R}$ as a function from the set of two elements to the real numbers. This viewpoint will be useful notationally at times.

We briefly note that the technical definition of a probability distribution is more involved. It is feasible to assign probability distributions to real-valued events. We will discuss such distributions later in the chapter.

Cross-entropy loss

Cross-entropy is a mathematical method for gauging the distance between two probability distributions:

$$H(p, q) = -\sum_x p(x) \log q(x)$$

Here p and q are two probability distributions. The notation $p(x)$ denotes the probability p accords to event x. This definition is worth discussing carefully. Like the L^2 norm, H provides a notion of distance. Note that in the case where $p = q$,

$$H(p, p) = -\sum_x p(x) \log p(x)$$

This quantity is the entropy of p and is usually written simply $H(p)$. It's a measure of how disordered the distribution is; the entropy is maximized when all events are equally likely. $H(p)$ is always less than or equal to $H(p, q)$. In fact, the "further away" distribution q is from p, the larger the cross-entropy gets. We won't dig deeply into the precise meanings of these statements, but the intuition of cross-entropy as a distance mechanism is worth remembering.

As an aside, note that unlike L^2 norm, H is asymmetric! That is, $H(p, q) \neq H(q, p)$. For this reason, reasoning with cross-entropy can be a little tricky and is best done with some caution.

Returning to concrete matters, now suppose that $p = (y, 1 - y)$ is the true data distribution for a discrete system with two outcomes, and $q = \left(y_{\text{pred}}, 1 - y_{\text{pred}}\right)$ is that predicted by a machine learning system. Then the cross-entropy loss is

$$H(p, q) = y \log y_{\text{pred}} + (1 - y) \log \left(1 - y_{\text{pred}}\right)$$

This form of the loss is used widely in machine learning systems to train classifiers. Empirically, minimizing $H(p, q)$ seems to construct classifiers that reproduce provided training labels well.

Gradient Descent

So far in this chapter, you have learned about the notion of function minimization as a proxy for machine learning. As a short recap, minimizing a suitable function is often sufficient to learn to solve a desired task. In order to use this framework, you need to use suitable loss functions, such as the L^2 or $H(p, q)$ cross-entropy in order to transform classification and regression problems into suitable loss functions.

Learnable Weights

So far in this chapter, we've explained that machine learning is the act of minimizing suitably defined loss function $\mathcal{L}(x, y)$. That is, we attempt to find arguments to the loss function $\mathcal{L}$ that minimize it. However, careful readers will recall that (x, y) are fixed quantities that cannot be changed. What arguments to $\mathcal{L}$ are we changing during learning then?

Enter learnable weights W. Suppose $f(x)$ is a differentiable function we wish to fit with our machine learning model. We will dictate that f be *parameterized* by choice of W. That is, our function actually has two arguments $f(W, x)$. Fixing the value of W results in a function that depends solely on datapoints x. These learnable weights are the quantities actually selected by minimization of the loss function. We will see later in the chapter how TensorFlow can be used to encode learnable weights using `tf.Variable`.

But now, suppose that we have encoded our learning problem with a suitable loss function. How can we actually find minima of this loss function in practice? The key trick we will use is minimization by gradient descent. Suppose that f is a function that depends on some weights W. Then ∇W denotes the direction change in W that would maximally increase f. It follows that taking a step in the opposite direction would get us closer to the minima of f.

Notation for Gradients

We have written the gradient for learnable weight W as ∇W. At times, it will be convenient to use the following alternative notation for the gradient:

$$\nabla W = \frac{\partial \mathcal{L}}{\partial W}$$

Read this equation as saying that gradient ∇W encodes the direction that maximally changes the loss $\mathcal{L}$.

TheI idea of gradient descent is to find the minima of functions by repeatedly following the negative gradient. Algorithmically, this update rule can be expressed as

$$W = W - \alpha \nabla W$$

where α is the *step-size* and dictates how much weight is given to new gradient ∇W. The idea is to take many little steps each in the direction of ∇W. Note that ∇W is itself a function of W, so the actual step changes at each iteration. Each step performs a little update to the weight matrix W. The iterative process of performing updates is typically called *learning* the weight matrix W.

Computing Gradients Efficiently with Minibatches

One issue is that computing ∇W can be very slow. Implicitly, ∇W depends on the loss function $\mathscr{L}$. Since $\mathscr{L}$ depends on the entire dataset, computing ∇W can become very slow for large datasets. In practice, people usually estimate ∇W on a fraction of the dataset called a *minibatch*. Each minibatch is of size typically 50–100. The size of the minibatch is a *hyperparameter* in a deep learning algorithm. The step-size for each step α is another hyperparameter. Deep learning algorithms typically have clusters of hyperparameters, which are not themselves learned via the stochastic gradient descent.

This tension between learnable parameters and hyperparameters is one of the weaknesses and strengths of deep architectures. The presence of hyperparameters provides much room for utilizing the expert's strong intuition, while the learnable parameters allow the data to speak for itself. However, this flexibility itself quickly becomes a weakness, with understanding of the behavior of hyperparameters something of a black art that blocks beginners from widely deploying deep learning. We will spend significant effort discussing hyperparameter optimization later in this book.

We end this section by introducing the notion of an *epoch*. An epoch is a full pass of the gradient descent algorithm over the data x. More particularly, an epoch consists of however many gradient descent steps are required to view all the data at a given mini-batch size. For example, suppose that a dataset has 1,000 datapoints and training uses a minibatch of size 50. Then an epoch will consist of 20 gradient descent updates. Each epoch of training increases the amount of useful knowledge the model has gained. Mathematically, this will correspond to reductions in the value of the loss function on the training set.

Early epochs will cause dramatic drops in the loss function. This process is often referred to as *learning the prior* on that dataset. While it appears that the model is learning rapidly, it is in fact only adjusting itself to reside in the portion of parameter space that is pertinent to the problem at hand. Later epochs will correspond to much smaller drops in the loss function, but it is often in these later epochs that meaningful learning will happen. A few epochs is usually too little time for a nontrivial model to learn anything useful; models are usually trained from 10–1,000 epochs or until convergence. While this appears large, it's important to note that the number of epochs required usually doesn't scale with the size of the dataset at hand. Consequently, gradient descent scales linearly with the size of data and not quadratically! This is one of the greatest strengths of the stochastic gradient descent method versus other learning algorithms. More complicated learning algorithms may only require a single pass over a dataset, but may use total compute that scales quadratically with the number of datapoints. In this era of big datasets, quadratic runtimes are a fatal weakness.

Tracking the drop in the loss function as a function of the number of epochs can be an extremely useful visual shorthand for understanding the learning process. These plots are often referred to as loss curves (see Figure 3-4). With time, an experienced practitioner can diagnose common failures in learning with just a quick glance at the loss curve. We will pay significant attention to the loss curves for various deep learning models over the course of this book. In particular, later in this chapter, we will introduce TensorBoard, a powerful visualization suite that TensorFlow provides for tracking quantities such as loss functions.

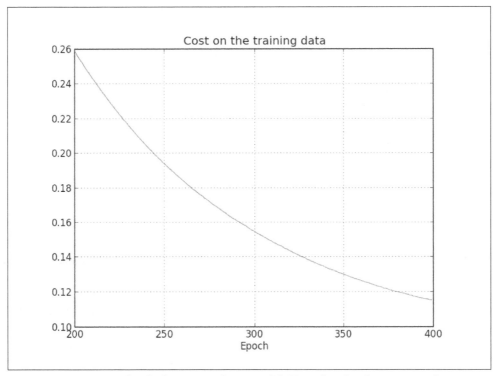

Figure 3-4. An example of a loss curve for a model. Note that this loss curve is from a model trained with the true gradient (that is, not a minibatch estimate) and is consequently smoother than other loss curves you will encounter later in this book.

Automatic Differentiation Systems

Machine learning is the art of defining loss functions suited to datasets and then minimizing them. In order to minimize loss functions, we need to compute their gradients and use the gradient descent algorithm to iteratively reduce the loss. However, we still need to discuss how gradients are actually computed. Until recently, the answer was "by hand." Machine learning experts would break out pen and paper and compute matrix derivatives by hand to compute the analytical formulas for all gradients in a learning system. These formulas would then be manually coded to implement the learning algorithm. This process was notoriously buggy, and more than one machine learning expert has stories of accidental gradient errors in published papers and production systems going undiscovered for years.

This state of affairs has changed significantly with the widespread availability of automatic differentiation engines. Systems like TensorFlow are capable of automatically computing gradients for almost all loss functions. This automatic differentiation is one of the greatest advantages of TensorFlow and similar systems, since machine learning practitioners no longer need to be experts at matrix calculus. However, it's still worth understanding at a high level how TensorFlow can automatically take derivatives of complex functions. For those readers who suffered through an introductory class in calculus, you might remember that taking derivatives of functions is surprisingly mechanical. There are a series of simple rules that can be applied to take derivatives of most functions. For example:

$$\frac{d}{dx}x^n = nx^{n-1}$$

$$\frac{d}{dx}e^x = e^x$$

These rules can be combined through the power of the chain rule:

$$\frac{d}{dx}f(g(x)) = f'(g(x))g'(x)$$

where f' is used to denote the derivative of f and g' that of g. With these rules, it's straightforward to envision how one might program an automatic differentiation engine for one-dimensional calculus. Indeed, the creation of such a differentiation engine is often a first-year programming exercise in Lisp-based classes. (It turns out that correctly parsing functions is a much trickier problem than taking derivatives. Lisp makes it trivial to parse formulas using its syntax, while in other languages, waiting to do this exercise until you take a course on compilers is often easier).

How might these rules be extended to calculus of higher dimensions? Getting the math right is trickier, since there are many more numbers to consider. For example, given $X = AB$ where X, A, B are all matrices, the formula comes out to be

$$\nabla A = \frac{\partial L}{\partial A} = \frac{\partial L}{\partial X}B^T = (\nabla X)B^T$$

Formulas like this can be combined to provide a symbolic differentiation system for vectorial and tensorial calculus.

Learning with TensorFlow

In the rest of this chapter, we will cover the concepts that you need to learn basic machine learning models with TensorFlow. We will start by introducing the concept of toy datasets, and will explain how to create meaningful toy datasets using common Python libraries. Next, we will discuss new TensorFlow ideas such as placeholders, feed dictionaries, name scopes, optimizers, and gradients. The next section will show you how to use these concepts to train simple regression and classification models.

Creating Toy Datasets

In this section, we will discuss how to create simple but meaningful synthetic datasets, or toy datasets, that we will use to train simple supervised classification and regression models.

An (extremely) brief introduction to NumPy

We will make heavy use of NumPy in order to define useful toy datasets. NumPy is a Python package that allows for manipulation of tensors (called `ndarrays` in NumPy). Example 3-1 shows some basics.

Example 3-1. Some examples of basic NumPy usage

```
>>> import numpy as np
>>> np.zeros((2,2))
array([[ 0.,  0.],
       [ 0.,  0.]])
>>> np.eye(3)
array([[ 1.,  0.,  0.],
       [ 0.,  1.,  0.],
       [ 0.,  0.,  1.]])
```

You may notice that NumPy `ndarray` manipulation looks remarkably similar to TensorFlow tensor manipulation. This similarity was purposefully designed by TensorFlow's architects. Many key TensorFlow utility functions have similar arguments and forms to analogous functions in NumPy. For this purpose, we will not attempt to introduce NumPy in great depth, and will trust readers to use experimentation to work out NumPy usage. There are numerous online resources that provide tutorial introductions to NumPy.

Why are toy datasets important?

In machine learning, it is often critical to learn to properly use toy datasets. Learning is challenging, and one of the most common mistakes beginners make is trying to learn nontrivial models on complex data too soon. These attempts often end in abject failure, and the would-be machine learner walks away dejected and convinced machine learning isn't for them.

The real culprit here of course isn't the student, but rather the fact that real-world datasets have many idiosyncrasies. Seasoned data scientists have learned that real-world datasets often require many clean-up and preprocessing transformations before becoming amenable to learning. Deep learning exacerbates this problem, since most deep learning models are notoriously sensitive to infelicities in data. Issues like a wide range of regression labels, or underlying strong noise patterns can throw off gradient-descent–based methods, even when other machine learning algorithms (such as random forests) would have no issues.

Luckily, it's almost always possible to deal with these issues, but doing so can require considerable sophistication on the part of the data scientist. These sensitivity issues are perhaps the biggest roadblock to the commoditization of machine learning as a technology. We will go into depth on data clean-up strategies, but for the time being, we recommend a much simpler alternative: use toy datasets!

Toy datasets are critical for understanding learning algorithms. Given very simple synthetic datasets, it is trivial to gauge whether the algorithm has learned the correct rule. On more complex datasets, this judgment can be highly challenging. Consequently, for the remainder of this chapter, we will only use toy datasets as we cover the fundamentals of gradient-descent–based learning with TensorFlow. We will dive deep into case studies with real-world data in the following chapters.

Adding noise with Gaussians

Earlier, we discussed discrete probability distributions as a tool for turning discrete choices into continuous values. We also alluded to the idea of a continuous probability distribution but didn't dive into it.

Continuous probability distributions (more accurately known as probability density functions) are a useful mathematical tool for modeling random events that may have a range of outcomes. For our purposes, it is enough to think of probability density functions as a useful tool for modeling some measurement error in gathering data. The Gaussian distribution is widely used for noise modeling.

As Figure 3-5 shows, note that Gaussians can have different *means μ* and *standard deviations σ*. The mean of a Gaussian is the average value it takes, while the standard deviation is a measure of the spread around this average value. In general, adding a Gaussian random variable onto some quantity provides a structured way to fuzz the quantity by making it vary slighty. This is a very useful trick for coming up with non-trivial synthetic datasets.

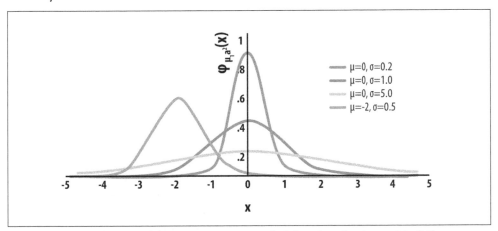

Figure 3-5. Illustrations of various Gaussian probability distributions with different means and standard deviations.

We quickly note that the Gaussian distribution is also called the Normal distribution. A Gaussian with mean μ and standard deviation σ is written $N(\mu, \sigma)$. This shorthand notation is convenient, and we will use it many times in the coming chapters.

Toy regression datasets

The simplest form of linear regression is learning the parameters for a one-dimensional line. Suppose that our datapoints x are one-dimensional. Then suppose that real-valued labels y are generated by a linear rule

$$y = wx + b$$

Here, w, b are the learnable parameters that must be estimated from data by gradient descent. In order to test that we can learn these parameters with TensorFlow, we will generate an artificial dataset consisting of points upon a straight line. To make the learning challenge a little more difficult, we will add a small amount of Gaussian noise to the dataset.

Let's write down the equation for our line perturbed by a small amount of Gaussian noise:

$$y = wx + b + N(0, \epsilon)$$

Here ϵ is the standard deviation of the noise term. We can then use NumPy to generate an artificial dataset drawn from this distribution, as shown in Example 3-2.

Example 3-2. Using NumPy to sample an artificial dataset

```
# Generate synthetic data
N = 100
w_true = 5
b_true = 2
noise_scale = .1
x_np = np.random.rand(N, 1)
noise = np.random.normal(scale=noise_scale, size=(N, 1))
# Convert shape of y_np to (N,)
y_np = np.reshape(w_true * x_np + b_true + noise, (-1))
```

We plot this dataset using Matplotlib in Figure 3-6. (you can find the code in the GitHub repo (*https://github.com/matroid/dlwithtf*) associated with this book to see the exact plotting code) to verify that synthetic data looks reasonable. As expected, the data distribution is a straight line, with a small amount of measurement error.

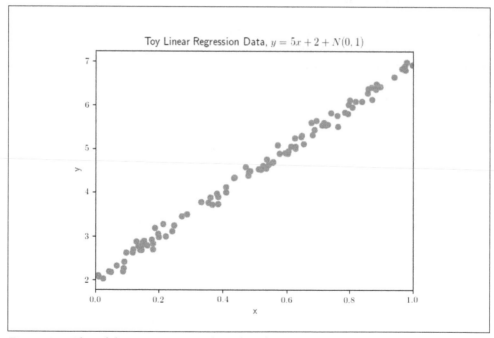

Figure 3-6. Plot of the toy regression data distribution.

Toy classification datasets

It's a little trickier to create a synthetic classification dataset. Logically, we want two distinct classes of points, which are easily separated. Suppose that the dataset consists of only two types of points, $(-1, -1)$ and $(1, 1)$. Then a learning algorithm would have to learn a rule that separates these two data values.

$$y_0 = (-1, -1)$$
$$y_1 = (1, 1)$$

As before, let's make the challenge a little more difficult by adding some Gaussian noise to both types of points:

$$y_0 = (-1, -1) + N(0, \epsilon)$$
$$y_1 = (1, 1) + N(0, \epsilon)$$

However, there's a slight bit of trickiness here. Our points are two-dimensional, while the Gaussian noise we introduced previously is one-dimensional. Luckily, there exists a multivariate extension of the Gaussian. We won't discuss the intricacies of the multivariate Gaussian here, but you do not need to understand the intricacies to follow our discussion.

The NumPy code to generate the synthetic dataset in Example 3-3 is slightly trickier than that for the linear regression problem since we have to use the stacking function np.vstack to combine the two different types of datapoints and associate them with different labels. (We use the related function np.concatenate to combine the one-dimensional labels.)

Example 3-3. Sample a toy classification dataset with NumPy

```
# Generate synthetic data
N = 100
# Zeros form a Gaussian centered at (-1, -1)
# epsilon is .1
x_zeros = np.random.multivariate_normal(
    mean=np.array((-1, -1)), cov=.1*np.eye(2), size=(N/2,))
y_zeros = np.zeros((N/2,))
# Ones form a Gaussian centered at (1, 1)
# epsilon is .1
x_ones = np.random.multivariate_normal(
    mean=np.array((1, 1)), cov=.1*np.eye(2), size=(N/2,))
y_ones = np.ones((N/2,))

x_np = np.vstack([x_zeros, x_ones])
y_np = np.concatenate([y_zeros, y_ones])
```

Figure 3-7 plots the data generated by this code with Matplotlib to verify that the distribution is as expected. We see that the data resides in two classes that are neatly separated.

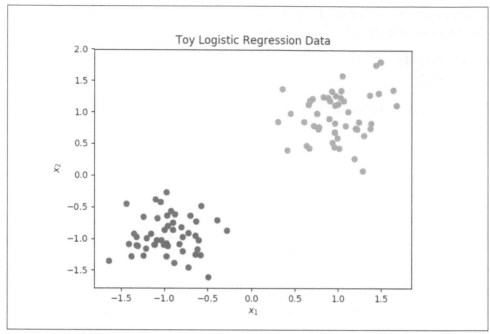

Figure 3-7. Plot of the toy classification data distribution.

New TensorFlow Concepts

Creating simple machine learning systems in TensorFlow will require that you learn some new TensorFlow concepts.

Placeholders

A placeholder is a way to input information into a TensorFlow computation graph. Think of placeholders as the input nodes through which information enters Tensor-Flow. The key function used to create placeholders is `tf.placeholder` (Example 3-4).

Example 3-4. Create a TensorFlow placeholder

```
>>> tf.placeholder(tf.float32, shape=(2,2))
<tf.Tensor 'Placeholder:0' shape=(2, 2) dtype=float32>
```

We will use placeholders to feed datapoints x and labels y to our regression and classification algorithms.

Feed dictionaries and Fetches

Recall that we can evaluate tensors in TensorFlow by using `sess.run(var)`. How do we feed in values for placeholders in our TensorFlow computations then? The answer is to construct *feed dictionaries*. Feed dictionaries are Python dictionaries that map TensorFlow tensors to `np.ndarray` objects that contain the concrete values for these placeholders. A feed dictionary is best viewed as an input to a TensorFlow computation graph. What then is an output? TensorFlow calls these outputs *fetches*. You have seen fetches already. We used them extensively in the previous chapter without calling them as such; the fetch is a tensor (or tensors) whose value is retrieved from the computation graph after the computation (using placeholder values from the feed dictionary) is run to completion (Example 3-5).

Example 3-5. Using fetches

```
>>> a = tf.placeholder(tf.float32, shape=(1,))
>>> b = tf.placeholder(tf.float32, shape=(1,))
>>> c = a + b
>>> with tf.Session() as sess:
        c_eval = sess.run(c, {a: [1.], b: [2.]})
        print(c_eval)
[ 3.]
```

Name scopes

In complicated TensorFlow programs, there will be many tensors, variables, and placeholders defined throughout the program. `tf.name_scope(name)` provides a simple scoping mechanism for managing these collections of variables (Example 3-6). All computational graph elements created within the scope of a `tf.name_scope(name)` call will have `name` prepended to their names.

This organizational tool is most useful when combined with TensorBoard, since it aids the visualization system in automatically grouping graph elements within the same name scope. You will learn more about TensorBoard further in the next section.

Example 3-6. Using namescopes to organize placeholders

```
>>> N = 5
>>> with tf.name_scope("placeholders"):
        x = tf.placeholder(tf.float32, (N, 1))
        y = tf.placeholder(tf.float32, (N,))
>>> x
<tf.Tensor 'placeholders/Placeholder:0' shape=(5, 1) dtype=float32>
```

Optimizers

The primitives introduced in the last two sections already hint at how machine learning is done in TensorFlow. You have learned how to add placeholders for datapoints and labels and how to use tensorial operations to define the loss function. The missing piece is that you still don't know how to perform gradient descent using TensorFlow.

While it is in fact possible to define optimization algorithms such as gradient descent directly in Python using TensorFlow primitives, TensorFlow provides a collection of optimization algorithms in the `tf.train` module. These algorithms can be added as nodes to the TensorFlow computation graph.

Which optimizer should I use?

There are many possible optimizers available in `tf.train`. For a short preview, this list includes `tf.train.GradientDescentOptim izer`, `tf.train.MomentumOptimizer`, `tf.train.AdagradOptim izer`, `tf.train.AdamOptimizer`, and many more. What's the difference between these various optimizers?

Almost all of these optimizers are based on the idea of gradient descent. Recall the simple gradient descent rule we previously introduced:

$$W = W - \alpha \nabla W$$

Mathematically, this update rule is primitive. There are a variety of mathematical tricks that researchers have discovered that enable faster optimization without using too much extra computation. In general, `tf.train.AdamOptimizer` is a good default that is relatively robust. (Many optimizer methods are very sensitive to hyperparameter choice. It's better for beginners to avoid trickier methods until they have a good grasp of the behavior of different optimization algorithms.)

Example 3-7 is a short bit of code that adds an optimizer to the computation graph that minimizes a predefined loss `l`.

Example 3-7. Adding an Adam optimizer to TensorFlow computation graph

```
learning_rate = .001
with tf.name_scope("optim"):
  train_op = tf.train.AdamOptimizer(learning_rate).minimize(l)
```

Taking gradients with TensorFlow

We mentioned previously that it is possible to directly implement gradient descent algorithms in TensorFlow. While most use cases don't need to reimplement the contents of `tf.train`, it can be useful to look at gradient values directly for debugging purposes. `tf.gradients` provides a useful tool for doing so (Example 3-8).

Example 3-8. Taking gradients directly

```
>>> W = tf.Variable((3,))
>>> l = tf.reduce_sum(W)
>>> gradW = tf.gradients(l, W)
>>> gradW
[<tf.Tensor 'gradients/Sum_grad/Tile:0' shape=(1,) dtype=int32>]
```

This code snippet symbolically pulls down the gradients of loss l with respect to learnable parameter (tf.Variable) W. tf.gradients returns a list of the desired gradients. Note that the gradients are themselves tensors! TensorFlow performs symbolic differentiation, which means that gradients themselves are parts of the computational graph. One neat side effect of TensorFlow's symbolic gradients is that it's possible to stack derivatives in TensorFlow. This can sometimes be useful for more advanced algorithms.

Summaries and file writers for TensorBoard

Gaining a visual understanding of the structure of a tensorial program can be very useful. The TensorFlow team provides the TensorBoard package for this purpose. TensorBoard starts a web server (on localhost by default) that displays various useful visualizations of a TensorFlow program. However, in order for TensorFlow programs to be inspected with TensorBoard, programmers must manually write logging statements. tf.train.FileWriter() specifies the logging directory for a TensorBoard program and tf.summary writes summaries of various TensorFlow variables to the specified logging directory. In this chapter, we will only use tf.summary.scalar, which summarizes a scalar quantity, to track the value of the loss function. tf.summary.merge_all() is a useful logging aid that merges multiple summaries into a single summary for convenience.

The code snippet in Example 3-9 adds a summary for the loss and specifies a logging directory.

Example 3-9. Adding a summary for the loss

```
with tf.name_scope("summaries"):
  tf.summary.scalar("loss", l)
  merged = tf.summary.merge_all()

train_writer = tf.summary.FileWriter('/tmp/lr-train', tf.get_default_graph())
```

Training models with TensorFlow

Suppose now that we have specified placeholders for datapoints and labels, and have defined a loss with tensorial operations. We have added an optimizer node train_op to the computational graph, which we can use to perform gradient descent steps (while we may actually use a different optimizer, we will refer to updates as gradient descent for convenience). How can we iteratively perform gradient descent to learn on this dataset?

The simple answer is that we use a Python for-loop. In each iteration, we use `sess.run()` to fetch the `train_op` along with the merged summary op `merged` and the loss `l` from the graph. We feed all datapoints and labels into `sess.run()` using a feed dictionary.

The code snippet in Example 3-10 demonstrates this simple learning method. Note that we don't make use of minibatches for pedagogical simplicity. Code in following chapters will use minibatches when training on larger datasets.

Example 3-10. A simple example of training a model

```
n_steps = 1000
with tf.Session() as sess:
  sess.run(tf.global_variables_initializer())
  # Train model
  for i in range(n_steps):
    feed_dict = {x: x_np, y: y_np}
    _, summary, loss = sess.run([train_op, merged, l], feed_dict=feed_dict)
    print("step %d, loss: %f" % (i, loss))
    train_writer.add_summary(summary, i)
```

Training Linear and Logistic Models in TensorFlow

This section ties together all the TensorFlow concepts introduced in the previous section to train linear and logistic regression models upon the toy datasets we introduced previously in the chapter.

Linear Regression in TensorFlow

In this section, we will provide code to define a linear regression model in TensorFlow and learn its weights. This task is straightforward and you can do it without TensorFlow easily. Nevertheless, it's a good exercise to do in TensorFlow since it will bring together the new concepts that we have introduced throughout the chapter.

Defining and training linear regression in TensorFlow

The model for a linear regression is straightforward:

$$y = wx + b$$

Here w and b are the weights we wish to learn. We transform these weights into `tf.Variable` objects. We then use tensorial operations to construct the L^2 loss:

$$\mathcal{L}(x, y) = (y - wx - b)^2$$

The code in Example 3-11 implements these mathematical operations in TensorFlow. It also uses `tf.name_scope` to group various operations, and adds a `tf.train.AdamOp timizer` for learning and `tf.summary` operations for TensorBoard usage.

Example 3-11. Defining a linear regression model

```
# Generate tensorflow graph
with tf.name_scope("placeholders"):
  x = tf.placeholder(tf.float32, (N, 1))
  y = tf.placeholder(tf.float32, (N,))
with tf.name_scope("weights"):
  # Note that x is a scalar, so W is a single learnable weight.
  W = tf.Variable(tf.random_normal((1, 1)))
  b = tf.Variable(tf.random_normal((1,)))
with tf.name_scope("prediction"):
  y_pred = tf.matmul(x, W) + b
with tf.name_scope("loss"):
  l = tf.reduce_sum((y - y_pred)**2)
# Add training op
with tf.name_scope("optim"):
  # Set learning rate to .001 as recommended above.
  train_op = tf.train.AdamOptimizer(.001).minimize(l)
with tf.name_scope("summaries"):
  tf.summary.scalar("loss", l)
  merged = tf.summary.merge_all()

train_writer = tf.summary.FileWriter('/tmp/lr-train', tf.get_default_graph())
```

Example 3-12 then trains this model as discussed previously (without using mini-batches).

Example 3-12. Training the linear regression model

```
n_steps = 1000
with tf.Session() as sess:
  sess.run(tf.global_variables_initializer())
  # Train model
  for i in range(n_steps):
    feed_dict = {x: x_np, y: y_np}
    _, summary, loss = sess.run([train_op, merged, l], feed_dict=feed_dict)
    print("step %d, loss: %f" % (i, loss))
    train_writer.add_summary(summary, i)
```

All code for this example is provided in the GitHub repository (*https://github.com/ matroid/dlwithtf*) associated with this book. We encourage all readers to run the full script for the linear regression example to gain a firsthand sense for how the learning algorithm functions. The example is small enough that readers will not need access to any special-purpose computing hardware to run.

Taking Gradients for Linear Regression

The equation for the linear system we're modeling is $y = wx + b$ where w, b are the learnable weights. As we mentioned previously, the loss for this system is $\mathcal{L} = (y - wx - b)^2$. Some matrix calculus can be used to compute the gradients of the learnable parameters directly for w:

$$\nabla w = \frac{\partial \mathcal{L}}{\partial w} = -2(y - wx - b)x^T$$

and for b

$$\nabla b = \frac{\partial \mathcal{L}}{\partial b} = -2(y - wx - b)$$

We place these equations here only for reference for curious readers. We will not attempt to systematically teach how to take the derivatives of the loss functions we encounter in this book. However, we will note that for complicated systems, taking the derivative of the loss function by hand helps build up an intuition for how the deep network learns. This intuition can serve as a powerful guide for the designer, so we encourage advanced readers to pursue this topic on their own.

Visualizing linear regression models with TensorBoard

The model defined in the previous section uses `tf.summary.FileWriter` to write logs to a logging directory */tmp/lr-train*. We can invoke TensorBoard on this logging directory with the command in Example 3-13 (TensorBoard is installed by default with TensorFlow).

Example 3-13. Invoking TensorBoard

```
tensorboard --logdir=/tmp/lr-train
```

This command will start TensorBoard on a port attached to localhost. Use your browser to open this port. The TensorBoard screen will look something like Figure 3-8. (The precise appearance may vary depending on your version of Tensor-Board.)

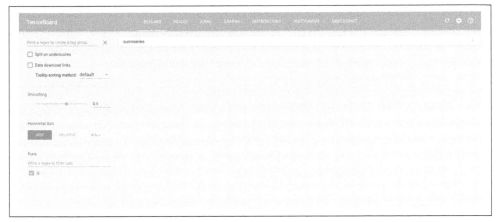

Figure 3-8. Screenshot of TensorBoard panel.

Navigate to the Graphs tab, and you will see a visualization of the TensorFlow architecture we have defined as illustrated in Figure 3-9.

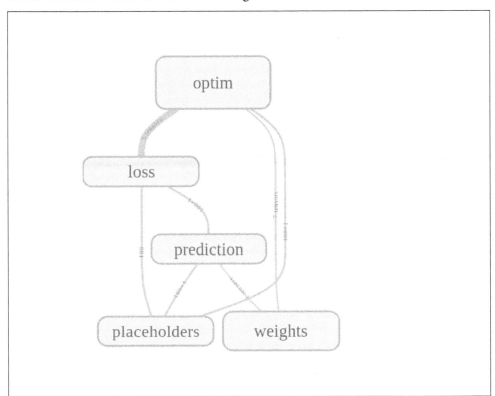

Figure 3-9. Visualization of linear regression architecture in TensorBoard.

Note that this visualization has grouped all computational graph elements belonging to various `tf.name_scopes`. Different groups are connected according to their dependencies in the computational graph. You can expand all of the grouped elements to view their contents. Figure 3-10 illustrates the expanded architecture.

As you can see, there are many hidden nodes that suddenly become visible! Tensor-Flow functions like `tf.train.AdamOptimizer` often hide many internal variables under a `tf.name_scope` of their own. Expanding in TensorBoard provides an easy way to peer underneath the hood to see what the system is actually creating. Although the visualization looks quite complex, most of these details are under the hood and not anything you need to worry about just yet.

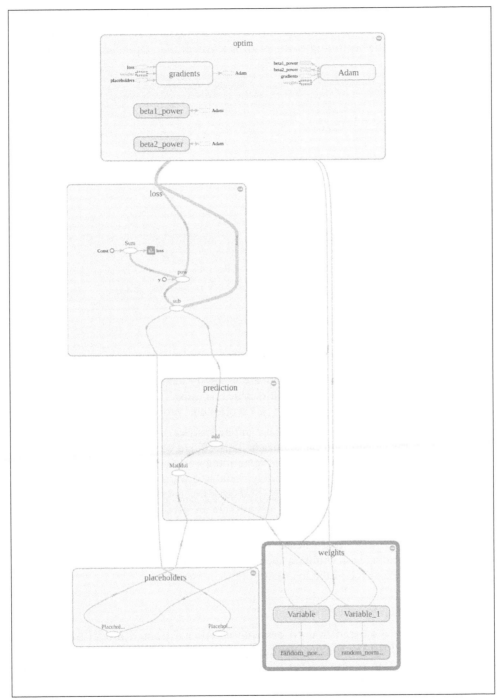

Figure 3-10. Expanded visualization of architecture.

Navigate back to the Home tab and open the Summaries section. You should now see a loss curve that looks something like Figure 3-11. Note the smooth falling shape. The loss falls rapidly at the beginning as the prior is learned, then tapers off and settles.

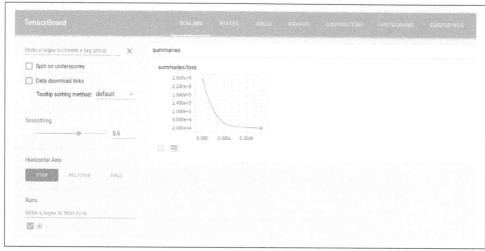

Figure 3-11. Viewing the loss curve in TensorBoard.

Visual and Nonvisual Debugging Styles

Is using a tool like TensorBoard necessary to get good use out of a system like TensorFlow? It depends. Is using a GUI or an interactive debugger necessary to be a professional programmer?

Different programmers have different styles. Some will find that the visualization capabilities of TensorBoard come to form a critical part of their tensorial programming workflows. Others will find that TensorBoard isn't terribly useful and will make greater use of print-statement debugging. Both styles of tensorial programming and debugging are valid, just as there are great programmers who swear by debuggers and others who loathe them.

In general, TensorBoard is quite useful for debugging and for building basic intuition about the dataset at hand. We recommend that you follow the style that works best for you.

Metrics for evaluating regression models

So far, we haven't discussed how to evaluate whether a trained model has actually learned anything. The first tool for evaluating whether a model has trained is by looking at the loss curve to ensure it has a reasonable shape. You learned how to do this in the previous section. What's the next thing to try?

We now want you to look at *metrics* associated with the model. A metric is a tool for comparing predicted labels to true labels. For regression problems, there are two common metrics: R^2 and RMSE (root-mean-squared error). The R^2 is a measure of the correlation between two variables that takes values between +1 and 0. +1 indicates perfect correlation, while 0 indicates no correlation. Mathematically, the R^2 for two datasets X and Y is defined as

$$R^2 = \frac{\text{cov}(X, Y)^2}{\sigma_X^2 \sigma_Y^2}$$

Where $\text{cov}(X, Y)$ is the covariance of X and Y, a measure of how the two datasets jointly vary, while σ_X and σ_Y are standard deviations, measures of how much each set individually varies. Intuitively, the R^2 measures how much of the independent variation in each set can be explained by their joint variation.

Multiple Types of R^2!

Note that there are two common definitions of R^2 used in practice. A common beginner (and expert) mistake is to confuse the two definitions. In this book, we will always use the squared Pearson correlation coefficient (Figure 3-12). The other definition is called the coefficient of determination. This other R^2 is often much more confusing to deal with since it doesn't have a lower bound of 0 like the squared Pearson correlation does.

In Figure 3-12, predicted and true values are highly correlated with an R^2 of nearly 1. It looks like learning has done a wonderful job on this system and succeeded in learning the true rule. *Not so fast.* You will note that the scale on the two axes in the figure isn't the same! It turns out that R^2 doesn't penalize for differences in scale. In order to understand what's happened on this system, we need to consider an alternate metric in Figure 3-13.

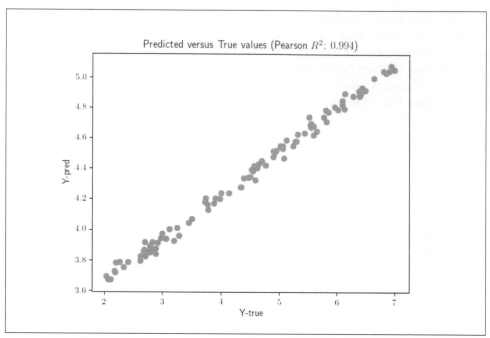

Figure 3-12. Plotting the Pearson correlation coefficient.

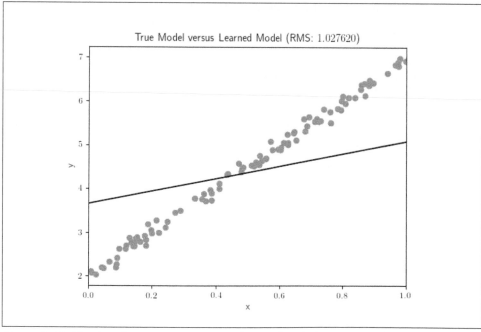

Figure 3-13. Plotting the root-mean-squared error (RMSE).

The RMSE is a measure of the average difference between predicted values and true values. In Figure 3-13 we plot predicted values and true labels as two separate functions using datapoints x as our x-axis. Note that the line learned isn't the true function! The RMSE is relatively high and diagnoses the error, unlike the R^2, which didn't pick up on this error.

What happened on this system? Why didn't TensorFlow learn the correct function despite being trained to convergence? This example provides a good illustration of one of the weaknesses of gradient descent algorithms. There is no guarantee of finding the true solution! The gradient descent algorithm can get trapped in *local minima*. That is, it can find solutions that look good, but are not in fact the lowest minima of the loss function $\mathscr{L}$.

Why use gradient descent at all then? For simple systems, it is indeed often better to avoid gradient descent and use other algorithms that have stronger performance guarantees. However, on complicated systems, such as those we will show you in later chapters, there do not yet exist alternative algorithms that perform better than gradient descent. We encourage you to remember this fact as we proceed further into deep learning.

Logistic Regression in TensorFlow

In this section, we will define a simple classifier using TensorFlow. It's worth first considering what the equation is for a classifier. The mathematical trick that is commonly used is exploiting the sigmoid function. The sigmoid, plotted in Figure 3-14, commonly denoted by σ, is a function from the real numbers $\mathbb{R}$ to $(0, 1)$. This property is convenient since we can interpret the output of a sigmoid as probability of an event happening. (The trick of converting discrete events into continuous values is a recurring theme in machine learning.)

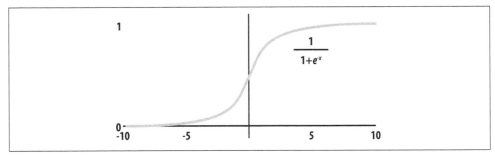

Figure 3-14. Plotting the sigmoid function.

The equations for predicting the probabilities of a discrete 0/1 variable follow. These equations define a simple logistic regression model:

$$y_0 = \sigma(wx + b)$$

$$y_1 = 1 - \sigma(wx + b)$$

TensorFlow provides utility functions to compute the cross-entropy loss for sigmoidal values. The simplest of these functions is `tf.nn.sigmoid_cross_entropy_with_logits`. (A logit is the inverse of the sigmoid. In practice, this simply means passing the argument to the sigmoid, $wx + b$, directly to TensorFlow instead of the sigmoidal value $\sigma(wx + b)$ itself). We recommend using TensorFlow's implementation instead of manually defining the cross-entropy, since there are tricky numerical issues that arise when computing the cross-entropy loss.

Example 3-14 defines a simple logistic regression model in TensorFlow.

Example 3-14. Defining a simple logistic regression model

```
# Generate tensorflow graph
with tf.name_scope("placeholders"):
  # Note that our datapoints x are 2-dimensional.
  x = tf.placeholder(tf.float32, (N, 2))
  y = tf.placeholder(tf.float32, (N,))
with tf.name_scope("weights"):
  W = tf.Variable(tf.random_normal((2, 1)))
  b = tf.Variable(tf.random_normal((1,)))
with tf.name_scope("prediction"):
  y_logit = tf.squeeze(tf.matmul(x, W) + b)
  # the sigmoid gives the class probability of 1
  y_one_prob = tf.sigmoid(y_logit)
  # Rounding P(y=1) will give the correct prediction.
  y_pred = tf.round(y_one_prob)

with tf.name_scope("loss"):
  # Compute the cross-entropy term for each datapoint
  entropy = tf.nn.sigmoid_cross_entropy_with_logits(logits=y_logit, labels=y)
  # Sum all contributions
  l = tf.reduce_sum(entropy)
with tf.name_scope("optim"):
  train_op = tf.train.AdamOptimizer(.01).minimize(l)

  train_writer = tf.summary.FileWriter('/tmp/logistic-train', tf.get_default_graph())
```

The training code for this model in Example 3-15 is identical to that for the linear regression model.

Example 3-15. Training a logistic regression model

```
n_steps = 1000
with tf.Session() as sess:
  sess.run(tf.global_variables_initializer())
  # Train model
  for i in range(n_steps):
    feed_dict = {x: x_np, y: y_np}
    _, summary, loss = sess.run([train_op, merged, l], feed_dict=feed_dict)
    print("loss: %f" % loss)
    train_writer.add_summary(summary, i)
```

Visualizing logistic regression models with TensorBoard

As before, you can use TensorBoard to visualize the model. Start by visualizing the
loss function as shown in Figure 3-15. Note that as before, the loss function follows a
neat pattern. There is a steep drop in the loss followed by a gradual smoothening.

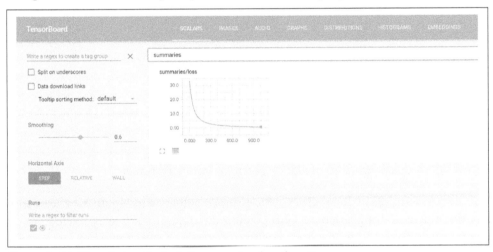

Figure 3-15. Visualizing the logistic regression loss function.

You can also view the TensorFlow graph in TensorBoard. Since the scoping structure
was similar to that used for linear regression, the simplified graph doesn't display
much differently, as shown in Figure 3-16.

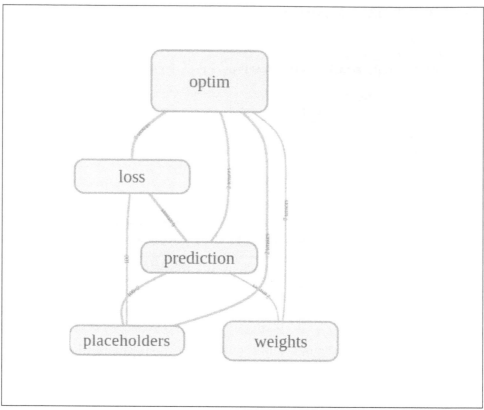

Figure 3-16. Visualizing the computation graph for logistic regression.

However, if you expand the nodes in this grouped graph, as in Figure 3-17, you will find that the underlying computational graph is different. In particular, the loss function is quite different from that used for linear regression (as it should be).

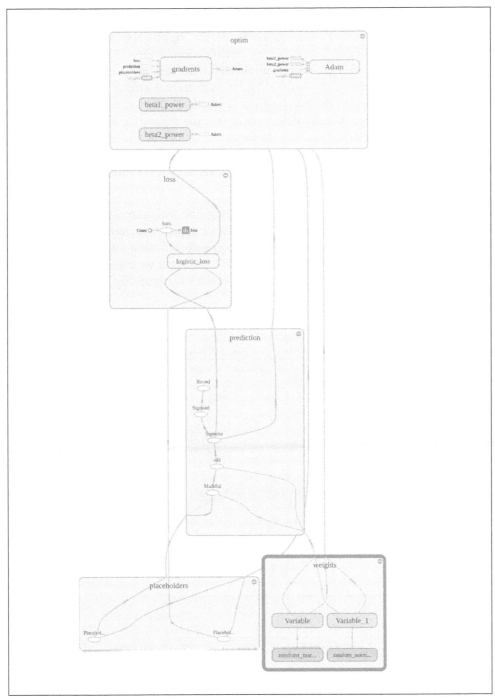

Figure 3-17. The expanded computation graph for logistic regression.

Metrics for evaluating classification models

Now that you have trained a classification model for logistic regression, you need to learn about metrics suitable for evaluating classification models. Although the equations for logistic regression are more complicated than they are for linear regression, the basic evaluation metrics are simpler. The classification accuracy simply checks for the fraction of datapoints that are classified correctly by the learned model. In fact, with a little more effort, it is possible to back out the *separating line* learned by the logistic regression model. This line displays the cutoff boundary the model has learned to separate positive and negative examples. (We leave the derivation of this line from the logistic regression equations as an exercise for the interested reader. The solution is in the code for this section.)

We display the learned classes and the separating line in Figure 3-18. Note that the line neatly separates the positive and negative examples and has perfect accuracy (1.0). This result raises an interesting point. Regression is often a harder problem to solve than classification. There are many possible lines that would neatly separate the datapoints in Figure 3-18, but only one that would have perfectly matched the data for the linear regression.

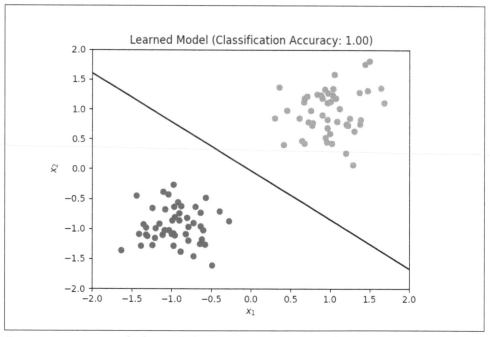

Figure 3-18. Viewing the learned classes and separating line for logistic regression.

Review

In this chapter, we've shown you how to build and train some simple learning systems in TensorFlow. We started by reviewing some foundational mathematical concepts including loss functions and gradient descent. We then introduced you to some new TensorFlow concepts such as placeholders, scopes, and TensorBoard. We ended the chapter with case studies that trained linear and logistic regression systems on toy datasets. We covered a lot of material in this chapter, and it's OK if you haven't yet internalized everything. The foundational material introduced here will be used throughout the remainder of this book.

In Chapter 4, we will introduce you to your first deep learning model and to fully connected networks, and will show you how to define and train fully connected networks in TensorFlow. In following chapters, we will explore more complicated deep networks, but all of these architectures will use the same fundamental learning principles introduced in this chapter.

Fully Connected Deep Networks

This chapter will introduce you to fully connected deep networks. Fully connected networks are the workhorses of deep learning, used for thousands of applications. The major advantage of fully connected networks is that they are "structure agnostic." That is, no special assumptions need to be made about the input (for example, that the input consists of images or videos). We will make use of this generality to use fully connected deep networks to address a problem in chemical modeling later in this chapter.

We delve briefly into the mathematical theory underpinning fully connected networks. In particular, we explore the concept that fully connected architectures are "universal approximators" capable of learning any function. This concept provides an explanation of the generality of fully connected architectures, but comes with many caveats that we discuss at some depth.

While being structure agnostic makes fully connected networks very broadly applicable, such networks do tend to have weaker performance than special-purpose networks tuned to the structure of a problem space. We will discuss some of the limitations of fully connected architectures later in this chapter.

What Is a Fully Connected Deep Network?

A fully connected neural network consists of a series of fully connected layers. A fully connected layer is a function from $\mathbb{R}^m$ to $\mathbb{R}^n$. Each output dimension depends on each input dimension. Pictorially, a fully connected layer is represented as follows in Figure 4-1.

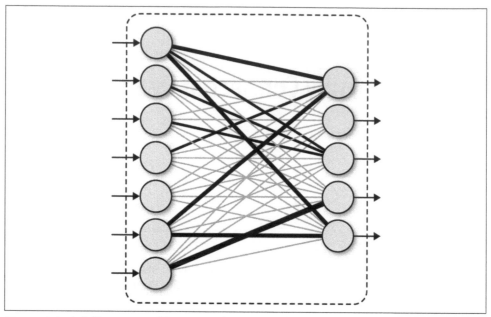

Figure 4-1. A fully connected layer in a deep network.

Let's dig a little deeper into what the mathematical form of a fully connected network is. Let $x \in \mathbb{R}^m$ represent the input to a fully connected layer. Let $y_i \in \mathbb{R}$ be the i-th output from the fully connected layer. Then $y_i \in \mathbb{R}$ is computed as follows:

$$y_i = \sigma(w_1 x_1 + \cdots + w_m x_m)$$

Here, σ is a nonlinear function (for now, think of σ as the sigmoid function introduced in the previous chapter), and the w_i are learnable parameters in the network. The full output y is then

$$y = \begin{pmatrix} \sigma(w_{1,1} x_1 + \cdots + w_{1,m} x_m) \\ \vdots \\ \sigma(w_{n,1} x_1 + \cdots + w_{n,m} x_m) \end{pmatrix}$$

Note that it's directly possible to stack fully connected networks. A network with multiple fully connected networks is often called a "deep" network as depicted in Figure 4-2.

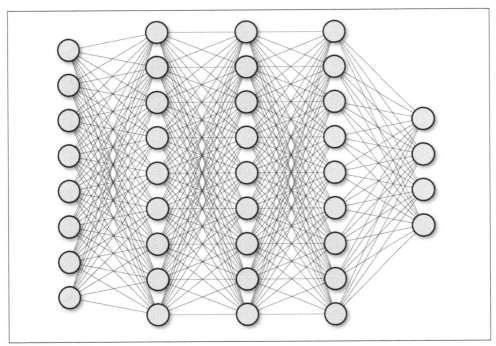

Figure 4-2. A multilayer deep fully connected network.

As a quick implementation note, note that the equation for a single neuron looks very similar to a dot-product of two vectors (recall the discussion of tensor basics). For a layer of neurons, it is often convenient for efficiency purposes to compute y as a matrix multiply:

$$y = \sigma(wx)$$

where sigma is a matrix in $\mathbb{R}^{n \times m}$ and the nonlinearity σ is applied componentwise.

"Neurons" in Fully Connected Networks

The nodes in fully connected networks are commonly referred to as "neurons." Consequently, elsewhere in the literature, fully connected networks will commonly be referred to as "neural networks." This nomenclature is largely a historical accident.

In the 1940s, Warren S. McCulloch and Walter Pitts published a first mathematical model of the brain that argued that neurons were capable of computing arbitrary functions on Boolean quantities. Successors to this work slightly refined this logical model by making mathematical "neurons" continuous functions that varied between zero and one. If the inputs of these functions grew large enough, the neuron "fired" (took on the value one), else was quiescent. With the addition of adjustable weights, this description matches the previous equations.

Is this how a real neuron behaves? Of course not! A real neuron (Figure 4-3) is an exceedingly complex engine, with over 100 trillion atoms, and tens of thousands of different signaling proteins capable of responding to varying signals. A microprocessor is a better analogy for a neuron than a one-line equation.

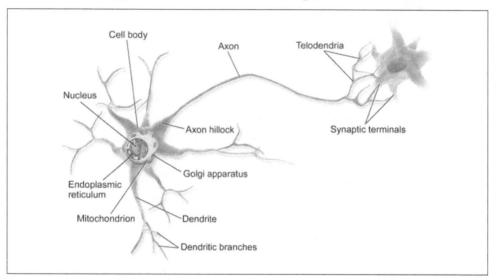

Figure 4-3. A more biologically accurate representation of a neuron.

In many ways, this disconnect between biological neurons and artificial neurons is quite unfortunate. Uninitiated experts read breathless press releases claiming artificial neural networks with billions of "neurons" have been created (while the brain has only 100 billion biological neurons) and reasonably come away believing scientists are close to creating human-level intelligences. Needless to say, state of the art in deep learning is decades (or centuries) away from such an achievement.

As you read further about deep learning, you may come across overhyped claims about artificial intelligence. Don't be afraid to call out these statements. Deep learning in its current form is a set of techniques for solving calculus problems on fast hardware. It is not a precursor to *Terminator* (Figure 4-4).

Figure 4-4. Unfortunately (or perhaps fortunately), this book won't teach you to build a Terminator!

AI Winters

Artificial intelligence has gone through multiple rounds of boom-and-bust development. This cyclical development is characteristic of the field. Each new advance in learning spawns a wave of optimism in which prophets claim that human-level (or superhuman) intelligences are incipient. After a few years, no such intelligences manifest, and disappointed funders pull out. The resulting period is called an AI winter.

There have been multiple AI winters so far. As a thought exercise, we encourage you to consider when the next AI winter will happen. The current wave of deep learning progress has solved many more practical problems than any previous wave of advances. Is it possible AI has finally taken off and exited the boom-and-bust cycle or do you think we're in for the "Great Depression" of AI soon?

Learning Fully Connected Networks with Backpropagation

The first version of a fully connected neural network was the Perceptron, (Figure 4-5), created by Frank Rosenblatt in the 1950s. These perceptrons are identical to the "neurons" we introduced in the previous equations.

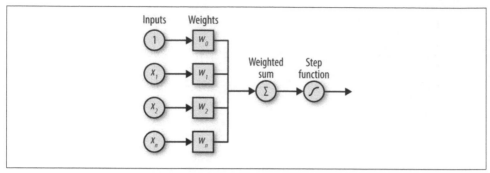

Figure 4-5. A diagrammatic representation of the perceptron.

Perceptrons were trained by a custom "perceptron" rule. While they were moderately useful solving simple problems, perceptrons were fundamentally limited. The book *Perceptrons* by Marvin Minsky and Seymour Papert from the end of the 1960s proved that simple perceptrons were incapable of learning the XOR function. Figure 4-6 illustrates the proof of this statement.

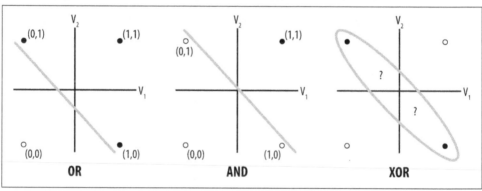

Figure 4-6. The perceptron's linear rule can't learn the perceptron.

This problem was overcome with the invention of the multilayer perceptron (another name for a deep fully connected network). This invention was a formidable achievement, since earlier simple learning algorithms couldn't learn deep networks effectively. The "credit assignment" problem stumped them; how does an algorithm decide which neuron learns what?

The full solution to this problem requires backpropagation. Backpropagation is a generalized rule for learning the weights of neural networks. Unfortunately, complicated explanations of backpropagation are epidemic in the literature. This situation is unfortunate since backpropagation is simply another word for automatic differentiation.

Let's suppose that $f(\theta, x)$ is a function that represents a deep fully connected network. Here x is the inputs to the fully connected network and θ is the learnable weights. Then the backpropagation algorithm simply computes $\frac{\partial f}{\partial \theta}$. The practical complexities arise in implementing backpropagation for all possible functions f that arise in practice. Luckily for us, TensorFlow takes care of this already!

Universal Convergence Theorem

The preceding discussion has touched on the ideas that deep fully connected networks are powerful approximations. McCulloch and Pitts showed that logical networks can code (almost) any Boolean function. Rosenblatt's Perceptron was the continuous analog of McCulloch and Pitt's logical functions, but was shown to be fundamentally limited by Minsky and Papert. Multilayer perceptrons looked to solve the limitations of simple perceptrons and empirically seemed capable of learning complex functions. However, it wasn't theoretically clear whether this empirical ability had undiscovered limitations. In 1989, George Cybenko demonstrated that multilayer perceptrons were capable of representing arbitrary functions. This demonstration provided a considerable boost to the claims of generality for fully connected networks as a learning architecture, partially explaining their continued popularity.

However, if both backpropagation and fully connected network theory were understood in the late 1980s, why didn't "deep" learning become more popular earlier? A large part of this failure was due to computational limitations; learning fully connected networks took an exorbitant amount of computing power. In addition, deep networks were very difficult to train due to lack of understanding about good hyperparameters. As a result, alternative learning algorithms such as SVMs that had lower computational requirements became more popular. The recent surge in popularity in deep learning is partly due to the increased availability of better computing hardware that enables faster computing, and partly due to increased understanding of good training regimens that enable stable learning.

Is Universal Approximation That Surprising?

Universal approximation properties are more common in mathematics than one might expect. For example, the Stone-Weierstrass theorem proves that any continuous function on a closed interval can be a suitable polynomial function. Loosening our criteria further, Taylor series and Fourier series themselves offer some universal approximation capabilities (within their domains of convergence). The fact that universal convergence is fairly common in mathematics provides partial justification for the empirical observation that there are many slight variants of fully connected networks that seem to share a universal approximation property.

Universal Approximation Doesn't Mean Universal Learning!

A critical subtlety exists in the universal approximation theorem. The fact that a fully connected network can represent any function doesn't mean that backpropagation can learn any function! One of the major limitations of backpropagation is that there is no guarantee the fully connected network "converges"; that is, finds the best available solution of a learning problem. This critical theoretical gap has left generations of computer scientists queasy with neural networks. Even today, many academics will prefer to work with alternative algorithms that have stronger theoretical guarantees.

Empirical research has yielded many practical tricks that allow backpropagation to find good solutions for problems. We will go into many of these tricks in significant depth in the remainder of this chapter. For the practicing data scientist, the universal approximation theorem isn't something to take too seriously. It's reassuring, but the art of deep learning lies in mastering the practical hacks that make learning work.

Why Deep Networks?

A subtlety in the universal approximation theorem is that it in fact holds true for fully connected networks with only one fully connected layer. What then is the use of "deep" learning with multiple fully connected layers? It turns out that this question is still quite controversial in academic and practical circles.

In practice, it seems that deeper networks can sometimes learn richer models on large datasets. (This is only a rule of thumb, however; every practitioner has a bevy of examples where deep fully connected networks don't do well.) This observation has led researchers to hypothesize that deeper networks can represent complex functions "more efficiently." That is, a deeper network may be able to learn more complex functions than shallower networks with the same number of neurons. For example, the ResNet architecture mentioned briefly in the first chapter, with 130 layers, seems to outperform its shallower competitors such as AlexNet. In general, for a fixed neuron budget, stacking deeper leads to better results.

A number of erroneous "proofs" for this "fact" have been given in the literature, but all of them have holes. It seems the question of depth versus width touches on profound concepts in complexity theory (which studies the minimal amount of resources required to solve given computational problems). At present day, it looks like theoretically demonstrating (or disproving) the superiority of deep networks is far outside the ability of our mathematicians.

Training Fully Connected Neural Networks

As we mentioned previously, the theory of fully connected networks falls short of practice. In this section, we will introduce you to a number of empirical observations about fully connected networks that aid practitioners. We strongly encourage you to use our code (introduced later in the chapter) to check our claims for yourself.

Learnable Representations

One way of thinking about fully connected networks is that each fully connected layer effects a transformation of the feature space in which the problem resides. The idea of transforming the representation of a problem to render it more malleable is a very old one in engineering and physics. It follows that deep learning methods are sometimes called "representation learning." (An interesting factoid is that one of the major conferences for deep learning is called the "International Conference on Learning Representations.")

Generations of analysts have used Fourier transforms, Legendre transforms, Laplace transforms, and so on in order to simplify complicated equations and functions to forms more suitable for handwritten analysis. One way of thinking about deep learning networks is that they effect a data-driven transform suited to the problem at hand.

The ability to perform problem-specific transformations can be immensely powerful. Standard transformation techniques couldn't solve problems of image or speech analysis, while deep networks are capable of solving these problems with relative ease due to the inherent flexibility of the learned representations. This flexibility comes with a price: the transformations learned by deep architectures tend to be much less general than mathematical transforms such as the Fourier transform. Nonetheless, having deep transforms in an analytic toolkit can be a powerful problem-solving tool.

There's a reasonable argument that deep learning is simply the first representation learning method that works. In the future, there may well be alternative representation learning methods that supplant deep learning methods.

Activations

We previously introduced the nonlinear function σ as the sigmoidal function. While the sigmoidal is the classical nonlinearity in fully connected networks, in recent years researchers have found that other activations, notably the rectified linear activation (commonly abbreviated ReLU or relu) $\sigma(x) = \max(x, 0)$ work better than the sigmoidal unit. This empirical observation may be due to the *vanishing gradient* problem in deep networks. For the sigmoidal function, the slope is zero for almost all values of its input. As a result, for deeper networks, the gradient would tend to zero. For the ReLU function, the slope is nonzero for a much greater part of input space, allowing nonzero gradients to propagate. Figure 4-7 illustrates sigmoidal and ReLU activations side by side.

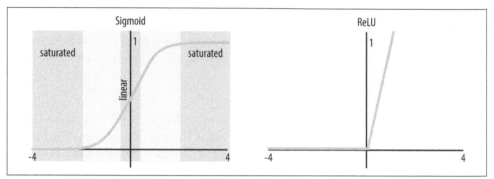

Figure 4-7. Sigmoidal and ReLU activation functions.

Fully Connected Networks Memorize

One of the striking aspects about fully connected networks is that they tend to memorize training data entirely given enough time. As a result, training a fully connected network to "convergence" isn't really a meaningful metric. The network will keep training and learning as long as the user is willing to wait.

For large enough networks, it is quite common for training loss to trend all the way to zero. This empirical observation is one the most practical demonstrations of the universal approximation capabilities of fully connected networks. Note however, that training loss trending to zero does not mean that the network has learned a more powerful model. It's rather likely that the model has started to memorize peculiarities of the training set that aren't applicable to any other datapoints.

It's worth digging into what we mean by peculiarities here. One of the interesting properties of high-dimensional statistics is that given a large enough dataset, there will be plenty of spurious correlations and patterns available for the picking. In practice, fully connected networks are entirely capable of finding and utilizing these spurious correlations. Controlling networks and preventing them from misbehaving in this fashion is critical for modeling success.

Regularization

Regularization is the general statistical term for a mathematical operation that limits memorization while promoting generalizable learning. There are many different types of regularization available, which we will cover in the next few sections.

Not Your Statistician's Regularization

Regularization has a long history in the statistical literature, with entire sheaves of papers written on the topic. Unfortunately, only some of this classical analysis carries over to deep networks. The linear models used widely in statistics can behave very differently from deep networks, and many of the intuitions built in that setting can be downright wrong for deep networks.

The first rule for working with deep networks, especially for readers with prior statistical modeling experience, is to trust empirical results over past intuition. Don't assume that past knowledge about techniques such as LASSO has much meaning for modeling deep architectures. Rather, set up an experiment to methodically test your proposed idea. We will return at greater depth to this methodical experimentation process in the next chapter.

Dropout

Dropout is a form of regularization that randomly drops some proportion of the nodes that feed into a fully connected layer (Figure 4-8). Here, dropping a node means that its contribution to the corresponding activation function is set to 0. Since there is no activation contribution, the gradients for dropped nodes drop to zero as well.

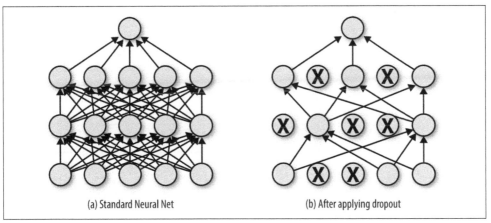

(a) Standard Neural Net   (b) After applying dropout

Figure 4-8. Dropout randomly drops neurons from a network while training. Empirically, this technique often provides powerful regularization for network training.

The nodes to be dropped are chosen at random during each step of gradient descent. The underlying design principle is that the network will be forced to avoid "co-adaptation." Briefly, we will explain what co-adaptation is and how it arises in non-regularized deep architectures. Suppose that one neuron in a deep network has learned a useful representation. Then other neurons deeper in the network will rapidly learn to depend on that particular neuron for information. This process will render the network brittle since the network will depend excessively on the features learned by that neuron, which might represent a quirk of the dataset, instead of learning a general rule.

Dropout prevents this type of co-adaptation because it will no longer be possible to depend on the presence of single powerful neurons (since that neuron might drop randomly during training). As a result, other neurons will be forced to "pick up the slack" and learn useful representations as well. The theoretical argument follows that this process should result in stronger learned models.

In practice, dropout has a pair of empirical effects. First, it prevents the network from memorizing the training data; with dropout, training loss will no longer tend rapidly toward 0, even for very large deep networks. Next, dropout tends to slightly boost the predictive power of the model on new data. This effect often holds for a wide range of datasets, part of the reason that dropout is recognized as a powerful invention, and not just a simple statistical hack.

You should note that dropout should be turned off when making predictions. Forgetting to turn off dropout can cause predictions to be much noisier and less useful than they would be otherwise. We discuss how to handle dropout for training and predictions correctly later in the chapter.

How Can Big Networks Not Overfit?

One of the most jarring points for classically trained statisticians is that deep networks may routinely have more internal degrees of freedom than are present in the training data. In classical statistics, the presence of these extra degrees of freedom would render the model useless, since there will no longer exist a guarantee that the model learned is "real" in the classical sense.

How then can a deep network with millions of parameters learn meaningful results on datasets with only thousands of exemplars? Dropout can make a big difference here and prevent brute memorization. But, there's also a deeper unexplained mystery in that deep networks will tend to learn useful facts even in the absence of dropout. This tendency might be due to some quirk of backpropagation or fully connected network structure that we don't yet understand.

Early stopping

As mentioned, fully connected networks tend to memorize whatever is put before them. As a result, it's often useful in practice to track the performance of the network on a held-out "validation" set and stop the network when performance on this validation set starts to go down. This simple technique is known as early stopping.

In practice, early stopping can be quite tricky to implement. As you will see, loss curves for deep networks can vary quite a bit in the course of normal training. Devising a rule that separates healthy variation from a marked downward trend can take significant effort. In practice, many practitioners just train models with differing (fixed) numbers of epochs, and choose the model that does best on the validation set. Figure 4-9 illustrates how training and test set accuracy typically change as training proceeds.

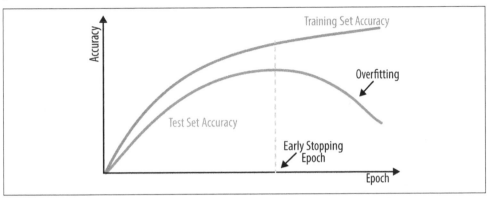

Figure 4-9. Model accuracy on training and test sets as training proceeds.

We will dig more into proper methods for working with validation sets in the following chapter.

Weight regularization

A classical regularization technique drawn from the statistical literature penalizes learned weights that grow large. Following notation from the previous chapter, let $\mathcal{L}(x, y)$ denote the loss function for a particular model and let θ denote the learnable parameters of this model. Then the regularized loss function is defined by

$$\mathcal{L}'(x, y) = \mathcal{L}(x, y) + \alpha \| \theta \|$$

where $\| \theta \|$ is the weight penalty and α is a tunable parameter. The two common choices for penalty are the L^1 and L^2 penalties

$$\| \theta \|_2 = \sqrt{\sum_{i = 1}^{N} \theta_i^2}$$

$$\| \theta \|_1 = \sum_{i = 1}^{N} |\theta_i|$$

where $\| \theta \|_2$ and $\| \theta \|_1$ denote the L^1 and L^2 penalties, respectively. From personal experience, these penalties tend to be less useful for deep models than dropout and early stopping. Some practitioners still make use of weight regularization, so it's worth understanding how to apply these penalties when tuning deep networks.

Training Fully Connected Networks

Training fully connected networks requires a few tricks beyond those you have seen so far in this book. First, unlike in the previous chapters, we will train models on larger datasets. For these datasets, we will show you how to use minibatches to speed up gradient descent. Second, we will return to the topic of tuning learning rates.

Minibatching

For large datasets (which may not even fit in memory), it isn't feasible to compute gradients on the full dataset at each step. Rather, practitioners often select a small chunk of data (typically 50–500 datapoints) and compute the gradient on these datapoints. This small chunk of data is traditionally called a minibatch.

In practice, minibatching seems to help convergence since more gradient descent steps can be taken with the same amount of compute. The correct size for a minibatch is an empirical question often set with hyperparameter tuning.

Learning rates

The learning rate dictates the amount of importance to give to each gradient descent step. Setting a correct learning rate can be tricky. Many beginning deep-learners set learning rates incorrectly and are surprised to find that their models don't learn or start returning NaNs. This situation has improved significantly with the development of methods such as ADAM that simplify choice of learning rate significantly, but it's worth tweaking the learning rate if models aren't learning anything.

Implementation in TensorFlow

In this section, we will show you how to implement a fully connected network in TensorFlow. We won't need to introduce many new TensorFlow primitives in this section since we have already covered most of the required basics.

Installing DeepChem

In this section, you will use the DeepChem machine learning toolchain for your experiments (full disclosure: one of the authors was the creator of DeepChem). Detailed installation directions (*https://deepchem.io*) for DeepChem can be found online, but briefly the Anaconda installation via the conda tool will likely be most convenient.

Tox21 Dataset

For our modeling case study, we will use a chemical dataset. Toxicologists are very interested in the task of using machine learning to predict whether a given compound will be toxic or not. This task is extremely complicated, since today's science has only a limited understanding of the metabolic processes that happen in a human body. However, biologists and chemists have worked out a limited set of experiments that provide indications of toxicity. If a compound is a "hit" in one of these experiments, it will likely be toxic for a human to ingest. However, these experiments are often costly to run, so data scientists aim to build machine learning models that can predict the outcomes of these experiments on new molecules.

One of the most important toxicological dataset collections is called Tox21. It was released by the NIH and EPA as part of a data science initiative and was used as the dataset in a model building challenge. The winner of this challenge used multitask fully connected networks (a variant of fully connected networks where each network predicts multiple quantities for each datapoint). We will analyze one of the datasets from the Tox21 collection. This dataset consists of a set of 10,000 molecules tested for interaction with the androgen receptor. The data science challenge is to predict whether new molecules will interact with the androgen receptor.

Processing this dataset can be tricky, so we will make use of the MoleculeNet dataset collection curated as part of DeepChem. Each molecule in Tox21 is processed into a bit-vector of length 1024 by DeepChem. Loading the dataset is then a few simple calls into DeepChem (Example 4-1).

Example 4-1. Load the Tox21 dataset

```
import deepchem as dc

_, (train, valid, test), _ = dc.molnet.load_tox21()
train_X, train_y, train_w = train.X, train.y, train.w
valid_X, valid_y, valid_w = valid.X, valid.y, valid.w
test_X, test_y, test_w = test.X, test.y, test.w
```

Here the X variables hold processed feature vectors, y holds labels, and w holds example weights. The labels are binary 1/0 for compounds that interact or don't interact with the androgen receptor. Tox21 holds *imbalanced* datasets, where there are far fewer positive examples than negative examples. w holds recommended per-example weights that give more emphasis to positive examples (increasing the importance of rare examples is a common technique for handling imbalanced datasets). We won't use these weights during training for simplicity. All of these variables are NumPy arrays.

Tox21 has more datasets than we will analyze here, so we need to remove the labels associated with these extra datasets (Example 4-2).

Example 4-2. Remove extra datasets from Tox21

```
# Remove extra tasks
train_y = train_y[:, 0]
valid_y = valid_y[:, 0]
test_y = test_y[:, 0]
train_w = train_w[:, 0]
valid_w = valid_w[:, 0]
test_w = test_w[:, 0]
```

Accepting Minibatches of Placeholders

In the previous chapters, we created placeholders that accepted arguments of fixed size. When dealing with minibatched data, it is often convenient to be able to feed batches of variable size. Suppose that a dataset has 947 elements. Then with a minibatch size of 50, the last batch will have 47 elements. This would cause the code in Chapter 3 to crash. Luckily, TensorFlow has a simple fix to the situation: using None as a dimensional argument to a placeholder allows the placeholder to accept tensors with arbitrary size in that dimension (Example 4-3).

Example 4-3. Defining placeholders that accept minibatches of different sizes

```
d = 1024
with tf.name_scope("placeholders"):
  x = tf.placeholder(tf.float32, (None, d))
  y = tf.placeholder(tf.float32, (None,))
```

Note d is 1024, the dimensionality of our feature vectors.

Implementing a Hidden Layer

The code to implement a hidden layer is very similar to code we've seen in the last chapter for implementing logistic regression, as shown in Example 4-4.

Example 4-4. Defining a hidden layer

```
with tf.name_scope("hidden-layer"):
  W = tf.Variable(tf.random_normal((d, n_hidden)))
  b = tf.Variable(tf.random_normal((n_hidden,)))
  x_hidden = tf.nn.relu(tf.matmul(x, W) + b)
```

We use a `tf.name_scope` to group together introduced variables. Note that we use the matricial form of the fully connected layer. We use the form xW instead of Wx in order to deal more conveniently with a minibatch of input at a time. (As an exercise, try working out the dimensions involved to see why this is so.) Finally, we apply the ReLU nonlinearity with the built-in `tf.nn.relu` activation function.

The remainder of the code for the fully connected layer is quite similar to that used for the logistic regression in the previous chapter. For completeness, we display the full code used to specify the network in Example 4-5. As a quick reminder, the full code for all models covered is available in the GitHub repo associated with this book. We strongly encourage you to try running the code for yourself.

Example 4-5. Defining the fully connected architecture

```
with tf.name_scope("placeholders"):
  x = tf.placeholder(tf.float32, (None, d))
  y = tf.placeholder(tf.float32, (None,))
with tf.name_scope("hidden-layer"):
  W = tf.Variable(tf.random_normal((d, n_hidden)))
  b = tf.Variable(tf.random_normal((n_hidden,)))
  x_hidden = tf.nn.relu(tf.matmul(x, W) + b)
with tf.name_scope("output"):
  W = tf.Variable(tf.random_normal((n_hidden, 1)))
  b = tf.Variable(tf.random_normal((1,)))
  y_logit = tf.matmul(x_hidden, W) + b
  # the sigmoid gives the class probability of 1
  y_one_prob = tf.sigmoid(y_logit)
  # Rounding P(y=1) will give the correct prediction.
  y_pred = tf.round(y_one_prob)
with tf.name_scope("loss"):
  # Compute the cross-entropy term for each datapoint
  y_expand = tf.expand_dims(y, 1)
  entropy = tf.nn.sigmoid_cross_entropy_with_logits(logits=y_logit, labels=y_expand)
  # Sum all contributions
  l = tf.reduce_sum(entropy)

with tf.name_scope("optim"):
  train_op = tf.train.AdamOptimizer(learning_rate).minimize(l)

with tf.name_scope("summaries"):
  tf.summary.scalar("loss", l)
  merged = tf.summary.merge_all()
```

Adding Dropout to a Hidden Layer

TensorFlow takes care of implementing dropout for us in the built-in primitive `tf.nn.dropout(x, keep_prob)`, where `keep_prob` is the probability that any given node is kept. Recall from our earlier discussion that we want to turn on dropout when training and turn off dropout when making predictions. To handle this correctly, we will introduce a new placeholder for `keep_prob`, as shown in Example 4-6.

Example 4-6. Add a placeholder for dropout probability

```
keep_prob = tf.placeholder(tf.float32)
```

During training, we pass in the desired value, often 0.5, but at test time we set keep_prob to 1.0 since we want predictions made with all learned nodes. With this setup, adding dropout to the fully connected network specified in the previous section is simply a single extra line of code (Example 4-7).

Example 4-7. Defining a hidden layer with dropout

```
with tf.name_scope("hidden-layer"):
  W = tf.Variable(tf.random_normal((d, n_hidden)))
  b = tf.Variable(tf.random_normal((n_hidden,)))
  x_hidden = tf.nn.relu(tf.matmul(x, W) + b)
  # Apply dropout
  x_hidden = tf.nn.dropout(x_hidden, keep_prob)
```

Implementing Minibatching

To implement minibatching, we need to pull out a minibatch's worth of data each time we call sess.run. Luckily for us, our features and labels are already in NumPy arrays, and we can make use of NumPy's convenient syntax for slicing portions of arrays (Example 4-8).

Example 4-8. Training on minibatches

```
step = 0
for epoch in range(n_epochs):
  pos = 0
  while pos < N:
    batch_X = train_X[pos:pos+batch_size]
    batch_y = train_y[pos:pos+batch_size]
    feed_dict = {x: batch_X, y: batch_y, keep_prob: dropout_prob}
    _, summary, loss = sess.run([train_op, merged, l], feed_dict=feed_dict)
    print("epoch %d, step %d, loss: %f" % (epoch, step, loss))
    train_writer.add_summary(summary, step)

    step += 1
    pos += batch_size
```

Evaluating Model Accuracy

To evaluate model accuracy, standard practice requires measuring the accuracy of the model on data not used for training (namely the validation set). However, the fact that the data is imbalanced makes this tricky. The classification accuracy metric we used in the previous chapter simply measures the fraction of datapoints that were labeled correctly. However, 95% of data in our dataset is labeled 0 and only 5% are labeled 1. As a result the all-0 model (which labels everything negative) would achieve 95% accuracy! This isn't what we want.

A better choice would be to increase the weights of positive examples so that they count for more. For this purpose, we use the recommended per-example weights from MoleculeNet to compute a weighted classification accuracy where positive samples are weighted 19 times the weight of negative samples. Under this weighted accuracy, the all-0 model would have 50% accuracy, which seems much more reasonable.

For computing the weighted accuracy, we use the function `accuracy_score(true, pred, sample_weight=given_sample_weight)` from `sklearn.metrics`. This function has a keyword argument `sample_weight`, which lets us specify the desired weight for each datapoint. We use this function to compute the weighted metric on both the training and validation sets (Example 4-9).

Example 4-9. Computing a weighted accuracy

```
train_weighted_score = accuracy_score(train_y, train_y_pred, sample_weight=train_w)
print("Train Weighted Classification Accuracy: %f" % train_weighted_score)
valid_weighted_score = accuracy_score(valid_y, valid_y_pred, sample_weight=valid_w)
print("Valid Weighted Classification Accuracy: %f" % valid_weighted_score)
```

While we could reimplement this function ourselves, sometimes it's easier (and less error prone) to use standard functions from the Python data science infrastructure. Learning about this infrastructure and available functions is part of being a practicing data scientist. Now, we can train the model (for 10 epochs in the default setting) and gauge its accuracy:

```
Train Weighted Classification Accuracy: 0.742045
Valid Weighted Classification Accuracy: 0.648828
```

In Chapter 5, we will show you methods to systematically improve this accuracy and tune our fully connected model more carefully.

Using TensorBoard to Track Model Convergence

Now that we have specified our model, let's use TensorBoard to inspect the model. Let's first check the graph structure in TensorBoard (Figure 4-10).

The graph looks similar to that for logistic regression, with the addition of a new hidden layer. Let's expand the hidden layer to see what's inside (Figure 4-11).

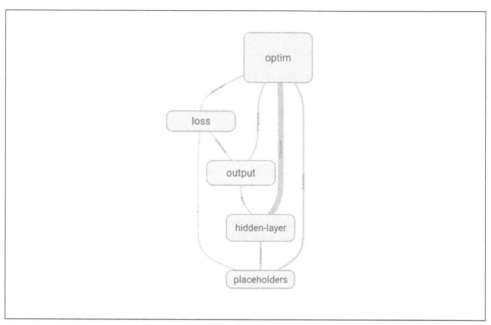

Figure 4-10. Visualizing the computation graph for a fully connected network.

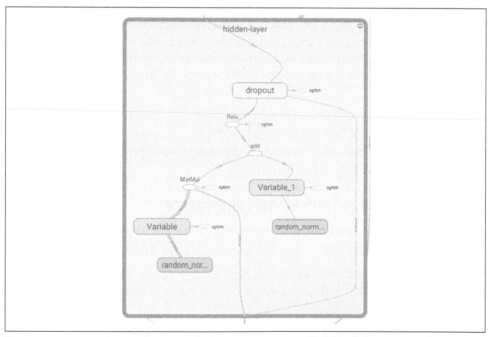

Figure 4-11. Visualizing the expanded computation graph for a fully connected network.

You can see how the new trainable variables and the dropout operation are represented here. Everything looks to be in the right place. Let's end now by looking at the loss curve over time (Figure 4-12).

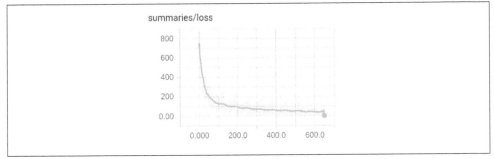

Figure 4-12. Visualizing the loss curve for a fully connected network.

The loss curve trends down as we saw in the previous section. But, let's zoom in to see what this loss looks like up close (Figure 4-13).

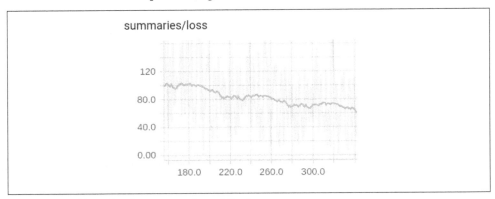

Figure 4-13. Zooming in on a section of the loss curve.

Note that loss looks much bumpier! This is one of the prices of using minibatch training. We no longer have the beautiful, smooth loss curves that we saw in the previous sections.

Review

In this chapter, we've introduced you to fully connected deep networks. We delved into the mathematical theory of these networks, and explored the concept of "universal approximation," which partially explains the learning power of fully connected networks. We ended with a case study, where you trained a deep fully connected architecture on the Tox21 dataset.

In this chapter, we haven't yet shown you how to tune the fully connected network to achieve good predictive performance. In Chapter 5, we will discuss "hyperparameter optimization," the process of tuning network parameters, and have you tune the parameters of the Tox21 network introduced in this chapter.

Hyperparameter Optimization

Training a deep model and training a good deep model are very different things. While it's easy enough to copy-paste some TensorFlow code from the internet to get a first prototype running, it's much harder to transform that prototype into a high-quality model. The process of taking a prototype to a high-quality model involves many steps. We'll explore one of these steps, hyperparameter optimization, in the rest of this chapter.

To first approximation, hyperparameter optimization is the process of tweaking all parameters of a model not learned by gradient descent. These quantities are called "hyperparameters." Consider fully connected networks from the previous chapter. While the weights of fully connected networks can be learned from data, the other settings of the network can't. These hyperparameters include the number of hidden layers, the number of neurons per hidden layer, the learning rate, and more. How can you systematically find good values for these quantities? Hyperparameter optimization methods provide our answer to this question.

Recall that we mentioned previously that model performance is tracked on a held-out "validation" set. Hyperparameter optimization methods systematically try multiple choices for hyperparameters on the validation set. The best-performing set of hyperparameter values is then evaluated on a second held-out "test" set to gauge the true model performance. Different hyperparameter optimization methods differ in the algorithm they use to propose new hyperparameter settings. These algorithms range from the obvious to quite sophisticated. We will only cover some of the simpler methods in these chapters, since the more sophisticated hyperparameter optimization techniques tend to require very large amounts of computational power.

As a case study, we will tune the Tox21 toxicity fully connected network introduced in Chapter 4 to achieve good performance. We strongly encourage you (as always) to run the hyperparameter optimization methods yourself using the code in the GitHub repo associated with this book (*https://github.com/matroid/dlwithtf*).

Hyperparameter Optimization Isn't Just for Deep Networks!

It's worth emphasizing that hyperparameter optimization isn't only for deep networks. Most forms of machine learning algorithms have parameters that can't be learned with the default learning methods. These parameters are also called hyperparameters. You will see some examples of hyperparameters for random forests (another common machine learning method) later in this chapter.

It's worth noting, however, that deep networks tend to be more sensitive to hyperparameter choice than other algorithms. While a random forest might underperform slightly with default choices for hyperparameters, deep networks might fail to learn entirely. For this reason, mastering hyperparameter optimization is a critical skill for a would-be deep learner.

Model Evaluation and Hyperparameter Optimization

In the previous chapters, we have only entered briefly into the question of how to tell whether a machine learning model is good or not. Any measurement of model performance must gauge the model's ability to generalize. That is, can the model make predictions on datapoints it has never seen before? The best test of model performance is to create a model, then evaluate *prospectively* on data that becomes available *after* the model was constructed. However, this sort of test is unwieldy to do regularly. During a design phase, a practicing data scientist may want to evaluate many different types of models or learning algorithms to find which is best.

The solution to this dilemma is to "hold-out" part of the available dataset as a validation set. This validation set will be used to measure the performance of different models (with differing hyperparameter choices). It's also good practice to have a second held-out set, the test set, for gauging the performance of the final model chosen by hyperparameter selection methods.

Let's assume you have a hundred datapoints. A simple procedure would be to use 80 of these datapoints to train prospective models with 20 held-out datapoints used to validate the model choice. The "goodness" of a proposed model can then be tracked by its "score" on the held-out 20 datapoints. Models can be iteratively improved by proposing new designs, and accepting only those that improve performance on the held-out set.

In practice, though, this procedure leads to *overfitting*. Practitioners quickly learn peculiarities of the held-out set and tweak model structure to artificially boost scores on the held-out set. To combat this, practitioners commonly break the held-out set into two parts: one part for validation of hyperparameters and the other for final model validation. In this case, let's say you reserve 10 datapoints for validation and 10 for final testing. This would be called an 80/10/10 data split.

Why Is the Test Set Necessary?

An important point worth noting is that hyperparameter optimization methods are themselves a form of learning algorithm. In particular, they are a learning algorithm for setting nondifferentiable quantities that aren't easily amenable to calculus-based analysis. The "training set" for the hyperparameter learning algorithm is simply the held-out validation set.

In general, it isn't very meaningful to gauge model performance on their training sets. As always, learned quantities must generalize and it is consequently necessary to test performance on a different set. Since the training set is used for gradient-based learning, and the validation set is used for hyperparameter learning, the test set is necessary to gauge how well learned hyperparameters generalize to new data.

Black-Box Learning Algorithms

Black-box learning algorithms assume no structural information about the systems they are trying to optimize. Most hyperparameter methods are black-box; they work for any type of deep learning or machine learning algorithm.

Black-box methods in general don't scale as well as white-box methods (such as gradient descent) since they tend to get lost in high-dimensional spaces. Due to the lack of directional information from a gradient, black-box methods can get lost in even 50 dimensional spaces (optimizing 50 hyperparameters is quite challenging in practice).

To understand why, suppose there are 50 hyperparameters, each with 3 potential values. Then the black-box algorithm must blindly search a space of size 3^{50}. This can be done, but performing the search will require lots of computational power in general.

Metrics, Metrics, Metrics

When choosing hyperparameters, you want to select those that make the models you design more accurate. In machine learning, a *metric* is a function that gauges the accuracy of predictions from a trained model. Hyperparameter optimization is done to optimize for hyperparameters that maximize (or minimize) this metric on the validation set. While this sounds simple up front, the notion of accuracy can in fact be quite subtle. Suppose you have a binary classifier. Is it more important to never mislabel false samples as true or to never mislabel true samples as false? How can you choose for model hyperparameters that satisfy the needs of your applications?

The answer turns out to be to choose the correct metric. In this section, we will discuss many different metrics for classification and regression problems. We will comment on the qualities each metric emphasizes. There is no best metric, but there are more suitable and less suitable metrics for different applications.

Metrics Aren't a Replacement for Common Sense!

Metrics are terribly blind. They only optimize for a single quantity. Consequently, blind optimization of metrics can lead to entirely unsuitable outcomes. On the web, media sites often choose to optimize the metric of "user clicks." Some enterprising young journalist or advertiser then realized that titles like "You'll never believe what happened when X" induced users to click at higher fractions. Lo and behold, clickbait was born. While clickbait headlines do indeed induce readers to click, they also turn off readers and lead them to avoid spending time on clickbait-filled sites. Optimizing for user clicks resulted in drops in user engagement and trust.

The lesson here is general. Optimizing for one metric often comes at the cost of a separate quantity. Make sure that the quantity you wish to optimize for is indeed the "right" quantity. Isn't it interesting how machine learning still seems to require human judgment at its core?

Binary Classification Metrics

Before introducing metrics for binary classification models, we think you will find it useful to learn about some auxiliary quantities. When a binary classifier makes predictions on a set of datapoints, you can split all these predictions into one of four categories (Table 5-1).

Table 5-1. Prediction categories

Category	Meaning
True Positive (TP)	Predicted true, Label true
False Positive (FP)	Predicted true, Label false
True Negative (TN)	Predicted false, Label false
False Negative (FN)	Predicted false, Label true

We will also find it useful to introduce the notation shown in Table 5-2.

Table 5-2. Positives and negatives

Category	Meaning
P	Number of positive labels
N	Number of negative labels

In general, minimizing the number of false positives and false negatives is highly desirable. However, for any given dataset, it is often not possible to minimize both false positives and false negatives due to limitations in the signal present. Consequently, there are a variety of metrics that provide various trade-offs between false positives and false negatives. These trade-offs can be quite important for applications. Suppose you are designing a medical diagnostic for breast cancer. Then a false positive would be to mark a healthy patient as having breast cancer. A false negative would be to mark a breast cancer sufferer as not having the disease. Neither of these outcomes is desirable, and designing the correct balance is a tricky question in bioethics.

We will now show you a number of different metrics that balance false positives and false negatives in different ratios (Table 5-3). Each of these ratios optimizes for a different balance, and we will dig into some of these in more detail.

Table 5-3. Binary metrics table

Metric	Definition
Accuracy	$(TP + TN)/(P + N)$
Precision	$TP/(TP + FP)$
Recall	$TP/(TP + FN) = TP/P$
Specificity	$TN/(FP + TN) = TN/N$
False Positive Rate (FPR)	$FP/(FP + TN) = FP/N$
False Negative Rate (FNR)	$FN/(TP + FN) = FN/P$

Accuracy is the simplest metric. It simply counts the fraction of predictions that were made correctly by the classifier. In straightforward applications, accuracy should be the first go-to metric for a practitioner. After accuracy, *precision* and *recall* are the most commonly measured metrics. Precision simply measures what fraction of the datapoints predicted positive were actually positive. Recall in its turn measures the fraction of positive labeled datapoints that the classifier labeled positive. *Specificity* measures the fraction of datapoints labeled negative that were correctly classified. The false positive rate measures the fraction of datapoints labeled negative that were misclassified as positive. False negative rate is the fraction of datapoints labeled positive that were falsely labeled as negatives.

These metrics all emphasize different aspects of a classifier's performance. They can also be useful in constructing some more sophisticated measurements of a binary classifier's performance. For example, suppose that your binary classifier outputs class probabilities, and not just raw predictions. Then, there rises the question of choosing a *cutoff*. That is, at what probability of positive do you label the output as actually positive? The most common answer is 0.5, but by choosing higher or lower cutoffs, it is often possible to manually vary the balance between precision, recall, FPR, and TPR. These trade-offs are often represented graphically.

The receiver operator curve (ROC) plots the trade-off between the true positive rate and the false positive rate as the cutoff probability is varied (see Figure 5-1).

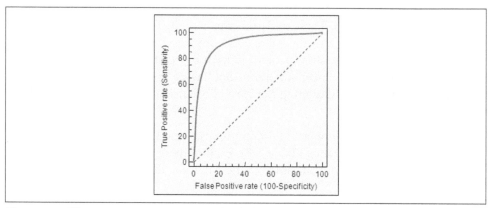

Figure 5-1. The receiver operator curve (ROC).

The area under curve (AUC) for the receiver operator curve (ROC-AUC) is a commonly measured metric. The ROC-AUC metric is useful since it provides a global picture of the binary classifier for all choices of cutoff. A perfect metric would have ROC-AUC 1.0 since the TPR would always be maximized. For comparison, a random classifier would have ROC-AUC 0.5. The ROC-AUC is often useful for imbalanced datasets, since the global view partially accounts for the imbalance in the dataset.

Multiclass Classification Metrics

Many common machine learning tasks require models to output classification labels that aren't just binary. The ImageNet challenge (ILSVRC) required entrants to build models that would recognize which of a thousand potential object classes were in provided images, for example. Or in a simpler example, perhaps you want to predict tomorrow's weather, where provided classes are "sunny," "rainy," and "cloudy." How do you measure the performance of such a model?

The simplest method is to use a straightforward generalization of accuracy that measures the fraction of datapoints correctly labeled (Table 5-4).

Table 5-4. Multiclass classification metrics

Metric	Definition
Accuracy	Num Correctly Labeled/Num Datapoints

We note that there do exist multiclass generalizations of quantities like precision, recall, and ROC-AUC, and we encourage you to look into these definitions if interested. In practice, there's a simpler visualization, the *confusion matrix*, which works well. For a multiclass problem with k classes, the confusion matrix is a $k \times k$ matrix. The (i, j)-th cell represents the number of datapoints labeled as class i with true label class j. Figure 5-2 illustrates a confusion matrix.

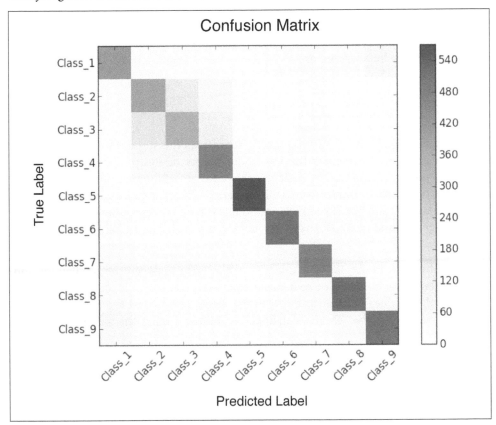

Figure 5-2. The confusion matrix for a 10-way classifier.

Don't underestimate the power of the human eye to catch systematic failure patterns from simple visualizations! Looking at the confusion matrix can provide quick understanding that dozens of more complex multiclass metrics might miss.

Regression Metrics

You learned about regression metrics a few chapters ago. As a quick recap, the Pearson R^2 and RMSE (root-mean-squared error) are good defaults.

We only briefly covered the mathematical definition of R^2 previously, but will delve into it more now. Let x_i represent predictions and y_i represent labels. Let $\bar{x}$ and $\bar{y}$ represent the mean of the predicted values and the labels, respectively. Then the Pearson R (note the lack of square) is

$$R = \frac{\Sigma_{i=1}^{N}(x_i - \bar{x})(y_i - \bar{y})}{\sqrt{\Sigma_{i=1}^{N}(x_i - \bar{x})^2}\sqrt{\Sigma_{i=1}^{N}(y_i - \bar{y})^2}}$$

This equation can be rewritten as

$$R = \frac{\text{cov}(x, y)}{\sigma(x)\sigma(y)}$$

where cov represents the covariance and σ represents the standard deviation. Intuitively, the Pearson R measures the joint fluctuations of the predictions and labels from their means normalized by their respective ranges of fluctuations. If predictions and labels differ, these fluctuations will happen at different points and will tend to cancel, making R^2 smaller. If predictions and labels tend to agree, the fluctuations will happen together and make R^2 larger. We note that R^2 is limited to a range between 0 and 1.

The RMSE measures the absolute quantity of the error between the predictions and the true quantities. It stands for root-mean-squared error, which is roughly analogous to the absolute value of the error between the true quantity and the predicted quantity. Mathematically, the RMSE is defined as follows (using the same notation as before):

$$\text{RMSE} = \sqrt{\frac{\Sigma_{i=1}^{N}(x_i - y_i)^2}{N}}$$

Hyperparameter Optimization Algorithms

As we mentioned earlier in the chapter, hyperparameter optimization methods are learning algorithms for finding values of the hyperparameters that optimize the chosen metric on the validation set. In general, this objective function cannot be differentiated, so any optimization method must by necessity be a black box. In this section, we will show you some simple black-box learning algorithms for choosing hyperparameter values. We will use the Tox21 dataset from Chapter 4 as a case study to demonstrate these black-box optimization methods. The Tox21 dataset is small enough to make experimentation easy, but complex enough that hyperparameter optimization isn't trivial.

We note before setting off that none of these black-box algorithms works perfectly. As you will soon see, in practice, much human input is required to optimize hyperparameters.

Can't Hyperparameter Optimization Be Automated?

One of the long-running dreams of machine learning has been to automate the process of selecting model hyperparameters. Projects such as the "automated statistician" and others have sought to remove some of the drudgery from the hyperparameter selection process and make model construction more easily available to non-experts. However, in practice, there has typically been a steep cost in performance for the added convenience.

In recent years, there has been a surge of work focused on improving the algorithmic foundations of model tuning. Gaussian processes, evolutionary algorithms, and reinforcement learning have all been used to learn model hyperparameters and architectures with very limited human input. Recent work has shown that with large amounts of computing power, these algorithms can exceed expert performance in model tuning! But the overhead is severe, with dozens to hundreds of times greater computational power required.

For now, automatic model tuning is still not practical. All algorithms we cover in this section require significant manual tuning However, as hardware quality improves, we anticipate that hyperparameter learning will become increasingly automated. In the near term, we recommend strongly that all practitioners master the intricacies of hyperparameter tuning. A strong ability to hyperparameter tune is the skill that separates the expert from the novice.

Setting Up a Baseline

The first step in hyperparameter tuning is finding a *baseline*. A baseline is performance achievable by a robust (non–deep learning usually) algorithm. In general, random forests are a superb choice for setting baselines. As shown in Figure 5-3, random forests are an ensemble method that train many decision tree models on subsets of the input data and input features. These individual trees then vote on the outcome.

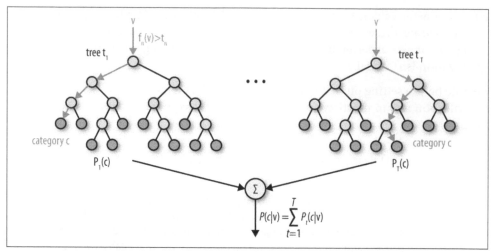

Figure 5-3. An illustration of a random forest. Here v is the input feature vector.

Random forests tend to be quite robust models. They are noise tolerant, and don't worry about the scale of their input features. (Although we don't have to worry about this for Tox21 since all our features are binary, in general deep networks are quite sensitive to their input range. It's healthy to normalize or otherwise scale the input range for good performance. We will return to this point in later chapters.) They also tend to have strong generalization and don't require much hyperparameter tuning to boot. For certain datasets, beating the performance of a random forest with a deep network can require considerable sophistication.

How can we create and train a random forest? Luckily for us, in Python, the scikit-learn library provides a high-quality implementation of a random forest. There are many tutorials and introductions to scikit-learn available, so we'll just display the training and prediction code needed to build a Tox21 random forest model here (Example 5-1).

Example 5-1. Defining and training a random forest on the Tox21 dataset

```
from sklearn.ensemble import RandomForestClassifier

# Generate tensorflow graph
sklearn_model = RandomForestClassifier(
    class_weight="balanced", n_estimators=50)
print("About to fit model on training set.")
sklearn_model.fit(train_X, train_y)

train_y_pred = sklearn_model.predict(train_X)
valid_y_pred = sklearn_model.predict(valid_X)
test_y_pred = sklearn_model.predict(test_X)
```

```
weighted_score = accuracy_score(train_y, train_y_pred, sample_weight=train_w)
print("Weighted train Classification Accuracy: %f" % weighted_score)
weighted_score = accuracy_score(valid_y, valid_y_pred, sample_weight=valid_w)
print("Weighted valid Classification Accuracy: %f" % weighted_score)
weighted_score = accuracy_score(test_y, test_y_pred, sample_weight=test_w)
print("Weighted test Classification Accuracy: %f" % weighted_score)
```

Here `train_X`, `train_y`, and so on are the Tox21 datasets defined in the previous chapter. Recall that all these quantities are NumPy arrays. `n_estimators` refers to the number of decision trees in our forest. Setting 50 or 100 trees often provides decent performance. Scikit-learn offers a simple object-oriented API with `fit(X, y)` and `predict(X)` methods. This model achieves the following accuracy with respect to our weighted accuracy metric:

```
Weighted train Classification Accuracy: 0.989845
Weighted valid Classification Accuracy: 0.681413
```

Recall that the fully connected network from Chapter 4 achieved performance:

```
Train Weighted Classification Accuracy: 0.742045
Valid Weighted Classification Accuracy: 0.648828
```

It looks like our baseline gets greater accuracy than our deep learning model! Time to roll up our sleeves and get to work.

Graduate Student Descent

The simplest method to try good hyperparameters is to simply try a number of different hyperparameter variants manually to see what works. This strategy can be surprisingly effective and educational. A deep learning practitioner needs to build up intuition about the structure of deep networks. Given the very weak state of theory, empirical work is the best way to learn how to build deep learning models. We highly recommend trying many variants of the fully connected model yourself. Be systematic; record your choices and results in a spreadsheet and systematically explore the space. Try to understand the effects of various hyperparameters. Which make network training proceed faster and which slower? What ranges of settings completely break learning? (These are quite easy to find, unfortunately.)

There are a few software engineering tricks that can make this search easier. Make a function whose arguments are the hyperparameter you wish to explore and have it print out the accuracy. Then trying new hyperparameter combinations requires only a single function call. Example 5-2 shows what this function signature would look like for our fully connected network from the Tox21 case study.

Example 5-2. A function mapping hyperparameters to different Tox21 fully connected networks

```
def eval_tox21_hyperparams(n_hidden=50, n_layers=1, learning_rate=.001,
                           dropout_prob=0.5, n_epochs=45, batch_size=100,
                           weight_positives=True):
```

Let's walk through each of these hyperparameters. n_hidden controls the number of neurons in each hidden layer of the network. n_layers controls the number of hidden layers. learning_rate controls the learning rate used in gradient descent, and dropout_prob is the probability neurons are not dropped during training steps. n_epochs controls the number of passes through the total data and batch_size controls the number of datapoints in each batch.

weight_positives is the only new hyperparameter here. For unbalanced datasets, it can often be helpful to weight examples of both classes to have equal weight. For the Tox21 dataset, DeepChem provides weights for us to use. We simply multiply the per-example cross-entropy terms by the weights to perform this weighting (Example 5-3).

Example 5-3. Weighting positive samples for Tox21

```
entropy = tf.nn.sigmoid_cross_entropy_with_logits(logits=y_logit, labels=y_expand)
# Multiply by weights
if weight_positives:
  w_expand = tf.expand_dims(w, 1)
  entropy = w_expand * entropy
```

Why is the method of picking hyperparameter values called graduate student descent? Machine learning, until recently, has been a primarily academic field. The tried-and-true method for designing a new machine learning algorithm has been describing the method desired to a new graduate student, and asking them to work out the details. This process is a bit of a rite of passage, and often requires the student to painfully try many design alternatives. On the whole, this is a very educational experience, since the only way to gain design aesthetic is to build up a memory of settings that work and don't work.

Grid Search

After having tried a few manual settings for hyperparameters, the process will begin to feel very tedious. Experienced programmers will be tempted to simply write a for loop that iterates over the choices of hyperparameters desired. This process is more or less the grid-search method. For each hyperparameter, pick a list of values that might be good hyperparameters. Write a nested for loop that tries all combinations of these values to find their validation accuracies, and keep track of the best performers.

There is one subtlety in the process, however. Deep networks can be fairly sensitive to the choice of random seed used to initialize the network. For this reason, it's worth repeating each choice of hyperparameter settings multiple times and averaging the results to damp the variance.

The code to do this is straightforward, as Example 5-4 shows.

Example 5-4. Performing grid search on Tox21 fully connected network hyperparameters

```
scores = {}
n_reps = 3
hidden_sizes = [50]
epochs = [10]
dropouts = [.5, 1.0]
num_layers = [1, 2]

for rep in range(n_reps):
  for n_epochs in epochs:
    for hidden_size in hidden_sizes:
      for dropout in dropouts:
        for n_layers in num_layers:
          score = eval_tox21_hyperparams(n_hidden=hidden_size, n_epochs=n_epochs,
                                  dropout_prob=dropout, n_layers=n_layers)
          if (hidden_size, n_epochs, dropout, n_layers) not in scores:
            scores[(hidden_size, n_epochs, dropout, n_layers)] = []
          scores[(hidden_size, n_epochs, dropout, n_layers)].append(score)
print("All Scores")
print(scores)

avg_scores = {}
for params, param_scores in scores.iteritems():
  avg_scores[params] = np.mean(np.array(param_scores))
print("Scores Averaged over %d repetitions" % n_reps)
```

Random Hyperparameter Search

For experienced practitioners, it will often be very tempting to reuse magical hyperparameter settings or search grids that worked in previous applications. These settings can be valuable, but they can also lead us astray. Each machine learning problem is slightly different, and the optimal settings might lie in a region of parameter space we haven't previously considered. For that reason, it's often worthwhile to try random settings for hyperparameters (where the random values are chosen from a reasonable range).

There's also a deeper reason to try random searches. In higher-dimensional spaces, regular grids can miss a lot of information, especially if the spacing between grid points isn't great. Selecting random choices for grid points can help us from falling into the trap of loose grids. Figure 5-4 illustrates this fact.

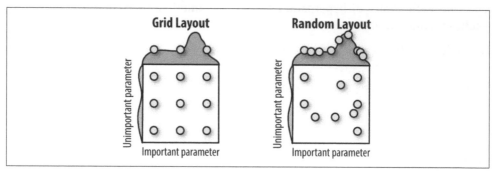

Figure 5-4. An illustration of why random hyperparameter search can be superior to grid search.

How can we implement random hyperparameter search in software? A neat software trick is to sample the random values desired up front and store them in a list. Then, random hyperparameter search simply turns into grid search over these randomly sampled lists. Here's an example. For learning rates, it's often useful to try a wide range from .1 to .000001 or so. Example 5-5 uses NumPy to sample some random learning rates.

Example 5-5. Sampling random learning rates

```
n_rates = 5
learning_rates = 10**(-np.random.uniform(low=1, high=6, size=n_rates))
```

We use a mathematical trick here. Note that $.1 = 10^{-1}$ and $.000001 = 10^{-6}$. Sampling real-valued numbers between ranges like 1 and 6 is easy with `np.random.uniform`. We can raise these sampled values to a power to recover our learning rates. Then `learning_rates` holds a list of values that we can feed into our grid search code from the previous section.

Challenge for the Reader

In this chapter, we've only covered the basics of hyperparameter tuning, but the tools covered are quite powerful. As a challenge, try tuning the fully connected deep network to achieve validation performance higher than that of the random forest. This might require a bit of work, but it's well worth the experience.

Review

In this chapter, we covered the basics of hyperparameter optimization, the process of selecting values for model parameters that can't be learned automatically on the training data. In particular, we introduced random and grid hyperparameter search and demonstrated the use of such code for optimizing models on the Tox21 dataset introduced in the last chapter.

In Chapter 6, we will return to our survey of deep architectures and introduce you to convolutional neural networks, one of the fundamental building blocks of modern deep architectures.

Convolutional Neural Networks

Convolutional neural networks allow deep networks to learn functions on structured spatial data such as images, video, and text. Mathematically, convolutional networks provide tools for exploiting the local structure of data effectively. Images satisfy certain natural statistical properties. Let's assume we represent an image as a two-dimensional grid of pixels. Parts of an image that are close to one other in the pixel grid are likely to vary together (for example, all pixels corresponding to a table in the image are probably brown). Convolutional networks learn to exploit this natural covariance structure in order to learn effectively.

Convolutional networks are a relatively old invention. Versions of convolutional networks have been proposed in the literature dating back to the 1980s. While the designs of these older convolutional networks were often quite sound, they required resources that exceeded hardware available at the time. As a result, convolutional networks languished in relative obscurity in the research literature.

This trend reversed dramatically following the 2012 ILSVRC challenge for object detection in images, where the convolutional AlexNet achieved error rates half that of its nearest competitors. AlexNet was able to use GPUs to train old convolutional architectures on dramatically larger datasets. This combination of old architectures with new hardware allowed AlexNet to dramatically outperform the state of the art in image object detection. This trend has only continued, with convolutional neural networks achieving tremendous boosts over other technologies for processing images. It isn't an exaggeration to say that nearly all modern image processing pipelines are now powered by convolutional neural networks.

There has also been a renaissance in convolutional network design that has moved convolutional networks well past the basic models from the 1980s. For one, networks have been getting much deeper with powerful state-of-the-art networks reaching hundreds of layers deep. Another broad trend has been toward generalizing convolutional architectures to work on new datatypes. For example, graph convolutional architectures allow convolutional networks to be applied to molecular data such as the Tox21 dataset we encountered a few chapters ago! Convolutional architectures are also making a mark in genomics and in text processing and even language translation.

In this chapter, we will introduce the basic concepts of convolutional networks. These will include the basic network components that constitute convolutional architectures and an introduction to the design principles that guide how these pieces are joined together. We will also provide an in-depth example that demonstrates how to use TensorFlow to train a convolutional network. The example code for this chapter was adapted from the TensorFlow documentation tutorial on convolutional neural networks. We encourage you to access the original tutorial (*https://www.tensor flow.org/tutorials/deep_cnn*) on the TensorFlow website if you're curious about the changes we've made. As always, we encourage you to work through the scripts for this chapter in the associated GitHub repo for this book (*https://github.com/matroid/dlwithtf*).

Introduction to Convolutional Architectures

Most convolutional architectures are made up of a number of basic primitives. These primitives include layers such as convolutional layers and pooling layers. There's also a set of associated vocabulary including local receptive field size, stride size, and number of filters. In this section, we will give you a brief introduction to the basic vocabulary and concepts underlying convolutional networks.

Local Receptive Fields

The local receptive field concept originates in neuroscience, where the receptive field of a neuron is the part of the body's sensory perception that affects the neuron's firing. Neurons have a certain field of "view" as they process sensory input that the brain sees. This field of view is traditionally called the local receptive field. This "field of view" could correspond to a patch of skin or to a segment of a person's visual field. Figure 6-1 illustrates a neuron's local receptive field.

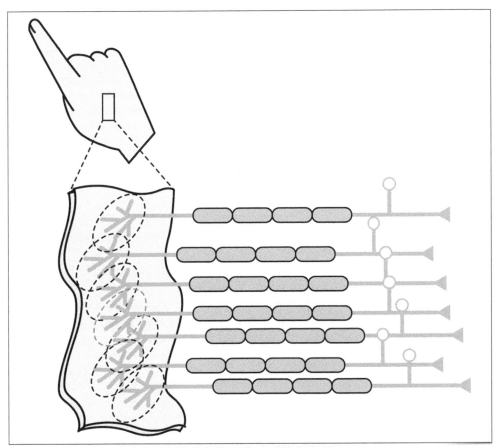

Figure 6-1. An illustration of a neuron's local receptive field.

Convolutional architectures borrow this latter concept with the computational notion of "local receptive fields." Figure 6-2 provides a pictorial representation of the local receptive field concept applied to image data. Each local receptive field corresponds to a patch of pixels in the image and is handled by a separate "neuron." These "neurons" are directly analogous to those in fully connected layers. As with fully connected layers, a nonlinear transformation is applied to incoming data (which originates from the local receptive image patch).

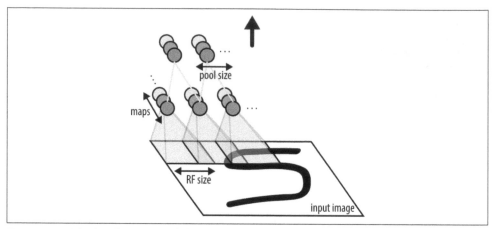

Figure 6-2. The local receptive field (RF) of a "neuron" in a convolutional network.

A layer of such "convolutional neurons" can be combined into a convolutional layer. This layer can viewed as a transformation of one spatial region into another. In the case of images, one batch of images is transformed into another by a convolutional layer. Figure 6-3 illustrates such a transformation. In the next section, we will show you more details about how a convolutional layer is constructed.

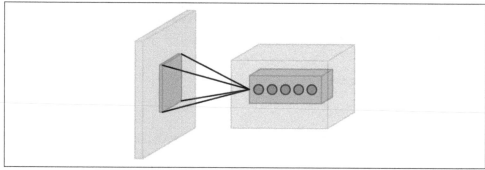

Figure 6-3. A convolutional layer performs an image transformation.

It's worth emphasizing that local receptive fields don't have to be limited to image data. For example, in stacked convolutional architectures, where the output of one convolutional layer feeds into the input of the next, the local receptive field will correspond to a "patch" of processed feature data.

Convolutional Kernels

In the last section, we mentioned that a convolutional layer applies nonlinear function to a local receptive field in its input. This locally applied nonlinearity is at the heart of convolutional architectures, but it's not the only piece. The second part of the convolution is what's called a "convolutional kernel." A convolutional kernel is just a matrix of weights, much like the weights associated with a fully connected layer. Figure 6-4 diagrammatically illustrates how a convolutional kernel is applied to inputs.

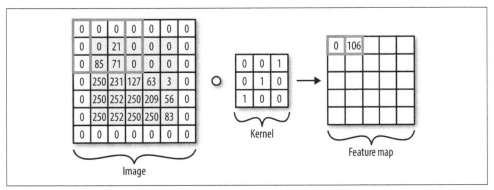

Figure 6-4. *A convolutional kernel is applied to inputs. The kernel weights are multiplied elementwise with the corresponding numbers in the local receptive field and the multiplied numbers are summed. Note that this corresponds to a convolutional layer without a nonlinearity.*

The key idea behind convolutional networks is that the same (nonlinear) transformation is applied to every local receptive field in the image. Visually, picture the local receptive field as a sliding window dragged over the image. At each positioning of the local receptive field, the nonlinear function is applied to return a single number corresponding to that image patch. As Figure 6-4 demonstrates, this transformation turns one grid of numbers into another grid of numbers. For image data, it's common to label the size of the local receptive field in terms of the number of pixels on each size of the receptive field. For example, 5 × 5 and 7 × 7 local receptive field sizes are commonly seen in convolutional networks.

What if we want to specify that local receptive fields should not overlap? The way to do this is to alter the *stride size* of the convolutional kernel. The stride size controls how the receptive field is moved over the input. Figure 6-4 demonstrates a one-dimensional convolutional kernel, with stride sizes 1 and 2, respectively. Figure 6-5 illustrates how altering the stride size changes how the receptive field is moved over the input.

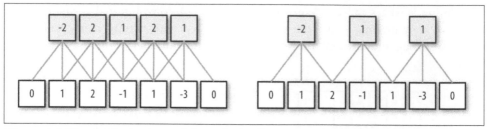

Figure 6-5. The stride size controls how the local receptive field "slides" over the input. This is easiest to visualize on a one-dimensional input. The network on the left has stride 1, while that on the right has stride 2. Note that each local receptive field computes the maximum of its inputs.

Now, note that the convolutional kernel we have defined transforms a grid of numbers into another grid of numbers. What if we want more than one grid of numbers output? It's easy enough; we simply need to add more convolutional kernels for processing the image. Convolutional kernels are also called *filters*, so the number of filters in a convolutional layer controls the number of transformed grids we obtain. A collection of convolutional kernels forms a *convolutional layer*.

Convolutional Kernels on Multidimensional Inputs

In this section, we primarily described convolutional kernels as transforming grids of numbers into other grids of numbers. Recalling our tensorial language from earlier chapters, convolutions transform matrices into matrices.

What if your input has more dimensions? For example, an RGB image typically has three color channels, so an RGB image is rightfully a rank-3 tensor. The simplest way to handle RGB data is to dictate that each local receptive field includes all the color channels associated with pixels in that patch. You might then say that the local receptive field is of size $5 \times 5 \times 3$ for a local receptive field of size 5×5 pixels with three color channels.

In general, you can generalize to tensors of higher dimension by expanding the dimensionality of the local receptive field correspondingly. This may also necessitate having multidimensional strides, especially if different dimensions are to be handled separately. The details are straightforward to work out, and we leave exploration of multidimensional convolutional kernels as an exercise for you to undertake.

Pooling Layers

In the previous section, we introduced the notion of convolutional kernels. These kernels apply learnable nonlinear transformations to local patches of inputs. These transformations are learnable, and by the universal approximation theorem, capable of learning arbitrarily complex input transformations on local patches. This flexibility gives convolutional kernels much of their power. But at the same time, having many learnable weights in a deep convolutional network can slow training.

Instead of using a learnable transformation, it's possible to instead use a fixed nonlinear transformation in order to reduce the computational cost of training a convolutional network. A popular fixed nonlinearity is "max pooling." Such layers select and output the maximally activating input within each local receptive patch. Figure 6-6 demonstrates this process. Pooling layers are useful for reducing the dimensionality of input data in a structured fashion. More mathematically, they take a local receptive field and replace the nonlinear activation function at each portion of the field with the max (or min or average) function.

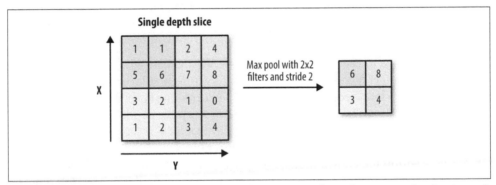

Figure 6-6. An illustration of a max pooling layer. Notice how the maximal value in each colored region (each local receptive field) is reported in the output.

Pooling layers have become less useful as hardware has improved. While pooling is still useful as a dimensionality reduction technique, recent research tends to avoid using pooling layers due to their inherent lossiness (it's not possible to back out of pooled data which pixel in the input originated the reported activation). Nonetheless, pooling appears in many standard convolutional architectures so it's worth understanding.

Constructing Convolutional Networks

A simple convolutional architecture applies a series of convolutional layers and pooling layers to its input to learn a complex function on the input image data. There are a lot of details in forming these networks, but at its heart, architecture design is simply an elaborate form of Lego stacking. Figure 6-7 demonstrates how a convolutional architecture might be built up out of constituent blocks.

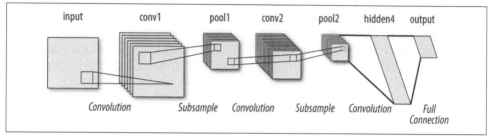

Figure 6-7. An illustration of a simple convolutional architecture constructed out of stacked convolutional and pooling layers.

Dilated Convolutions

Dilated or atrous convolutions are a newly popular form of convolutional layer. The insight here is to leave gaps in the local receptive field for each neuron (atrous means *a trous*, or "with holes" in French). The basic concept is an old one in signal processing that has recently found some good traction in the convolutional literature.

The core advantage to the atrous convolution is the increase in visible area for each neuron. Let's consider a convolution architecture whose first layer is a vanilla convolutional with 3 × 3 local receptive fields. Then a neuron one layer deeper in the architecture in a second vanilla convolutional layer has receptive depth 5 × 5 (each neuron in a local receptive field of the second layer itself has a local receptive field in the first layer). Then, a neuron two layers deeper has receptive view 7 × 7. In general, a neuron N layers within the convolutional architecture has receptive view of size $(2N + 1)$ × $(2N + 1)$. This linear growth in receptive view is fine for smaller images, but quickly becomes a liability for large images.

The atrous convolution enables exponential growth in the visible receptive field by leaving gaps in its local receptive fields. A "1-dilated" convolution leaves no gaps, while a "2-dilated" convolution leaves one gap between each local receptive field element. Stacking dilated layers leads to exponentially increasing local receptive field sizes. Figure 6-8 illustrates this exponential increase.

Dilated convolutions can be very useful for large images. For example, medical images can stretch thousands of pixels in every dimension. Creating vanilla convolutional networks that have global understanding could require unreasonably deep networks. Using dilated convolutions could enable networks to better understand the global structure of such images.

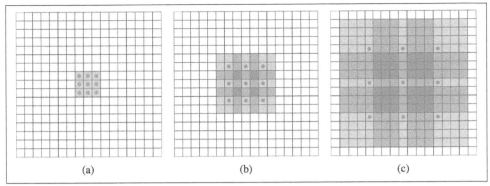

Figure 6-8. A dilated (or atrous) convolution. Gaps are left in the local receptive field for each neuron. Diagram (a) depicts a 1-dilated 3 × 3 convolution. Diagram (b) depicts the application of a 2-dilated 3 × 3 convolution to (a). Diagram (c) depicts the application of a 4-dilated 3 × 3 convolution to (b). Notice that the (a) layer has receptive field of width 3, the (b) layer has receptive field of width 7, and the (c) layer has receptive field of width 15.

Applications of Convolutional Networks

In the previous section, we covered the mechanics of convolutional networks and introduced you to many of the components that make up these networks. In this section, we describe some applications that convolutional architectures enable.

Object Detection and Localization

Object detection is the task of detecting the objects (or entities) present in a photograph. Object localization is the task of identifying where in the image the objects exist and drawing a "bounding box" around each occurrence. Figure 6-9 demonstrates what detection and localization on standard images looks like.

Figure 6-9. Objects detected and localized with bounding boxes in some example images.

Why is detection and localization important? One very useful localization task is detecting pedestrians in images taken from a self-driving car. Needless to say, it's extremely important that a self-driving car be able to identify all nearby pedestrians. Other applications of object detection could be used to find all instances of friends in photos uploaded to a social network. Yet another application could be to identify potential collision dangers from a drone.

This wealth of applications has made detection and localization the focus of tremendous amounts of research activity. The ILSVRC challenge mentioned multiple times in this book focused on detecting and localizing objects found in the ImagetNet collection.

Image Segmentation

Image segmentation is the task of labeling each pixel in an image with the object it belongs to. Segmentation is related to object localization, but is significantly harder since it requires precisely understanding the boundaries between objects in images. Until recently, image segmentation was often done with graphical models, an alternate form of machine learning (as opposed to deep networks), but recently convolutional segmentations have risen to prominence and allowed image segmentation algorithms to achieve new accuracy and speed records. Figure 6-10 displays an example of image segmentation applied to data for self-driving car imagery.

Figure 6-10. Objects in an image are "segmented" into various categories. Image segmentation is expected to prove very useful for applications such as self-driving cars and robotics since it will enable fine-grained scene understanding.

Graph Convolutions

The convolutional algorithms we've shown you thus far expect rectangular tensors as their inputs. Such inputs could come in the form of images, videos, or even sentences. Is it possible to generalize convolutions to apply to irregular inputs?

The fundamental idea underlying convolutional layers is the notion of a local receptive field. Each neuron computes upon the inputs in its local receptive field, which typically constitute adjacent pixels in an image input. For irregular inputs, such as the undirected graph in Figure 6-11, this simple notion of a local receptive field doesn't make sense; there are no adjacent pixels. If we can define a more general local receptive field for an undirected graph, it stands to reason that we should be able to define convolutional layers that accept undirected graphs.

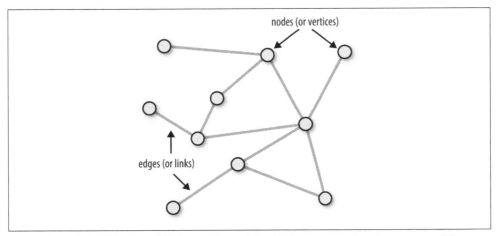

Figure 6-11. An illustration of an undirected graph consisting of nodes connected by edges.

As Figure 6-11 shows, a graph is made up of a collection of nodes connected by edges. One potential definition of a local receptive field might be to define it to constitute a node and its collection of neighbors (where two nodes are considered neighbors if they are connected by an edge). Using this definition of local receptive fields, it's possible to define generalized notions of convolutional and pooling layers. These layers can be assembled into graph convolutional architectures.

Where might such graph convolutional architectures prove useful? In chemistry, it turns out molecules can be modeled as undirected graphs where atoms form nodes and chemical bonds form edges. As a result, graph convolutional architectures are particularly useful in chemical machine learning. For example, Figure 6-12 demonstrates how graph convolutional architectures can be applied to process molecular inputs.

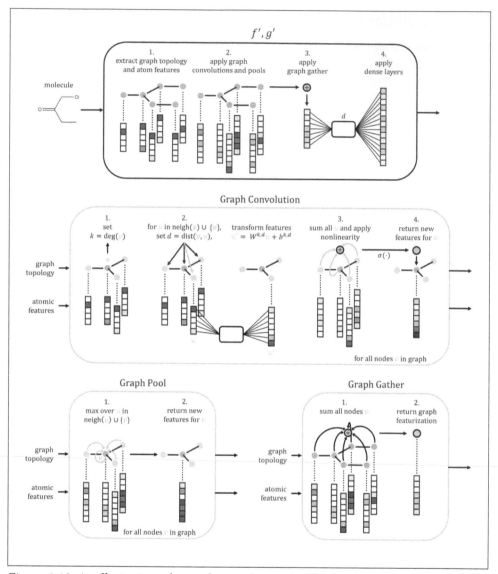

Figure 6-12. An illustration of a graph convolutional architecture processing a molecular input. The molecule is modeled as an undirected graph with atoms forming nodes and chemical bond edges. The "graph topology" is the undirected graph corresponding to the molecule. "Atom features" are vectors, one per atom, summarizing local chemistry. Adapted from "Low Data Drug Discovery with One-Shot Learning."

Generating Images with Variational Autoencoders

The applications we've described thus far are all supervised learning problems. There are well-defined inputs and outputs, and the task remains (using a convolutional network) to learn a sophisticated function mapping input to output. Are there unsupervised learning problems that can be solved with convolutional networks? Recall that unsupervised learning requires "understanding" the structure of input datapoints. For image modeling, a good measure of understanding the structure of input images is being able to "sample" new images that come from the input distribution.

What does "sampling" an image mean? To explain, let's suppose we have a dataset of dog images. Sampling a new dog image requires the generation of a new image of a dog that *is not in the training data!* The idea is that we would like a picture of a dog that could have reasonably been included with the training data, but was not. How could we solve this task with convolutional networks?

Perhaps we could train a model to take in word labels like "dog" and predict dog images. We might possibly be able to train a supervised model to solve this prediction problem, but the issue remains that our model could generate only one dog picture given the input label "dog." Suppose now that we could attach a random tag to each dog—say "dog3422" or "dog9879." Then all we'd need to do to get a new dog image would be to attach a new random tag, say "dog2221," to get out a new picture of a dog.

Variational autoencoders formalize these intuitions. Variational autoencoders consist of two convolutional networks: the encoder and decoder network. The encoder network is used to transform an image into a flat "embedded" vector. The decoder network is responsible for transforming the embedded vector into images. Noise is added to ensure that different images can be sampled by the decoder. Figure 6-13 illustrates a variational autoencoder.

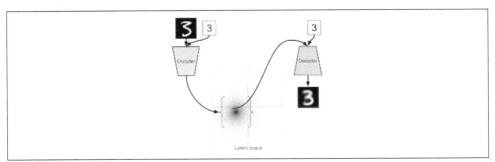

Figure 6-13. A diagrammatic illustration of a variational autoencoder. A variational autoencoder consists of two convolutional networks, the encoder and decoder.

There are more details involved in an actual implementation, but variational autoencoders are capable of sampling images. However, naive variational encoders seem to generate blurry image samples, as Figure 6-14 demonstrates. This blurriness may be because the L^2 loss doesn't penalize image blurriness sharply (recall our discussion about L^2 not penalizing small deviations). To generate crisp image samples, we will need other architectures.

Figure 6-14. Images sampled from a variational autoencoder trained on a dataset of faces. Note that sampled images are quite blurry.

Adversarial models

The L2 loss sharply penalizes large local deviations, but doesn't severely penalize many small local deviations, causing blurriness. How could we design an alternate loss function that penalizes blurriness in images more sharply? It turns out that it's quite challenging to write down a loss function that does the trick. While our eyes can quickly spot blurriness, our analytical tools aren't quite so fast to capture the problem.

What if we could somehow "learn" a loss function? This idea sounds a little nonsensical at first; where would we get training data? But it turns out that there's a clever idea that makes it feasible.

Suppose we could train a separate network that learns the loss. Let's call this network the discriminator. Let's call the network that makes the images the generator. The generator can be set to duel against the discriminator until the generator is capable of producing images that are photorealistic. This form of architecture is commonly called a generative adversarial network, or GAN.

Faces generated by a GAN (Figure 6-15) are considerably crisper than those generated by the naive variational autoencoder (Figure 6-14)! There are a number of other promising results that have been achieved by GANs. The CycleGAN, for example, appears capable of learning complex image transformations such as transmuting horses into zebras and vice versa. Figure 6-16 shows some CycleGAN image transformations.

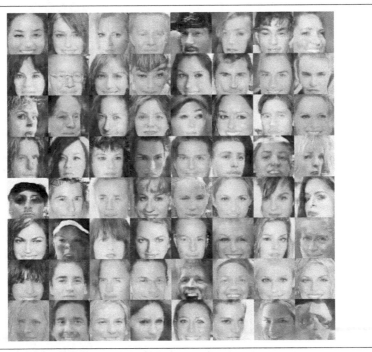

Figure 6-15. Images sampled from a generative adversarial network (GAN) trained on a dataset of faces. Note that sampled images are less blurry than those from the variational autoencoder.

Figure 6-16. The CycleGAN is capable of performing complex image transformations, such as transforming images of horses into those of zebras (and vice versa).

Unfortunately, generative adversarial networks are still challenging to train in practice. Making generators and discriminators learn reasonable functions requires a deep bag of tricks. As a result, while there have been many exciting GAN demonstrations, GANs have not yet matured into a state where they can be widely deployed in industrial applications.

Training a Convolutional Network in TensorFlow

In this section we consider a code sample for training a simple convolutional neural network. In particular, our code sample will demonstrate how to train a LeNet-5 convolutional architecture on the MNIST dataset using TensorFlow. As always, we recommend that you follow along by running the full code sample from the GitHub repo associated with the book (*https://github.com/matroid/dlwithtf*).

The MNIST Dataset

The MNIST dataset consists of images of handwritten digits. The machine learning challenge associated with MNIST consists of creating a model trained on the training set of digits that generalizes to the validation set. Figure 6-17 shows some images drawn from the MNIST dataset.

Figure 6-17. Some images of handwritten digits from the MNIST dataset. The learning challenge is to predict the digit from the image.

MNIST was a very important dataset for the development of machine learning methods for computer vision. The dataset is challenging enough that obvious, non-learning methods don't tend to do well. At the same time, MNIST is small enough that experimenting with new architectures doesn't require very large amounts of computing power.

However, the MNIST dataset has mostly become obsolete. The best models achieve near one hundred percent test accuracy. Note that this fact doesn't mean that the problem of handwritten digit recognition is solved! Rather, it is likely that human scientists have overfit architectures to the MNIST dataset and capitalized on its quirks to achieve very high predictive accuracies. As a result, it's no longer good practice to use MNIST to design new deep architectures. That said, MNIST is still a superb dataset for pedagogical purposes.

Loading MNIST

The MNIST codebase is located online on Yann LeCun's website (*http://yann.lecun.com/exdb/mnist/*). The download script pulls down the raw file from the website. Notice how the script caches the download so repeated calls to download() won't waste effort.

As a more general note, it's quite common to store ML datasets in the cloud and have user code retrieve it before processing for input into a learning algorithm. The Tox21 dataset we accessed via the DeepChem library in Chapter 4 followed this same design pattern. In general, if you would like to host a large dataset for analysis, hosting on the cloud and downloading to a local machine for processing as necessary seems good practice. (This breaks down for very large datasets however, where network transfer times become exorbitantly expensive.) See Example 6-1.

Example 6-1. This function downloads the MNIST dataset

```python
def download(filename):
  """Download the data from Yann's website, unless it's already here."""
  if not os.path.exists(WORK_DIRECTORY):
    os.makedirs(WORK_DIRECTORY)
  filepath = os.path.join(WORK_DIRECTORY, filename)
  if not os.path.exists(filepath):
    filepath, _ = urllib.request.urlretrieve(SOURCE_URL + filename, filepath)
    size = os.stat(filepath).st_size
    print('Successfully downloaded', filename, size, 'bytes.')
  return filepath
```

This download checks for the existence of WORK_DIRECTORY. If this directory exists, it assumes that the MNIST dataset has already been downloaded. Else, the script uses the urllib Python library to perform the download and prints the number of bytes downloaded.

The MNIST dataset is stored as a raw string of bytes encoding pixel values. In order to easily process this data, we need to convert it into a NumPy array. The function np.frombuffer provides a convenience that allows the conversion of a raw byte buffer into a numerical array (Example 6-2). As we have noted elsewhere in this book, deep networks can be destabilized by input data that occupies wide ranges. For stable gradient descent, it is often necessary to constrain inputs to span a bounded range. The original MNIST dataset contains pixel values ranging from 0 to 255. For stability, this range needs to be shifted to have mean zero and unit range (from –0.5 to +0.5).

Example 6-2. Extracting images from a downloaded dataset into NumPy arrays

```python
def extract_data(filename, num_images):
  """Extract the images into a 4D tensor [image index, y, x, channels].

  Values are rescaled from [0, 255] down to [-0.5, 0.5].
  """
  print('Extracting', filename)
  with gzip.open(filename) as bytestream:
    bytestream.read(16)
    buf = bytestream.read(IMAGE_SIZE * IMAGE_SIZE * num_images * NUM_CHANNELS)
    data = numpy.frombuffer(buf, dtype=numpy.uint8).astype(numpy.float32)
```

```
data = (data - (PIXEL_DEPTH / 2.0)) / PIXEL_DEPTH
data = data.reshape(num_images, IMAGE_SIZE, IMAGE_SIZE, NUM_CHANNELS)
return data
```

The labels are stored in a simple file as a string of bytes. There is a header consisting of 8 bytes, with the remainder of the data containing labels (Example 6-3).

Example 6-3. This function extracts labels from the downloaded dataset into an array of labels

```
def extract_labels(filename, num_images):
  """Extract the labels into a vector of int64 label IDs."""
  print('Extracting', filename)
  with gzip.open(filename) as bytestream:
    bytestream.read(8)
    buf = bytestream.read(1 * num_images)
    labels = numpy.frombuffer(buf, dtype=numpy.uint8).astype(numpy.int64)
  return labels
```

Given the functions defined in the previous examples, it is now feasible to download and process the MNIST training and test dataset (Example 6-4).

Example 6-4. Using the functions defined in the previous examples, this code snippet downloads and processes the MNIST train and test datasets

```
# Get the data.
train_data_filename = download('train-images-idx3-ubyte.gz')
train_labels_filename = download('train-labels-idx1-ubyte.gz')
test_data_filename = download('t10k-images-idx3-ubyte.gz')
test_labels_filename = download('t10k-labels-idx1-ubyte.gz')

# Extract it into NumPy arrays.
train_data = extract_data(train_data_filename, 60000)
train_labels = extract_labels(train_labels_filename, 60000)
test_data = extract_data(test_data_filename, 10000)
test_labels = extract_labels(test_labels_filename, 10000)
```

The MNIST dataset doesn't explicitly define a validation dataset for hyperparameter tuning. Consequently, we manually designate the final 5,000 datapoints of the training dataset as validation data (Example 6-5).

Example 6-5. Extract the final 5,000 datasets of the training data for hyperparameter validation

```
VALIDATION_SIZE = 5000  # Size of the validation set.

# Generate a validation set.
validation_data = train_data[:VALIDATION_SIZE, ...]
```

```
validation_labels = train_labels[:VALIDATION_SIZE]
train_data = train_data[VALIDATION_SIZE:, ...]
train_labels = train_labels[VALIDATION_SIZE:]
```

Choosing the Correct Validation Set

In Example 6-5, we use the final fragment of training data as a validation set to gauge the progress of our learning methods. In this case, this method is relatively harmless. The distribution of data in the test set is well represented by the distribution of data in the validation set.

However, in other situations, this type of simple validation set selection can be disastrous. In molecular machine learning (the use of machine learning to predict properties of molecules), it is almost always the case that the test distribution is dramatically different from the training distribution. Scientists are most interested in *prospective* prediction. That is, scientists would like to predict the properties of molecules that have never been tested for the property at hand. In this case, using the last fragment of training data for validation, or even a random subsample of the training data, will lead to misleadingly high accuracies. It's quite common for a molecular machine learning model to have 90% accuracy on validation and, say, 60% on test.

To correct for this error, it becomes necessary to design validation set selection methods that take pains to make the validation dissimilar from the training set. A variety of such algorithms exist for molecular machine learning, most of which use various mathematical estimates of graph dissimilarity (treating a molecule as a mathematical graph with atoms as nodes and chemical bonds as edges).

This issue crops up in many other areas of machine learning as well. In medical machine learning or in financial machine learning, relying on historical data to make forecasts can be disastrous. For each application, it's important to critically reason about whether performance on the selected validation set is actually a good proxy for true performance.

TensorFlow Convolutional Primitives

We start by introducing the TensorFlow primitives that are used to construct our convolutional networks (Example 6-6).

Example 6-6. Defining a 2D convolution in TensorFlow

```
tf.nn.conv2d(
    input,
    filter,
    strides,
    padding,
    use_cudnn_on_gpu=None,
    data_format=None,
    name=None
)
```

The function `tf.nn.conv2d` is the built-in TensorFlow function that defines convolutional layers. Here, `input` is assumed to be a tensor of shape (`batch`, `height`, `width`, `channels`) where `batch` is the number of images in a minibatch.

Note that the conversion functions defined previously read the MNIST data into this format. The argument `filter` is a tensor of shape (`filter_height`, `filter_width`, `channels`, `out_channels`) that specifies the learnable weights for the nonlinear transformation learned in the convolutional kernel. `strides` contains the filter strides and is a list of length 4 (one for each input dimension).

`padding` controls whether the input tensors are padded (with extra zeros as in Figure 6-18) to guarantee that output from the convolutional layer has the same shape as the input. If `padding="SAME"`, then `input` is padded to ensure that the convolutional layer outputs an image tensor of the same shape as the original input image tensor. If `padding="VALID"` then extra padding is not added.

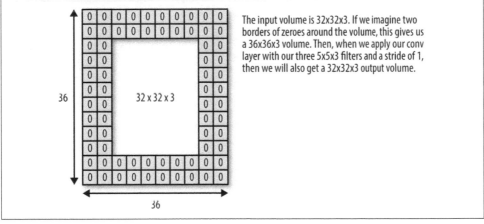

Figure 6-18 text: The input volume is 32x32x3. If we imagine two borders of zeroes around the volume, this gives us a 36x36x3 volume. Then, when we apply our conv layer with our three 5x5x3 filters and a stride of 1, then we will also get a 32x32x3 output volume.

Figure 6-18. Padding for convolutional layers ensures that the output image has the same shape as the input image.

The code in Example 6-7 defines max pooling in TensorFlow.

Example 6-7. Defining max pooling in TensorFlow

```
tf.nn.max_pool(
    value,
    ksize,
    strides,
    padding,
    data_format='NHWC',
    name=None
)
```

The `tf.nn.max_pool` function performs max pooling. Here `value` has the same shape as `input` for `tf.nn.conv2d`, (`batch, height, width, channels`). `ksize` is the size of the pooling window and is a list of length 4. `strides` and `padding` behave as for `tf.nn.conv2d`.

The Convolutional Architecture

The architecture defined in this section will closely resemble LeNet-5, the original architecture used to train convolutional neural networks on the MNIST dataset. At the time the LeNet-5 architecture was invented, it was exorbitantly expensive computationally, requiring multiple weeks of compute to complete training. Today's laptops thankfully are more than sufficient to train LeNet-5 models. Figure 6-19 illustrates the structure of the LeNet-5 architecture.

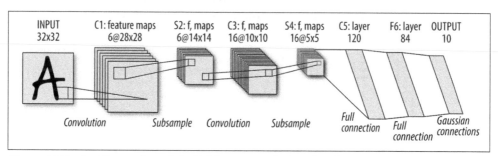

Figure 6-19. An illustration of the LeNet-5 convolutional architecture.

Where Would More Compute Make a Difference?

The LeNet-5 architecture is decades old, but is essentially the right architecture for the problem of digit recognition. However, its computational requirements forced the architecture into relative obscurity for decades. It's interesting to ask, then, what research problems today are similarly solved but limited solely by lack of adequate computational power?

One good contender is video processing. Convolutional models are quite good at processing video. However, it is unwieldy to store and train models on large video datasets, so most academic papers don't report results on video datasets. As a result, it's not so easy to hack together a good video processing system.

This situation will likely change as computing capabilities increase and it's likely that video processing systems will become much more commonplace. However, there's one critical difference between today's hardware improvements and those of past decades. Unlike in years past, Moore's law has slowed dramatically. As a result, improvements in hardware require more than natural transistor shrinkage and often require considerable ingenuity in architecture design. We will return to this topic in later chapters and discuss the architectural needs of deep networks.

Let's define the weights needed to train our LeNet-5 network. We start by defining some basic constants that are used to define our weight tensors (Example 6-8).

Example 6-8. Defining basic constants for the LeNet-5 model

```
NUM_CHANNELS = 1
IMAGE_SIZE = 28
NUM_LABELS = 10
```

The architecture we define will use two convolutional layers interspersed with two pooling layers, topped off by two fully connected layers. Recall that pooling requires no learnable weights, so we simply need to create weights for the convolutional and fully connected layers. For each `tf.nn.conv2d`, we need to create a learnable weight tensor corresponding to the `filter` argument for `tf.nn.conv2d`. In this particular architecture, we will also add a convolutional bias, one for each output channel (Example 6-9).

Example 6-9. Defining learnable weights for the convolutional layers

```
conv1_weights = tf.Variable(
    tf.truncated_normal([5, 5, NUM_CHANNELS, 32],  # 5x5 filter, depth 32.
                        stddev=0.1,
                        seed=SEED, dtype=tf.float32))
conv1_biases = tf.Variable(tf.zeros([32], dtype=tf.float32))
conv2_weights = tf.Variable(tf.truncated_normal(
    [5, 5, 32, 64], stddev=0.1,
    seed=SEED, dtype=tf.float32))
conv2_biases = tf.Variable(tf.constant(0.1, shape=[64], dtype=tf.float32))
```

Note that the convolutional weights are 4-tensors, while the biases are 1-tensors. The first fully connected layer converts the outputs of the convolutional layer to a vector of size 512. The input images start with size `IMAGE_SIZE=28`. After the two pooling layers (each of which reduces the input by a factor of 2), we end with images of size `IMAGE_SIZE//4`. We create the shape of the fully connected weights accordingly.

The second fully connected layer is used to provide the 10-way classification output, so it has weight shape `(512,10)` and bias shape `(10)`, shown in Example 6-10.

Example 6-10. Defining learnable weights for the fully connected layers

```
fc1_weights = tf.Variable(  # fully connected, depth 512.
    tf.truncated_normal([IMAGE_SIZE // 4 * IMAGE_SIZE // 4 * 64, 512],
                        stddev=0.1,
                        seed=SEED,
                        dtype=tf.float32))
fc1_biases = tf.Variable(tf.constant(0.1, shape=[512], dtype=tf.float32))
fc2_weights = tf.Variable(tf.truncated_normal([512, NUM_LABELS],
                                              stddev=0.1,
                                              seed=SEED,
                                              dtype=tf.float32))
fc2_biases = tf.Variable(tf.constant(
    0.1, shape=[NUM_LABELS], dtype=tf.float32))
```

With all the weights defined, we are now free to define the architecture of the network. The architecture has six layers in the pattern conv-pool-conv-pool-full-full (Example 6-11).

Example 6-11. Defining the LeNet-5 architecture. Calling the function defined in this example will instantiate the architecture.

```
def model(data, train=False):
  """The Model definition."""
  # 2D convolution, with 'SAME' padding (i.e. the output feature map has
  # the same size as the input). Note that {strides} is a 4D array whose
```

```
# shape matches the data layout: [image index, y, x, depth].
conv = tf.nn.conv2d(data,
                    conv1_weights,
                    strides=[1, 1, 1, 1],
                    padding='SAME')
# Bias and rectified linear non-linearity.
relu = tf.nn.relu(tf.nn.bias_add(conv, conv1_biases))
# Max pooling. The kernel size spec {ksize} also follows the layout of
# the data. Here we have a pooling window of 2, and a stride of 2.
pool = tf.nn.max_pool(relu,
                    ksize=[1, 2, 2, 1],
                    strides=[1, 2, 2, 1],
                    padding='SAME')
conv = tf.nn.conv2d(pool,
                    conv2_weights,
                    strides=[1, 1, 1, 1],
                    padding='SAME')
relu = tf.nn.relu(tf.nn.bias_add(conv, conv2_biases))
pool = tf.nn.max_pool(relu,
                    ksize=[1, 2, 2, 1],
                    strides=[1, 2, 2, 1],
                    padding='SAME')
# Reshape the feature map cuboid into a 2D matrix to feed it to the
# fully connected layers.
pool_shape = pool.get_shape().as_list()
reshape = tf.reshape(
    pool,
    [pool_shape[0], pool_shape[1] * pool_shape[2] * pool_shape[3]])
# Fully connected layer. Note that the '+' operation automatically
# broadcasts the biases.
hidden = tf.nn.relu(tf.matmul(reshape, fc1_weights) + fc1_biases)
# Add a 50% dropout during training only. Dropout also scales
# activations such that no rescaling is needed at evaluation time.
if train:
  hidden = tf.nn.dropout(hidden, 0.5, seed=SEED)
return tf.matmul(hidden, fc2_weights) + fc2_biases
```

As noted previously, the basic architecture of the network intersperses tf.nn.conv2d, tf.nn.max_pool, with nonlinearities, and a final fully connected layer. For regularization, a dropout layer is applied after the final fully connected layer, but only during training. Note that we pass in the input as an argument data to the function model().

The only part of the network that remains to be defined are the placeholders (Example 6-12). We need to define two placeholders for inputting the training images and the training labels. In this particular network, we also define a separate placeholder for evaluation that allows us to input larger batches when evaluating.

Example 6-12. Define placeholders for the architecture

```
BATCH_SIZE = 64
EVAL_BATCH_SIZE = 64

train_data_node = tf.placeholder(
    tf.float32,
    shape=(BATCH_SIZE, IMAGE_SIZE, IMAGE_SIZE, NUM_CHANNELS))
train_labels_node = tf.placeholder(tf.int64, shape=(BATCH_SIZE,))
eval_data = tf.placeholder(
    tf.float32,
    shape=(EVAL_BATCH_SIZE, IMAGE_SIZE, IMAGE_SIZE, NUM_CHANNELS))
```

With these definitions in place, we now have the data processed, inputs and weights specified, and the model constructed. We are now prepared to train the network (Example 6-13).

Example 6-13. Training the LeNet-5 architecture

```
# Create a local session to run the training.
start_time = time.time()
with tf.Session() as sess:
  # Run all the initializers to prepare the trainable parameters.
  tf.global_variables_initializer().run()
  # Loop through training steps.
  for step in xrange(int(num_epochs * train_size) // BATCH_SIZE):
    # Compute the offset of the current minibatch in the data.
    # Note that we could use better randomization across epochs.
    offset = (step * BATCH_SIZE) % (train_size - BATCH_SIZE)
    batch_data = train_data[offset:(offset + BATCH_SIZE), ...]
    batch_labels = train_labels[offset:(offset + BATCH_SIZE)]
    # This dictionary maps the batch data (as a NumPy array) to the
    # node in the graph it should be fed to.
    feed_dict = {train_data_node: batch_data,
                 train_labels_node: batch_labels}
    # Run the optimizer to update weights.
    sess.run(optimizer, feed_dict=feed_dict)
```

The structure of this fitting code looks quite similar to other code for fitting we've seen so far in this book. In each step, we construct a feed dictionary, and then run a step of the optimizer. Note that we use minibatch training as before.

Evaluating Trained Models

We now have a model training. How can we evaluate the accuracy of the trained model? A simple method is to define an error metric. As in previous chapters, we shall use a simple classification metric to gauge accuracy (Example 6-14).

Example 6-14. Evaluating the error of trained architectures

```
def error_rate(predictions, labels):
  """Return the error rate based on dense predictions and sparse labels."""
  return 100.0 - (
      100.0 *
      numpy.sum(numpy.argmax(predictions, 1) == labels) /
      predictions.shape[0])
```

We can use this function to evaluate the error of the network as we train. Let's introduce an additional convenience function that evaluates predictions on any given dataset in batches (Example 6-15). This convenience is necessary since our network can only handle inputs with fixed batch sizes.

Example 6-15. Evaluating a batch of data at a time

```
def eval_in_batches(data, sess):
  """Get predictions for a dataset by running it in small batches."""
  size = data.shape[0]
  if size < EVAL_BATCH_SIZE:
    raise ValueError("batch size for evals larger than dataset: %d"
                     % size)
  predictions = numpy.ndarray(shape=(size, NUM_LABELS),
                              dtype=numpy.float32)
  for begin in xrange(0, size, EVAL_BATCH_SIZE):
    end = begin + EVAL_BATCH_SIZE
    if end <= size:
      predictions[begin:end, :] = sess.run(
          eval_prediction,
          feed_dict={eval_data: data[begin:end, ...]})
    else:
      batch_predictions = sess.run(
          eval_prediction,
          feed_dict={eval_data: data[-EVAL_BATCH_SIZE:, ...]})
      predictions[begin:, :] = batch_predictions[begin - size:, :]
  return predictions
```

We can now add a little instrumentation (in the inner for-loop of training) that periodically evaluates the model's accuracy on the validation set. We can end training by scoring test accuracy. Example 6-16 shows the full fitting code with instrumentation added in.

Example 6-16. The full code for training the network, with instrumentation added

```
# Create a local session to run the training.
start_time = time.time()
with tf.Session() as sess:
  # Run all the initializers to prepare the trainable parameters.
  tf.global_variables_initializer().run()
```

```
# Loop through training steps.
for step in xrange(int(num_epochs * train_size) // BATCH_SIZE):
  # Compute the offset of the current minibatch in the data.
  # Note that we could use better randomization across epochs.
  offset = (step * BATCH_SIZE) % (train_size - BATCH_SIZE)
  batch_data = train_data[offset:(offset + BATCH_SIZE), ...]
  batch_labels = train_labels[offset:(offset + BATCH_SIZE)]
  # This dictionary maps the batch data (as a NumPy array) to the
  # node in the graph it should be fed to.
  feed_dict = {train_data_node: batch_data,
               train_labels_node: batch_labels}
  # Run the optimizer to update weights.
  sess.run(optimizer, feed_dict=feed_dict)
  # print some extra information once reach the evaluation frequency
  if step % EVAL_FREQUENCY == 0:
    # fetch some extra nodes' data
    l, lr, predictions = sess.run([loss, learning_rate,
                                   train_prediction],
                                  feed_dict=feed_dict)
    elapsed_time = time.time() - start_time
    start_time = time.time()
    print('Step %d (epoch %.2f), %.1f ms' %
          (step, float(step) * BATCH_SIZE / train_size,
           1000 * elapsed_time / EVAL_FREQUENCY))
    print('Minibatch loss: %.3f, learning rate: %.6f' % (l, lr))
    print('Minibatch error: %.1f%%'
          % error_rate(predictions, batch_labels))
    print('Validation error: %.1f%%' % error_rate(
          eval_in_batches(validation_data, sess), validation_labels))
    sys.stdout.flush()
# Finally print the result!
test_error = error_rate(eval_in_batches(test_data, sess),
                        test_labels)
print('Test error: %.1f%%' % test_error)
```

Challenge for the Reader

Try training the network yourself. You should be able to achieve test error of < 1%!

Review

In this chapter, we have shown you the basic concepts of convolutional network design. These concepts include convolutional and pooling layers that constitute core building blocks of convolutional networks. We then discussed applications of convolutional architectures such as object detection, image segmentation, and image generation. We ended the chapter with an in-depth case study that showed you how to train a convolutional architecture on the MNIST handwritten digit dataset.

In Chapter 7, we will cover recurrent neural networks, another core deep learning architecture. Unlike convolutional networks, which were designed for image processing, recurrent architectures are powerfully suited to handling sequential data such as natural language datasets.

Recurrent Neural Networks

So far in this book, we've introduced you to the use of deep learning to process various types of inputs. We started from simple linear and logistic regression on fixed dimensional feature vectors, and then followed up with a discussion of fully connected deep networks. These models take in arbitrary feature vectors with fixed, predetermined sizes. These models make no assumptions about the type of data encoded into these vectors. On the other hand, convolutional networks place strong assumptions upon the structure of their data. Inputs to convolutional networks have to satisfy a locality assumption that allows for the definition of a local receptive field.

How could we use the networks that we've described thus far to process data like sentences? Sentences do have some locality properties (nearby words are typically related), and it is indeed possible to use a one-dimensional convolutional network to process sentence data. That said, most practitioners resort to a different type of architecture, the recurrent neural network, in order to handle sequences of data.

Recurrent neural networks (RNNs) are designed natively to allow deep networks to process sequences of data. RNNs assume that incoming data takes the form of a sequence of vectors or tensors. If we transform each word in a sentence into a vector (more on how to do this later), sentences can be fed into RNNs. Similarly, video (considered as a sequence of images) can similarly be processed by an RNN. At each sequence position, an RNN applies an arbitrary nonlinear transformation to the input at that sequence location. This nonlinear transformation is shared for all sequence steps.

The description in the previous paragraph is a little abstract, but turns out to be immensely powerful. In this chapter, you will learn more details about how RNNs are structured and about how to implement RNNs in TensorFlow. We will also discuss how RNNs can be used in practice to perform tasks like sampling new sentences or generating text for applications such as chatbots.

The case study for this chapter trains a recurrent neural network language model on the Penn Treebank corpus, a body of sentences extracted from *Wall Street Journal* articles. This tutorial was adapted from the TensorFlow official documentation tutorial on recurrent networks. (We encourage you to access the original tutorial on the TensorFlow website if you're curious about the changes we've made.) As always, we recommend that you follow along with the code in the GitHub repo associated with this book (*https://github.com/matroid/dlwithtf*).

Overview of Recurrent Architectures

Recurrent architectures are useful for modeling very complex time varying datasets. Time varying datasets are traditionally called *time-series*. Figure 7-1 displays a number of time-series datasets.

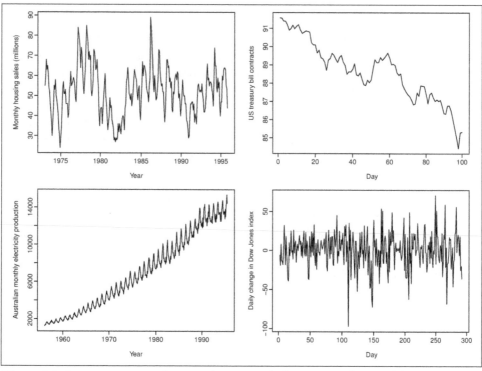

Figure 7-1. Some time-series datasets that we might be interested in modeling.

In time-series modeling, we design learning systems that are capable of learning the evolution rule that models how the future of the system at hand evolves depending on the past. Mathematically, let's suppose that at each time step, we receive a datapoint x_t where t is the current time. Then, time-series methods seek to learn some function f such that

$$x_{t+1} = f(x_1, \cdots, x_t)$$

The idea is that f encodes the underlying dynamics of the system well and learning it from data would enable a learning system to predict the future of the system at hand. In practice, it's too unwieldy to learn a function that depends on all past inputs, so learning systems often assume that all information about last datapoints $x_1, \cdots, x_{t-1}$ can be encoded into some fixed vector h_t. Then, the update equation simplifies into the format

$$x_{t+1}, h_{t+1} = f(x_t, h_t)$$

Notice that we assume that the same function f here applies for all timesteps t. That is, we assume the time-series to be *stationary* (Figure 7-2). This assumption is broken for many systems, notably including the stock market where today's rules need not hold tomorrow.

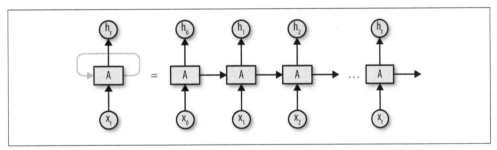

Figure 7-2. A mathematical model of a time-series with a stationary evolution rule. Recall that a stationary system is one whose underlying dynamics don't shift over time.

What does this equation have to do with recurrent neural nets? The basic answer derives from the universal approximation theorem that we introduced in Chapter 4. The function f can be arbitrarily complex, so using a fully connected deep network to learn f seems like a reasonable idea. This intuition essentially defines the RNN. A simple recurrent network can be viewed as a fully connected network that is applied repeatedly to each time step of the data.

In fact, recurrent neural networks really become interesting only for complex high-dimensional time-series. For simpler systems, there are classical signal processing time-series methods that often do a good job of modeling time dynamics. However, for complex systems, such as speech (see the speech spectrogram in Figure 7-3), RNNs come into their own and offer capabilities that other methods can't.

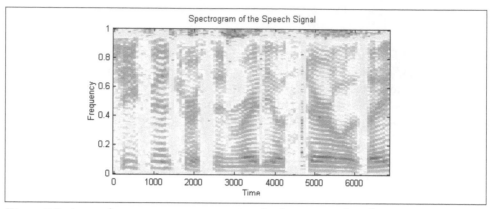

Figure 7-3. A speech spectrogram representing the frequencies found in a speech sample.

Recurrent Cells

Gradient Instability

Recurrent networks tend to degrade signal over time. Think of it as attenuating a signal by a multiplicative factor at each timestep. As a result, after 50 timesteps, the signal is quite degraded.

As a result of this instability, it has been challenging to train recurrent neural networks on longer time-series. A number of methods have arisen to combat this instability, which we will discuss in the remainder of this section.

There are a number of elaborations on the concept of a simple recurrent neural network that have proven significantly more successful in practical applications. In this section, we will briefly review some of these variations.

Long Short-Term Memory (LSTM)

Part of the challenge with the standard recurrent cell is that signals from the distant past attenuate rapidly. As a result, RNNs can fail to learn models of complex dependencies. This failure becomes particularly notable in applications such as language modeling, where words can have complex dependencies on earlier phrases.

One potential solution to this issue is to allow states from the past to pass through unmodified. The long short-term memory (LSTM) architecture proposes a mechanism to allow past state to pass through to the present with minimal modifications. Empirically using an LSTM "cell" (shown in Figure 7-4) seems to offer superior learning performance when compared to simple recurrent neural networks using fully connected layers.

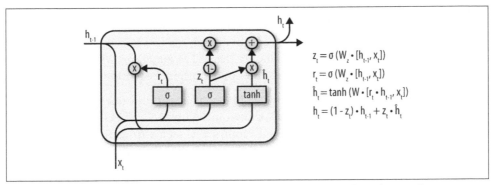

$$z_t = \sigma (W_z \cdot [h_{t-1}, x_t])$$
$$r_t = \sigma (W_z \cdot [h_{t-1}, x_t])$$
$$\hat{h}_t = \tanh (W \cdot [r_t \cdot h_{t-1}, x_t])$$
$$h_t = (1 - z_t) \cdot h_{t-1} + z_t \cdot \hat{h}_t$$

Figure 7-4. A long short-term memory (LSTM) cell. LSTMs perform better than standard recurrent neural networks at preserving long-range dependencies in inputs. As a result, LSTMs are often preferred for complex sequential data, such as natural language.

So Many Equations!

The LSTM equations involve many sophisticated terms. If you are interested in understanding precisely the mathematical intuitions behind the LSTM, we encourage you to play with the equations with pencil and paper and trying to take derivatives of the LSTM cell.

However, for other readers who are primarily interested in using recurrent architectures to solve practical problems, we believe it isn't absolutely necessary to delve into the nitty-gritty details of how LSTMs work. Rather, keep the high-level intuition that past state is allowed to pass through, and work through the example code for this chapter in some depth.

Optimizing Recurrent Networks

Unlike fully connected networks or convolutional networks, LSTMs involve some sophisticated mathematical operations and control-flow operations. As a result, training large recurrent networks at scale has proven to be challenging, even with modern GPU hardware.

Significant effort has been put into optimizing RNN implementations to run quickly on GPU hardware. In particular, Nvidia has incorporated RNNs into their CuDNN library that provides specially optimized code for training deep networks on GPUs. Luckily for TensorFlow users, integration with libraries such as CuDNN is performed within TensorFlow itself so you don't need to worry too much about code optimization (unless of course, you're working on very large-scale datasets). We will discuss hardware needs for deep neural networks at greater depth in Chapter 9.

Gated Recurrent Units (GRU)

The complexity, both conceptual and computational, for LSTM cells has motivated a number of researchers to attempt to simplify the LSTM equations while retaining the performance gains and modeling capabilities of the original equations.

There are a number of contenders for LSTM replacement, but one of the frontrunners is the gated recurrent unit (GRU), shown in Figure 7-5. The GRU removes one of the subcomponents of the LSTM but empirically seems to achieve performance similar to that of the LSTM. The GRU might be a suitable replacement for LSTM cells on sequence modeling projects.

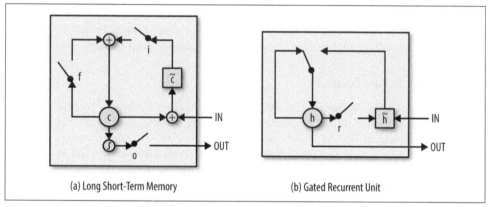

(a) Long Short-Term Memory   *(b) Gated Recurrent Unit*

Figure 7-5. A gated recurrent unit (GRU) cell. GRUs preserve many of the benefits of LSTMs at lower computational cost.

Applications of Recurrent Models

While recurrent neural networks are useful tools for modeling time-series datasets, there are a host of other applications of recurrent networks. These include applications such as natural language modeling, machine translation, chemical retrosynthesis, and arbitrary computation with Neural Turing machines. In this section, we provide a brief tour of some of these exciting applications.

Sampling from Recurrent Networks

So far, we've taught you how recurrent networks can learn to model the time evolution of sequences of data. It stands to reason that if you understand the evolution rule for a set of sequences, you ought to be able to sample new sequences from the distribution of training sequences. And indeed, it turns out that that good sequences can be sampled from trained models. The most useful application thus far is in language modeling. Being able to generate realistic sentences is a very useful tool that underpins systems such as autocomplete and chatbots.

Why Don't We Use GANs for Sequences?

In Chapter 6, we discussed the problem of generating new images. We discussed models such as variational autoencoders that produced only blurry images and introduced the technology of generative adversarial networks that proves capable of producing sharp images. The question remains, though: if we need GANs for good image samples, why don't we use them for good sentences?

It turns out that today's generative adversarial models are mediocre at sampling sequences. It's not clear why this is the case. Theoretical understanding of GANs remains very weak (even by the standards of deep learning theory), but something about the game theoretic equilibrium discovery seems to perform worse for sequences than for images.

Seq2seq Models

Sequence-to-sequence (seq2seq) models are powerful tools that enable models to transform one sequence into another. The core idea of a sequence-to-sequence model is to use an encoding recurrent network that embeds input sequences into vector spaces alongside a decoding network that enables sampling of output sequences as described in previous sentences. Figure 7-6 illustrates a seq2seq model.

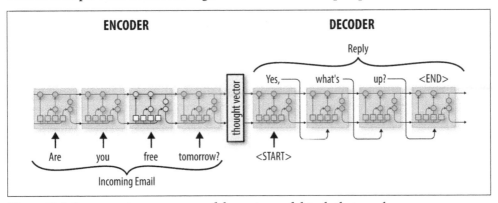

Figure 7-6. Sequence-to-sequence models are powerful tools that can learn sequence transformations. They have been applied to machine translation (for example, transforming a sequence of English words to Mandarin) and chemical retrosynthesis (transforming a sequence of chemical products into a sequence of reactants).

Things get interesting since encoder and decoder layers can themselves be deep. (RNN layers can be stacked in a natural fashion.) The Google neural machine translation (GNMT) system has many stacked encoding and decoding layers. As a result of this powerful representational capacity, it is capable of performing state-of-the-art translations far beyond the capabilities of its nearest nondeep competitors. Figure 7-7 illustrates the GNMT architecture.

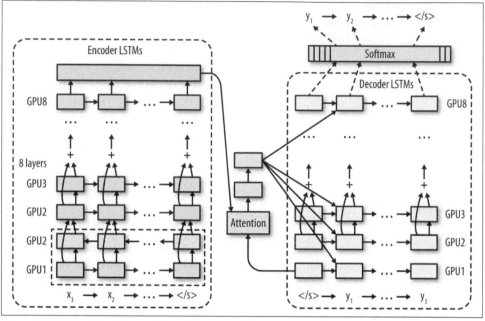

Figure 7-7. The Google neural machine translation (GNMT) architecture is a deep seq2seq model that learns to perform machine translation.

While so far we've mainly discussed applications to natural language processing, the seq2seq architecture has myriad applications in other domains. One of the authors has used seq2seq architectures to perform chemical retrosynthesis, the act of deconstructing molecules into simpler constituents. Figure 7-8 illustrates.

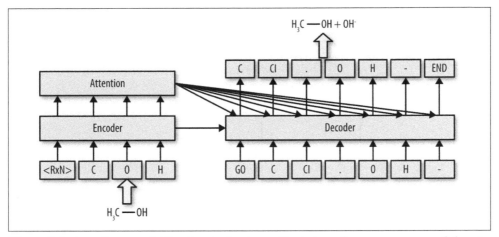

Figure 7-8. A seq2seq model for chemical retrosynthesis transforms a sequence of chemical products into a sequence of chemical reactants.

Neural Turing Machines

The dream of machine learning has been to move further up the abstraction stack: moving from learning short pattern-matching engines to learning to perform arbitrary computations. The Neural Turing machine is a powerful step in this evolution.

The Turing machine was a seminal contribution to the mathematical theory of computation. It was the first mathematical model of a machine capable of performing any computation. The Turing machine maintains a "tape" that provides a memory of the performed computation. The second part of the machine is a "head" that performs transformations on single tape cells. The insight of the Turing machine was that the "head" didn't need to be very complicated in order to perform arbitrarily complicated calculations.

The Neural Turing machine (NTM) is a very clever attempt to transmute a Turing machine itself into a neural network. The trick in this transmutation is to turn discrete actions into soft continuous functions (this is a trick that pops up in deep learning repeatedly, so take note!)

The Turing machine head is quite similar to the RNN cell! As a result, the NTM can be trained end-to-end to learn to perform arbitrary computations, in principle at least (Figure 7-9). In practice, there are severe limitations to the set of computations that the NTM can perform. Gradient flow instabilities (as always) limit what can be learned. More research and experimentation will be needed to devise successors to NTMs capable of learning more useful functions.

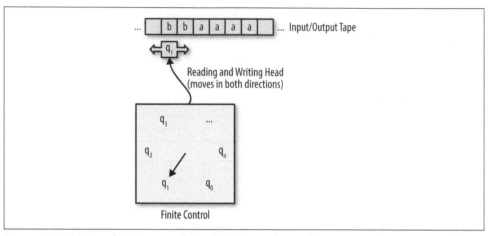

... | b | b | a | a | a | a | ... Input/Output Tape

q_1

Reading and Writing Head
(moves in both directions)

q_3 ...

q_2 q_n

q_1 q_0

Finite Control

Figure 7-9. A Neural Turing machine (NTM) is a learnable version of a Turing machine. It maintains a tape where it can store the outputs of intermediate computations. While NTMs have many practical limitations, it's possible that their intellectual descendants will be capable of learning powerful algorithms.

Turing Completeness

The concept of Turing completeness is an important notion in computer science. A programming language is said to be Turing complete if it is capable of performing any computation that can be performed by a Turing machine. The Turing machine itself was invented to provide a mathematical model of what it means for a function to be "computable." The machine provides the capability to read, write, and store in memory various instructions, abstract primitives that underlie all computing machines.

Over time, a large body of work has shown that the Turing machine closely models the set of computations performable in the physical world. To a first approximation, if it can be shown that a Turing machine is incapable of performing a computation, no computing device is capable of it either. On the other side, if it can be shown that a computing system can perform the basic operations of a Turing machine, it is then "Turing complete" and capable of performing in principle any computation that can be performed at all. A number of surprising systems are Turing complete. We encourage you to read more about this topic if interested.

Recurrent Networks Are Turing Complete

Perhaps unsurprisingly, NTMs are capable of performing any computation a Turing machine can and are consequently Turing complete. However, a less known fact is that vanilla recurrent neural networks are themselves Turing complete! Put another way, in principle, a recurrent neural network is capable of learning to perform arbitrary computation.

The basic idea is that the transition operator can learn to perform basic reading, writing, and storage operations. The unrolling of the recurrent network over time allows for the performance of complex computations. In some sense, this fact shouldn't be too surprising. The universal approximation theorem already demonstrates that fully connected networks are capable of learning arbitrary functions. Chaining arbitrary functions together over time leads to arbitrary computations. (The technical details required to formally prove this are formidable, though.)

Working with Recurrent Neural Networks in Practice

In this section, you will learn about the use of recurrent neural networks for language modeling on the Penn Treebank dataset, a natural language dataset built from *Wall Street Journal* articles. We will introduce the TensorFlow primitives needed to perform this modeling and will also walk you through the data handling and preprocessing steps needed to prepare data for training. We encourage you to follow along and try running the code in the GitHub repo associated with the book (*https://github.com/matroid/dlwithtf*).

Processing the Penn Treebank Corpus

The Penn Treebank contains a million-word corpus of *Wall Street Journal* articles. This corpus can be used for either character-level or word-level modeling (the tasks of predicting the next character or word in a sentence given those preceding). The efficacy of models is measured using the perplexity of trained models (more on this metric later).

The Penn Treebank corpus consists of sentences. How can we transform sentences into a form that can be fed to machine learning systems such as recurrent language models? Recall that machine learning models accept tensors (with recurrent models accepting sequences of tensors) as input. Consequently, we need to transform words into tensors for machine learning.

The simplest method of transforming words into vectors is to use "one-hot" encoding. In this encoding, let's suppose that our language dataset uses a vocabulary that has $|V|$ words. Then each word is transformed into a vector of shape ($|V|$). All the entries of this vector are zero, except for one entry, at the index that corresponds to the current word. For an example of this embedding, see Figure 7-10.

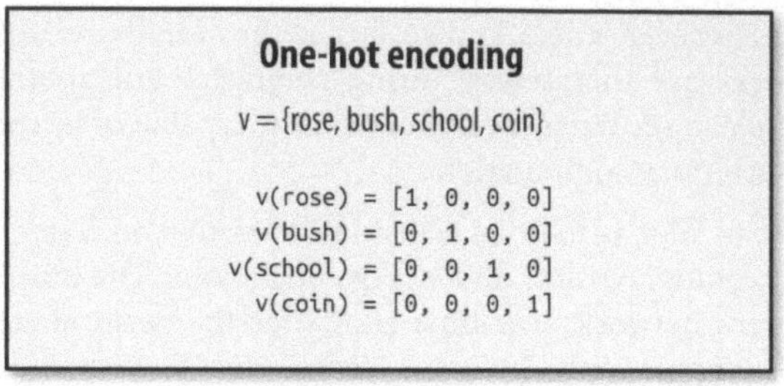

One-hot encoding

v = {rose, bush, school, coin}

```
v(rose)   = [1, 0, 0, 0]
v(bush)   = [0, 1, 0, 0]
v(school) = [0, 0, 1, 0]
v(coin)   = [0, 0, 0, 1]
```

Figure 7-10. One-hot encodings transform words into vectors with only one nonzero entry (which is typically set to one). Different indices in the vector uniquely represent words in a language corpus.

It's also possible to use more sophisticated embeddings. The basic idea is similar to that for the one-hot encoding. Each word is associated with a unique vector. However, the key difference is that it's possible to learn this encoding vector directly from data to obtain a "word embedding" for the word in question that's meaningful for the dataset at hand. We will show you how to learn word embeddings later in this chapter.

In order to process the Penn Treebank data, we need to find the vocabulary of words used in the corpus, then transform each word into its associated word vector. We will then show how to feed the processed data into a TensorFlow model.

Penn Treebank Limitations

The Penn Treebank is a very useful dataset for language modeling, but it no longer poses a challenge for state-of-the-art language models; researchers have already overfit models on the peculiarities of this collection. State-of-the-art research would use larger datasets such as the billion-word-corpus language benchmark. However, for our exploratory purposes, the Penn Treebank easily suffices.

Code for Preprocessing

The snippet of code in Example 7-1 reads in the raw files associated with the Penn Treebank corpus. The corpus is stored with one sentence per line. Some Python string handling is done to replace "\n" newline markers with fixed-token "<eos>" and then split the file into a list of tokens.

Example 7-1. This function reads in the raw Penn Treebank file

```
def _read_words(filename):
  with tf.gfile.GFile(filename, "r") as f:
    if sys.version_info[0] >= 3:
      return f.read().replace("\n", "<eos>").split()
    else:
      return f.read().decode("utf-8").replace("\n", "<eos>").split()
```

With _read_words defined, we can build the vocabulary associated with a given file using function _build_vocab defined in Example 7-2. We simply read in the words in the file, and count the number of unique words in the file using Python's collec tions library. For convenience, we construct a dictionary object mapping words to their unique integer identifiers (their positions in the vocabulary). Tying it all together, _file_to_word_ids transforms a file into a list of word identifiers (Example 7-3).

Example 7-2. This function builds a vocabulary consisting of all words in the specified file

```
def _build_vocab(filename):
  data = _read_words(filename)

  counter = collections.Counter(data)
  count_pairs = sorted(counter.items(), key=lambda x: (-x[1], x[0]))

  words, _ = list(zip(*count_pairs))
  word_to_id = dict(zip(words, range(len(words))))

  return word_to_id
```

Example 7-3. This function transforms words in a file into id numbers

```
def _file_to_word_ids(filename, word_to_id):
  data = _read_words(filename)
  return [word_to_id[word] for word in data if word in word_to_id]
```

With these utilities in place, we can process the Penn Treebank corpus with function ptb_raw_data (Example 7-4). Note that training, validation, and test datasets are pre-specified, so we need only read each file into a list of unique indices.

Example 7-4. This function loads the Penn Treebank data from the specified location

```
def ptb_raw_data(data_path=None):
  """Load PTB raw data from data directory "data_path".

  Reads PTB text files, converts strings to integer ids,
```

and performs mini-batching of the inputs.

The PTB dataset comes from Tomas Mikolov's webpage:
http://www.fit.vutbr.cz/~imikolov/rnnlm/simple-examples.tgz

```
Args:
  data_path: string path to the directory where simple-examples.tgz
             has been extracted.

Returns:
  tuple (train_data, valid_data, test_data, vocabulary)
  where each of the data objects can be passed to PTBIterator.
"""


train_path = os.path.join(data_path, "ptb.train.txt")
valid_path = os.path.join(data_path, "ptb.valid.txt")
test_path = os.path.join(data_path, "ptb.test.txt")


word_to_id = _build_vocab(train_path)
train_data = _file_to_word_ids(train_path, word_to_id)
valid_data = _file_to_word_ids(valid_path, word_to_id)
test_data = _file_to_word_ids(test_path, word_to_id)
vocabulary = len(word_to_id)
return train_data, valid_data, test_data, vocabulary
```

tf.GFile and tf.Flags

TensorFlow is a large project that contains many bits and pieces. While most of the library is devoted to machine learning, there's also a large proportion that's dedicated to loading and massaging data. Some of these functions provide useful capabilities that aren't found elsewhere. Other parts of the loading functionality are less useful, however.

tf.GFile and tf.FLags provide functionality that is more or less identical to standard Python file handling and argparse. The provenance of these tools is historical. With Google, custom file handlers and flag handling are required by internal code standards. For the rest of us, though, it's better style to use standard Python tools whenever possible. It's much better for readability and stability.

Loading Data into TensorFlow

In this section, we cover the code needed to load our processed indices into Tensor-Flow. To do so, we will introduce you to a new bit of TensorFlow machinery. Until now, we've used feed dictionaries to pass data into TensorFlow. While feed dictionaries are fine for small toy datasets, they are often not good choices for larger datasets, since large Python overheads involving packing and unpacking dictionaries are introduced. For more performant code, it's better to use TensorFlow queues.

`tf.Queue` provides a way to load data asynchronously. This allows decoupling of the GPU compute thread from the CPU-bound data preprocessing thread. This decoupling is particularly useful for large datasets where we want to keep the GPU maximally active.

It's possible to feed `tf.Queue` objects into TensorFlow placeholders to train models and achieve greater performance. We will demonstrate how to do so later in this chapter.

The function `ptb_producer` introduced in Example 7-5 transforms raw lists of indices into `tf.Queues` that can pass data into a TensorFlow computational graph. Let's start by introducing some of the computational primitives we use. `tf.train.range_input_producer` is a convenience operation that produces a `tf.Queue` from an input tensor. The method `tf.Queue.dequeue()` pulls a tensor from the queue for training. `tf.strided_slice` extracts the part of this tensor that corresponds to the data for the current minibatch.

Example 7-5. This function loads the Penn Treebank data from the specified location

```
def ptb_producer(raw_data, batch_size, num_steps, name=None):
  """Iterate on the raw PTB data.

  This chunks up raw_data into batches of examples and returns
  Tensors that are drawn from these batches.

  Args:
    raw_data: one of the raw data outputs from ptb_raw_data.
    batch_size: int, the batch size.
    num_steps: int, the number of unrolls.
    name: the name of this operation (optional).

  Returns:
    A pair of Tensors, each shaped [batch_size, num_steps]. The
    second element of the tuple is the same data time-shifted to the
    right by one.

  Raises:
    tf.errors.InvalidArgumentError: if batch_size or num_steps are
    too high.
  """
  with tf.name_scope(name, "PTBProducer",
                     [raw_data, batch_size, num_steps]):
    raw_data = tf.convert_to_tensor(raw_data, name="raw_data",
                                    dtype=tf.int32)

    data_len = tf.size(raw_data)
    batch_len = data_len // batch_size
    data = tf.reshape(raw_data[0 : batch_size * batch_len],
                      [batch_size, batch_len])
```

```
epoch_size = (batch_len - 1) // num_steps
assertion = tf.assert_positive(
    epoch_size,
    message="epoch_size == 0, decrease batch_size or num_steps")
with tf.control_dependencies([assertion]):
  epoch_size = tf.identity(epoch_size, name="epoch_size")

i = tf.train.range_input_producer(epoch_size,
                                  shuffle=False).dequeue()
x = tf.strided_slice(data, [0, i * num_steps],
                     [batch_size, (i + 1) * num_steps])
x.set_shape([batch_size, num_steps])
y = tf.strided_slice(data, [0, i * num_steps + 1],
                     [batch_size, (i + 1) * num_steps + 1])
y.set_shape([batch_size, num_steps])
return x, y
```

tf.data

TensorFlow (from version 1.4 onward) supports a new module `tf.data` with a new class `tf.data.Dataset` that provides an explicit API for representing streams of data. It's likely that `tf.data` will eventually supersede queues as the preferred input modality, especially since it has a well-thought-out functional API.

At the time of writing, the `tf.data` module was just released and remained relatively immature compared with other parts of the API, so we decided to stick with queues for the examples. However, we encourage you to learn about `tf.data` yourself.

The Basic Recurrent Architecture

We will use an LSTM cell for modeling the Penn Treebank, since LSTMs often offer superior performance for language modeling challenges. The function `tf.con trib.rnn.BasicLSTMCell` implements the basic LSTM cell for us already, so no need to implement it ourselves (Example 7-6).

Example 7-6. This function wraps an LSTM cell from tf.contrib

```
def lstm_cell():
  return tf.contrib.rnn.BasicLSTMCell(
      size, forget_bias=0.0, state_is_tuple=True,
      reuse=tf.get_variable_scope().reuse)
```

Is Using TensorFlow Contrib Code OK?

Note that the LSTM implementation we use is drawn from `tf.con trib`. Is it acceptable to use code from `tf.contrib` for industrial-strength projects? The jury still appears to be out on this one. From our personal experience, code in `tf.contrib` tends to be a bit shakier than code in the core TensorFlow library, but is usually still pretty solid. There are often many useful libraries and utilities that are only available as part of `tf.contrib`. Our recommendation is to use pieces from `tf.contrib` as necessary, but make note of the pieces you use and replace them if an equivalent in the core TensorFlow library becomes available.

The snippet in Example 7-7 instructs TensorFlow to learn a word embedding for each word in our vocabulary. The key function for us is `tf.nn.embedding_lookup`, which allows us to perform the correct tensorial lookup operation. Note that we need to manually define the embedding matrix as a TensorFlow variable.

Example 7-7. Learn a word embedding for each word in the vocabulary

```
with tf.device("/cpu:0"):
  embedding = tf.get_variable(
      "embedding", [vocab_size, size], dtype=tf.float32)
  inputs = tf.nn.embedding_lookup(embedding, input_.input_data)
```

With our word vectors in hand, we simply need to apply the LSTM cell (using function `lstm_cell`) to each word vector in our sequence. To do this, we simply use a Python `for`-loop to construct the needed set of calls to `cell()`. There's only one trick here: we need to make sure we reuse the same variables at each timestep, since the LSTM cell should perform the same operation at each timestep. Luckily, the method `reuse_variables()` for variable scopes allows us to do so without much effort. See Example 7-8.

Example 7-8. Apply LSTM cell to each word vector in input sequence

```
outputs = []
state = self._initial_state
with tf.variable_scope("RNN"):
  for time_step in range(num_steps):
    if time_step > 0: tf.get_variable_scope().reuse_variables()
    (cell_output, state) = cell(inputs[:, time_step, :], state)
    outputs.append(cell_output)
```

All that remains now is to define the loss associated with the graph in order to train it. Conveniently, TensorFlow offers a loss for training language models in tf.contrib. We need only make a call to tf.contrib.seq2seq.sequence_loss (Example 7-9). Underneath the hood, this loss turns out to be a form of perplexity.

Example 7-9. Add the sequence loss

```
# use the contrib sequence loss and average over the batches
loss = tf.contrib.seq2seq.sequence_loss(
    logits,
    input_.targets,
    tf.ones([batch_size, num_steps], dtype=tf.float32),
    average_across_timesteps=False,
    average_across_batch=True
)
# update the cost variables
self._cost = cost = tf.reduce_sum(loss)
```

Perplexity

Perplexity is often used for language modeling challenges. It is a variant of the binary cross-entropy that is useful for measuring how close the learned distribution is to the true distribution of data. Empirically, perplexity has proven useful for many language modeling challenges and we make use of it here in that capacity (since the sequence_loss just implements perplexity specialized to sequences inside).

We can then train this graph using a standard gradient descent method. We leave out some of the messy details of the underlying code, but suggest you check GitHub if curious. Evaluating the quality of the trained model turns out to be straightforward as well, since the perplexity is used both as the training loss and the evaluation metric. As a result, we can simply display self._cost to gauge how the model is training. We encourage you to train the model for yourself!

Challenge for the Reader

Try lowering perplexity on the Penn Treebank by experimenting with different model architectures. Note that these experiments might be time-consuming without a GPU.

Review

This chapter introduced you to recurrent neural networks (RNNs), a powerful architecture for learning on sequential data. RNNs are capable of learning the underlying evolution rule that governs a sequence of data. While RNNs can be used for modeling simple time-series, they are most powerful when modeling complex sequential data such as speech and natural language.

We introduced you to a number of RNN variants such as LSTMs and GRUs, which perform better on data with complex long-range interactions, and also took a brief detour to discuss the exciting prospect of Neural Turing machines. We ended the chapter with an in-depth case study that applied LSTMs to model the Penn Treebank.

In Chapter 8, we will introduce you to reinforcement learning, a powerful technique for learning to play games.

Reinforcement Learning

The learning techniques we've covered so far in this book fall into the categories of supervised or unsupervised learning. In both cases, solving a given problem requires a data scientist to design a deep architecture that handles and processes input data and to connect the output of the architecture to a loss function suitable for the problem at hand. This framework is widely applicable, but not all applications fall neatly into this style of thinking. Let's consider the challenge of training a machine learning model to win a game of chess. It seems reasonable to process the board as spatial input using a convolutional network, but what would the loss entail? None of our standard loss functions such as cross-entropy or L^2 loss quite seem to apply.

Reinforcement learning provides a mathematical framework well suited to solving games. The central mathematical concept is that of the *Markov decision process*, a tool for modeling AI agents that interact with *environments* that offer *rewards* upon completion of certain *actions*. This framework proves to be flexible and general, and has found a number of applications in recent years. It's worth noting that reinforcement learning as a field is quite mature and has existed in recognizable form since the 1970s. However, until recently, most reinforcement learning systems were only capable of solving toy problems. Recent work has revealed that these limitations were likely due to the lack of sophisticated data intake mechanisms; hand-engineered features for many games or robotic environments often did not suffice. Deep representation extractions trained end-to-end on modern hardware seem to break through the barriers of earlier reinforcement learning systems and have achieved notable results in recent years.

Arguably, the first breakthrough in deep reinforcement learning was on ATARI arcade games. ATARI arcade games were traditionally played in video game arcades and offered users simple games that don't typically require sophisticated strategizing but might require good reflexes. Figure 8-1 shows a screenshot from the popular

ATARI game Breakout. In recent years, due to the development of good ATARI emulation software, ATARI games have become a testbed for gameplay algorithms. At first, reinforcement learning algorithms applied to ATARI didn't achieve superb results; the requirement that the algorithm understand a visual game state frustrated most attempts. However, as convolutional networks matured, researchers at Deep-Mind realized that convolutional networks could be combined with existing reinforcement learning techniques and trained end-to-end.

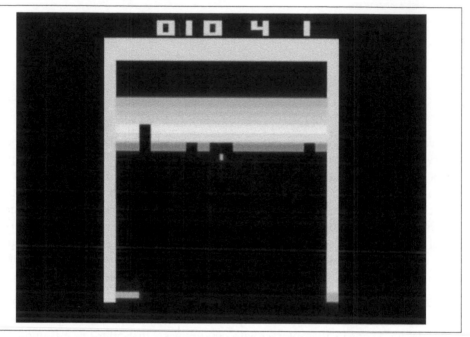

Figure 8-1. A screenshot of the ATARI arcade game Breakout. Players have to use the paddle at the bottom of the screen to bounce a ball that breaks the tiles at the top of the screen.

The resulting system achieved superb results, and learned to play many ATARI games (especially those dependent on quick reflexes) at superhuman standards. Figure 8-2 lists ATARI scores achieved by DeepMind's DQN algorithm. This breakthrough result spurred tremendous growth in the field of deep reinforcement learning and inspired legions of researchers to explore the potential of deep reinforcement learning techniques. At the same time, DeepMind's ATARI results showed reinforcement learning techniques were capable of solving systems dependent on short-term movements. These results didn't demonstrate that deep reinforcement learning systems were capable of solving games that required greater strategic planning.

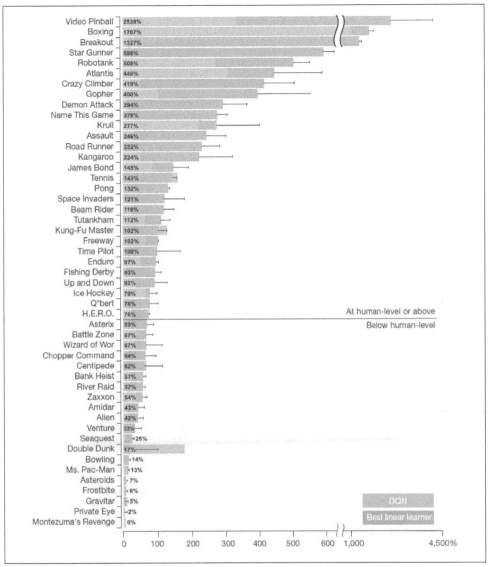

Figure 8-2. Results of DeepMind's DQN reinforcement learning algorithm on various ATARI games. 100% is the score of a strong human player. Note that DQN achieves superhuman performance on many games, but is quite weak on others.

Computer Go

In 1994, IBM revealed the system Deep Blue, which later succeeded in defeating Garry Kasparov in a highly publicized chess match. This system relied on brute force computation to expand the tree of possible chess moves (with some help from handcrafted chess heuristics) to play master-level chess.

Computer scientists attempted to apply similar techniques to other games such as Go. Unfortunately for early experimenters, Go's 19 × 19 game board is significantly larger than chess's 8 × 8 board. As a result, trees of possible moves explode much more quickly than for chess, and simple back-of-the-envelope calculations indicated that Moore's law would take a very long time to enable brute force solution of Go in the style of Deep Blue. Complicating matters, there existed no simple heuristic for evaluating who's winning in a half-played Go game (determining whether black or white is ahead is a notoriously noisy art for the best human analysts). As a result, until very recently, many prominent computer scientists believed that strong computer Go play was a decade away at the least.

To demonstrate the prowess of its reinforcement learning algorithms, DeepMind took on the challenge of learning to play Go, a game that requires complex strategic planning. In a tour-de-force paper, DeepMind revealed its deep reinforcement learning engine, AlphaGo, which combined convolutional networks with tree-based search to defeat the human Go master Lee Sedol (Figure 8-3).

Figure 8-3. Human Go champion Lee Sedol battles AlphaGo. Lee Sedol eventually lost the match 1–4, but succeeded in winning one game. It's unlikely that this victory can be replicated against the vastly improved successors of AlphaGo such as AlphaZero.

AlphaGo convincingly demonstrated that deep reinforcement learning techniques were capable of learning to solve complex strategic games. The heart of the breakthrough was the realization that convolutional networks could learn to estimate whether black or white was ahead in a half-played game, which enabled game trees to be truncated at reasonable depths. (AlphaGo also estimates which moves are most fruitful, enabling a second pruning of the game tree space.) AlphaGo's victory really launched deep reinforcement learning into prominence, and a host of researchers are working to transform AlphaGo-style systems into practical use.

In this chapter, we discuss reinforcement learning algorithms and specifically deep reinforcement learning architectures. We then show readers how to successfully apply reinforcement learning to the game of tic-tac-toe. Despite the simplicity of the game, training a successful reinforcement learner for tic-tac-toe requires significant sophistication, as you will soon see.

The code for this chapter was adapted from the DeepChem reinforcement learning library, and in particular from example code created by Peter Eastman and Karl Leswing. Thanks to Peter for debugging and tuning help on this chapter's example code.

Markov Decision Processes

Before launching into a discussion of reinforcement learning algorithms, it will be useful to pin down the family of problems that reinforcement learning methods seek to solve. The mathematical framework of Markov decision processes (MDPs) is very useful for formulating reinforcement learning methods. Traditionally, MDPs are introduced with a battery of Greek symbols, but we will instead try to proceed by providing some basic intuition.

The heart of MDPs is the pair of an *environment* and an *agent*. An environment encodes a "world" in which the agent seeks to act. Example environments could include game worlds. For example, a Go board with master Lee Sedol sitting opposite is a valid environment. Another potential environment could be the environment surrounding a small robot helicopter. In a prominent early reinforcement learning success, a team at Stanford led by Andrew Ng trained a helicopter to fly upside down using reinforcement learning as shown in Figure 8-4.

Figure 8-4. Andrew Ng's team at Stanford, from 2004 to 2010, trained a helicopter to learn to fly upside down using reinforcement learning. This work required the construction of a sophisticated physically accurate simulator.

The agent is the learning entity that acts within the environment. In our first example, AlphaGo itself is the agent. In the second, the robot helicopter (or more accurately, the control algorithm in the robot helicopter) is the agent. Each agent has a set of actions that it can take within the environment. For AlphaGo, these constitute valid Go moves. For the robot helicopter, these include control of the main and secondary rotors.

Actions the agent takes are presumed to have an effect on the environment. In the case of AlphaGo, this effect is deterministic (AlphaGo deciding to place a Go stone results in the stone being placed). In the case of the helicopter, the effect is likely probabilistic (changes in helicopter position may depend on wind conditions, which can't be modeled effectively).

The final piece of the model is the notion of reward. Unlike supervised learning where explicit labels are present to learn from, or unsupervised learning where the challenge is to learn the underlying structure of the data, reinforcement learning operates in a setting of partial, sparse rewards. In Go, rewards are achieved at the end of the game upon victory or defeat, while in helicopter flight, rewards might be presented for successful flights or completion of trick moves.

Reward Function Engineering Is Hard

One of the largest challenges in reinforcement learning is designing rewards that induce agents to learn desired behaviors. For even simple win/loss games such as Go or tic-tac-toe, this can be surprisingly difficult. How much should a loss be punished and how much should a win be rewarded? There don't yet exist good answers.

For more complex behaviors, this can be extremely challenging. A number of studies have demonstrated that simple rewards can result in agents learning unexpected and even potentially damaging behaviors. These systems spur fears of future agents with greater autonomy wreaking havoc when unleashed in the real world after having been trained to optimize bad reward functions.

In general, reinforcement learning is less mature than supervised learning techniques, and we caution that decisions to deploy reinforcement learning in production systems should be taken very carefully. Given uncertainty over learned behavior, make sure to thoroughly test any deployed reinforcement learned system.

Reinforcement Learning Algorithms

Now that we've introduced you to the core mathematical structures underlying reinforcement learning, let's consider how to design algorithms that learn intelligent behaviors for reinforcement learning agents. At a high level, reinforcement learning algorithms can be separated into the buckets of *model-based* and *model-free* algorithms. The central difference is whether the algorithm seeks to learn an internal model of how its environment acts. For simpler environments, such as tic-tac-toe, the model dynamics are trivial. For more complex environments, such as helicopter flight or even ATARI games, the underlying environment is likely extraordinarily complex. Avoiding the construction of an explicit model of the environment in favor of an implicit model that advises the agent on how to act may well be more pragmatic.

Simulations and Reinforcement Learning

Any reinforcement learning algorithm requires iteratively improving the performance of the current agent by evaluating the agent's current behavior and changing it to improve received rewards. These updates to the agent structure often include some gradient descent update, as we will see in the following sections. However, as you know intimately from previous chapters, gradient descent is a slow training algorithm! Millions or even billions of gradient descent steps may be required to learn an effective model.

This poses a problem if the learning environment is in the real world; how can an agent interact millions of times with the real world? In most cases it can't. As a result, most sophisticated reinforcement learning systems depend critically on simulators that allow interaction with a simulation computational version of the environment. For the helicopter flight environment, one of the hardest challenges researchers faced was building an accurate helicopter physics simulator that allowed learning of effective flight policies computationally.

Q-Learning

In the framework of Markov decision processes, agents take actions in an environment and obtain rewards that are (presumably) tied to agent actions. The Q function predicts the expected reward for taking a given action in a particular environment state. This concept seems very straightforward, but the trickiness arises when this expected reward includes discounted rewards from future actions.

Discounting Rewards

The notion of a discounted reward is widespread, and is often introduced in the context of finances. Suppose a friend says he'll pay you $10 next week. That future 10 dollars is worth less to you than 10 dollars in your hand right now (what if the payment never happens, for one?). So mathematically, it's common practice to introduce a discounting factor γ (typically between 0 and 1) that lowers the "present-value" of future payments. For example, say your friend is somewhat untrustworthy. You might decide to set $\gamma = 0.5$ and value your friend's promise as worth $10\gamma = 5$ dollars today to account for uncertainty in rewards.

However, these future rewards depend on actions taken by the agent in the future. As a result, the Q function must be formulated recursively in terms of itself, since expected rewards for one state depend on those for another state. This recursive definition makes learning the Q function tricky. This recursive relationship can be formulated explicitly for simple environments with discrete state spaces and solved with dynamic programming methods. For more general environments, Q-learning methods were not very useful until recently.

Recently, Deep Q-networks (DQN) were introduced by DeepMind and used to solve ATARI games as mentioned earlier. The key insight underlying DQN is once again the universal approximation theorem; since Q may be arbitrarily complex, we should model it with a universal approximator such as a deep network. While using neural networks to model Q had been done before, DeepMind also introduced the notion of experience replay for these networks, which let them train DQN models effectively at scale. Experience replay stores observed game outcomes and transitions from past games, and resamples them while training (in addition to training on new games) to ensure that lessons from the past are not forgotten by the network.

Catastrophic Forgetting

Neural networks quickly forget the past. In fact, this phenomenon, termed *catastrophic forgetting*, can occur very rapidly; a few mini-batch updates can be sufficient for the network to forget a complex behavior it previously knew. As a result, without techniques like experience replay that ensure the network always trains on episodes from past matches, it wouldn't be possible to learn complex behaviors.

Designing a training algorithm for deep networks that doesn't suffer from catastrophic forgetting is still a major open problem today. Humans notably don't suffer from catastrophic forgetting; even if you haven't ridden a bike in years, it's likely you still remember how to do so. Creating a neural network that has similar resilience might involve the addition of long-term external memory, along the lines of the Neural Turing machine. Unfortunately, none of the attempts thus far at designing resilient architectures has really worked well.

Policy Learning

In the previous section, you learned about Q-learning, which seeks to understand the expected rewards for taking given actions in given environment states. Policy learning is an alternative mathematical framework for learning agent behavior. It introduces the policy function π that assigns a probability to each action that an agent can take in a given state.

Note that a policy is sufficient for defining agent behavior entirely. Given a policy, an agent can act just by sampling a suitable action for the current environment state. Policy learning is convenient, since policies can be learned directly through an algorithm called policy gradient. This algorithm uses a couple mathematical tricks to enable policy gradients to be computed directly via backpropagation for deep networks. The key concept is the *rollout*. Let an agent act in an environment according to its current policy and observe all rewards that come in. Then backpropagate to increase the likelihood of those actions that led to more fruitful rewards. This description is accurate at a high level, but we will see more implementation details later in the chapter.

A policy is often associated with a *value function V*. This function returns the expected discounted reward for following policy π starting from the current state of the environment. V and Q are closely related functions since both provide estimates of future rewards starting from present state, but V does not specify an action to be taken and assumes rather that actions are sampled from π.

Another commonly defined function is the *advantage A*. This function defines the difference in expected reward due to taking a particular action a in a given environment state s, as opposed to following the base policy π. Mathematically, A is defined in terms of Q and V:

$$A(s, a) = Q(s, a) - V(s)$$

The advantage is useful in policy-learning algorithms, since it lets an algorithm quantify how a particular action may have been better suited than the present recommendation of the policy.

Policy Gradient Outside Reinforcement Learning

Although we have introduced policy gradient as a reinforcement learning algorithm, it can equally be viewed as a tool for learning deep networks with nondifferentiable submodules. What does this mean when we unpack the mathematical jargon?

Let's suppose we have a deep network that calls an external program within the network itself. This external program is a black box; it could be a network call or an invocation of a 1970s COBOL routine. How can we learn the rest of the deep network when this module has no gradient?

It turns out that policy gradient can be repurposed to estimate an "effective" gradient for the system. The simple intuition is that multiple "rollouts" can be run, which are used to estimate gradients. Expect to see research over the next few years extending this idea to create large networks with nondifferential modules.

Asynchronous Training

A disadvantage of the policy gradient methods presented in the previous section is that performing the rollout operations requires evaluating agent behavior in some (likely simulated) environment. Most simulators are complicated pieces of software that can't be run on the GPU. As a result, taking a single learning step will require running long CPU-bound calculations. This can lead to unreasonably slow training.

Asynchronous reinforcement learning methods seek to speed up this process by using multiple asynchronous CPU threads to perform rollouts independently. These worker threads will perform rollouts, estimate gradient updates to the policy locally, and then periodically synchronize with the global set of parameters. Empirically, asynchronous training appears to significantly speed up reinforcement learning and allows for fairly sophisticated policies to be learned on laptops. (Without GPUs! The majority of computational power is used on rollouts, so gradient update steps are often not the rate limiting aspect of reinforcement learning training.) The most popular algorithm for asynchronous reinforcement learning currently is the asynchronous actor advantage critic (A3C) algorithm.

CPU or GPU?

GPUs are necessary for most large deep learning applications, but reinforcement learning currently appears to be an exception to this general rule. The reliance of reinforcement learning algorithms to perform many rollouts seems to currently bias reinforcement learning implementations toward multicore CPU systems. It's likely that in specific applications, individual simulators can be ported to work more quickly on GPUs, but CPU-based simulations will likely continue to dominate for the near future.

Limits of Reinforcement Learning

The framework of Markov decision processes is immensely general. For example, behavioral scientists routinely use Markov decision processes to understand and model human decision making. The mathematical generality of this framework has spurred scientists to posit that solving reinforcement learning might spur the creation of artificial general intelligences (AGIs). The stunning success of AlphaGo against Lee Sedol amplified this belief, and indeed research groups such as OpenAI and Deep-Mind aiming to build AGIs focus much of their efforts on developing new reinforcement learning techniques.

Nonetheless, there are major weaknesses to reinforcement learning as it currently exists. Careful benchmarking work has shown that reinforcement learning techniques are very susceptible to choice of hyperparameters (even by the standards of deep learning, which is already much finickier than other techniques like random forests).

As we have mentioned, reward function engineering is very immature. Humans are capable of internally designing their own reward functions or effectively learning to copy reward functions from observation. Although "inverse reinforcement learning" algorithms that learn reward functions directly have been proposed, these algorithms have many limitations in practice.

In addition to these fundamental limitations, there are still many practical scaling issues. Humans are capable of playing games that combine high-level strategizing with thousands of "micro" moves. For example, master-level play of the strategy game StarCraft (see Figure 8-5) requires sophisticated strategic ploys combined with careful control of hundreds of units. Games can require thousands of local moves to be played to completion. In addition, unlike Go or chess, StarCraft has a "fog of war" where players cannot see the entire game state. This combination of large game state and uncertainty has foiled reinforcement learning attempts on StarCraft. As a result, teams of AI researchers at DeepMind and other groups are focusing serious effort on solving StarCraft with deep reinforcement learning methods. Despite some serious effort, though, the best StarCraft bots remain at amateur level.

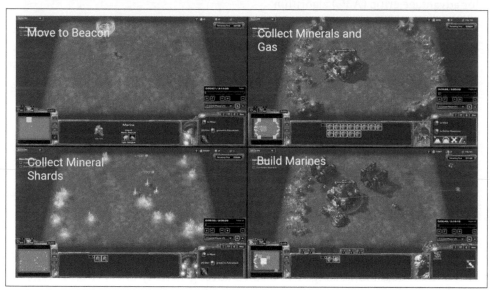

Figure 8-5. A collection of subtasks required for playing the real-time strategy game Star-Craft. In this game, players must build an army that they can use to defeat the opposing force. Successful StarCraft play requires mastery of resource planning, exploration, and complex strategy. The best computer StarCraft agents remain at amateur level.

In general, there's wide consensus that reinforcement learning is a useful technique that's likely to be deeply influential over the next few decades, but it's also clear that the many practical limitations of reinforcement learning methods will mean that most work will continue to be done in research labs for the near future.

Playing Tic-Tac-Toe

Tic-tac-toe is a simple two-player game. Players place Xs and Os on a 3 × 3 game board until one player succeeds in placing three of her pieces in a row. The first player to do so wins. If neither player succeeds in obtaining three in a row before the board is filled up, the game ends in a draw. Figure 8-6 illustrates a tic-tac-toe game board.

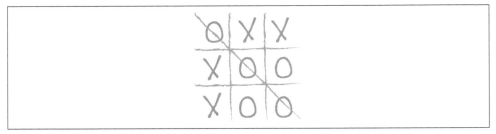

Figure 8-6. A tic-tac-toe game board.

Tic-tac-toe is a nice testbed for reinforcement learning techniques. The game is simple enough that exorbitant amounts of computational power aren't required to train effective agents. At the same time, despite tic-tac-toe's simplicity, learning an effective agent requires considerable sophistication. The TensorFlow code for this section is arguably the most sophisticated example found in this book. We will walk you through the design of a TensorFlow tic-tac-toe asynchronous reinforcement learning agent in the remainder of this section.

Object Orientation

The code we've introduced thus far in this book has primarily consisted of scripts augmented by smaller helper functions. In this chapter, however, we will swap to an object-oriented programming style. This style of programming might be new to you, especially if you hail from the scientific world rather than from the tech world. Briefly, an object-oriented program defines *objects* that model aspects of the world. For example, you might want to define `Environment` or `Agent` or `Reward` objects that directly correspond to these mathematical concepts. A *class* is a template for objects that can be used to *instantiate* (or create) many new objects. For example, you will shortly see an `Environment` class definition we will use to define many particular `Environment` objects.

Object orientation is particularly powerful for building complex systems, so we will use it to simplify the design of our reinforcement learning system. In practice, your real-world deep learning (or reinforcement learning) systems will likely need to be object oriented as well, so we encourage taking some time to master object-oriented design. There are many superb books that cover the fundamentals of object-oriented design, and we recommend that you check them out as necessary.

Abstract Environment

Let's start by defining an abstract `Environment` object that encodes the state of a system in a list of NumPy objects (Example 8-1). This `Environment` object is quite general (adapted from DeepChem's reinforcement learning engine) so it can easily serve as a template for other reinforcement learning projects you might seek to implement.

Example 8-1. This class defines a template for constructing new environments

```
class Environment(object):
  """An environment in which an actor performs actions to accomplish a task.

  An environment has a current state, which is represented as either a single NumPy
  array, or optionally a list of NumPy arrays.  When an action is taken, that causes
  the state to be updated.  Exactly what is meant by an "action" is defined by each
  subclass.  As far as this interface is concerned, it is simply an arbitrary object.
  The environment also computes a reward for each action, and reports when the task
  has been terminated (meaning that no more actions may be taken).
  """

  def __init__(self, state_shape, n_actions, state_dtype=None):
    """Subclasses should call the superclass constructor in addition to doing their
      own initialization."""
    self.state_shape = state_shape
    self.n_actions = n_actions
    if state_dtype is None:
      # Assume all arrays are float32.
      if isinstance(state_shape[0], collections.Sequence):
        self.state_dtype = [np.float32] * len(state_shape)
      else:
        self.state_dtype = np.float32
    else:
      self.state_dtype = state_dtype
```

Tic-Tac-Toe Environment

We need to specialize the `Environment` class to create a `TicTacToeEnvironment` suitable for our needs. To do this, we construct a *subclass* of `Environment` that adds on more features, while retaining the core functionality of the original *superclass*. In Example 8-2, we define `TicTacToeEnvironment` as a subclass of `Environment` that adds details specific to tic-tac-toe.

Example 8-2. The TicTacToeEnvironment class defines a template for constructing new tic-tac-toe environments

```
class TicTacToeEnvironment(dc.rl.Environment):
  """
  Play tictactoe against a randomly acting opponent
```

```
"""
X = np.array([1.0, 0.0])
O = np.array([0.0, 1.0])
EMPTY = np.array([0.0, 0.0])

ILLEGAL_MOVE_PENALTY = -3.0
LOSS_PENALTY = -3.0
NOT_LOSS = 0.1
DRAW_REWARD = 5.0
WIN_REWARD = 10.0

def __init__(self):
  super(TicTacToeEnvironment, self).__init__([(3, 3, 2)], 9)
  self.terminated = None
  self.reset()
```

The first interesting tidbit to note here is that we define the board state as a NumPy array of shape (3, 3, 2). We use a one-hot encoding of X and O (one-hot encodings aren't only useful for natural language processing!).

The second important thing to note is that the environment explicitly defines the reward function by setting penalties for illegal moves and losses, and rewards for draws and wins. This snippet powerfully illustrates the arbitrary nature of reward function engineering. Why these particular numbers?

Empirically, these choices appear to result in stable behavior, but we encourage you to experiment with alternate reward settings to observe results. In this implementation, we specify that the agent always plays X, but randomize whether X or O goes first. The function get_O_move() simply places an O on a random open tile on the game board. TicTacToeEnvironment encodes an opponent that plays O while always selecting a random move. The reset() function simply clears the board, and places an O tile randomly if O is going first during this game. See Example 8-3.

Example 8-3. More methods from the TicTacToeEnvironment class

```
def reset(self):
  self.terminated = False
  self.state = [np.zeros(shape=(3, 3, 2), dtype=np.float32)]

  # Randomize who goes first
  if random.randint(0, 1) == 1:
    move = self.get_O_move()
    self.state[0][move[0]][move[1]] = TicTacToeEnvironment.O

def get_O_move(self):
  empty_squares = []
  for row in range(3):
    for col in range(3):
      if np.all(self.state[0][row][col] == TicTacToeEnvironment.EMPTY):
```

```
      empty_squares.append((row, col))
  return random.choice(empty_squares)
```

The utility function `game_over()` reports that the game has ended if all tiles are filled. `check_winner()` checks whether the specified player has achieved three in a row and won the game (Example 8-4).

Example 8-4. Utility methods from the TicTacToeEnvironment class for detecting when the game has ended and who won

```
def check_winner(self, player):
  for i in range(3):
    row = np.sum(self.state[0][i][:], axis=0)
    if np.all(row == player * 3):
      return True
    col = np.sum(self.state[0][:][i], axis=0)
    if np.all(col == player * 3):
      return True

  diag1 = self.state[0][0][0] + self.state[0][1][1] + self.state[0][2][2]
  if np.all(diag1 == player * 3):
    return True
  diag2 = self.state[0][0][2] + self.state[0][1][1] + self.state[0][2][0]
  if np.all(diag2 == player * 3):
    return True
  return False

def game_over(self):
  for i in range(3):
    for j in range(3):
      if np.all(self.state[0][i][j] == TicTacToeEnvironment.EMPTY):
        return False
  return True
```

In our implementation, an action is simply a number between 0 and 8 specifying the tile on which the X tile is placed. The `step()` method checks whether this tile is occupied (returning a penalty if so), then places the tile. If X has won, a reward is returned. Else, the random O opponent is allowed to make a move. If O won, then a penalty is returned. If the game has ended as a draw, then a penalty is returned. Else, the game continues with a `NOT_LOSS` reward. See Example 8-5.

Example 8-5. This method performs a step of the simulation

```
def step(self, action):
  self.state = copy.deepcopy(self.state)
  row = action // 3
  col = action % 3
```

```python
# Illegal move -- the square is not empty
if not np.all(self.state[0][row][col] == TicTacToeEnvironment.EMPTY):
  self.terminated = True
  return TicTacToeEnvironment.ILLEGAL_MOVE_PENALTY

# Move X
self.state[0][row][col] = TicTacToeEnvironment.X

# Did X Win
if self.check_winner(TicTacToeEnvironment.X):
  self.terminated = True
  return TicTacToeEnvironment.WIN_REWARD

if self.game_over():
  self.terminated = True
  return TicTacToeEnvironment.DRAW_REWARD

move = self.get_O_move()
self.state[0][move[0]][move[1]] = TicTacToeEnvironment.O

# Did O Win
if self.check_winner(TicTacToeEnvironment.O):
  self.terminated = True
  return TicTacToeEnvironment.LOSS_PENALTY

if self.game_over():
  self.terminated = True
  return TicTacToeEnvironment.DRAW_REWARD

return TicTacToeEnvironment.NOT_LOSS
```

The Layer Abstraction

Running an asynchronous reinforcement learning algorithm such as A3C requires that each thread have access to a separate copy of the policy model. These copies of the model have to be periodically re-synced with one another for training to proceed. What is the easiest way we can construct multiple copies of the TensorFlow graph that we can distribute to each thread?

One simple possibility is to create a function that creates a copy of the model in a separate TensorFlow graph. This approach works well, but gets to be a little messy, especially for sophisticated networks. Using a little bit of object orientation can significantly simplify this process. Since our reinforcement learning code is adapted from the DeepChem library, we use a simplified version of the TensorGraph framework from DeepChem (see *https://deepchem.io* for information and docs). This framework is similar to other high-level TensorFlow frameworks such as Keras. The core abstraction in all such models is the introduction of a Layer object that encapsulates a portion of a deep network.

A `Layer` is a portion of a TensorFlow graph that accepts a list `in_layers` of input layers. In this abstraction, a deep architecture consists of a *directed graph* of layers. Directed graphs are similar to the undirected graphs you saw in Chapter 6, but have directions on their edges. In this case, the `in_layers` have edges to the new `Layer`, with the direction pointing toward the new layer. You will learn more about this concept in the next section.

We use `tf.register_tensor_conversion_function`, a utility that allows arbitrary classes to register themselves as tensor convertible. This registration will mean that a `Layer` can be converted into a TensorFlow tensor via a call to `tf.convert_to_tensor`. The `_get_input_tensors()` private method is a utility that uses `tf.convert_to_ten sor` to transform input layers into input tensors. Each `Layer` is responsible for implementing a `create_tensor()` method that specifies the operations to add to the TensorFlow computational graph. See Example 8-6.

Example 8-6. The Layer object is the fundamental abstraction in object-oriented deep architectures. It encapsulates a part of the netwok such as a fully connected layer or a convolutional layer. This example defines a generic superclass for all such layers.

```
class Layer(object):

  def __init__(self, in_layers=None, **kwargs):
    if "name" in kwargs:
      self.name = kwargs["name"]
    else:
      self.name = None
    if in_layers is None:
      in_layers = list()
    if not isinstance(in_layers, Sequence):
      in_layers = [in_layers]
    self.in_layers = in_layers
    self.variable_scope = ""
    self.tb_input = None

  def create_tensor(self, in_layers=None, **kwargs):
    raise NotImplementedError("Subclasses must implement for themselves")

  def _get_input_tensors(self, in_layers):
    """Get the input tensors to his layer.

    Parameters
    ----------
    in_layers: list of Layers or tensors
      the inputs passed to create_tensor().  If None, this layer's inputs will
      be used instead.
    """
    if in_layers is None:
      in_layers = self.in_layers
```

```
  if not isinstance(in_layers, Sequence):
    in_layers = [in_layers]
  tensors = []
  for input in in_layers:
    tensors.append(tf.convert_to_tensor(input))
  return tensors

def _convert_layer_to_tensor(value, dtype=None, name=None, as_ref=False):
  return tf.convert_to_tensor(value.out_tensor, dtype=dtype, name=name)

tf.register_tensor_conversion_function(Layer, _convert_layer_to_tensor)
```

The preceding description is abstract, but in practice easy to use. Example 8-7 shows a `Squeeze` layer that wraps `tf.squeeze` with a `Layer` (you will find this class convenient later). Note that `Squeeze` is a subclass of `Layer`.

Example 8-7. The Squeeze layer squeezes its input

```
class Squeeze(Layer):

  def __init__(self, in_layers=None, squeeze_dims=None, **kwargs):
    self.squeeze_dims = squeeze_dims
    super(Squeeze, self).__init__(in_layers, **kwargs)

  def create_tensor(self, in_layers=None, **kwargs):
    inputs = self._get_input_tensors(in_layers)
    parent_tensor = inputs[0]
    out_tensor = tf.squeeze(parent_tensor, squeeze_dims=self.squeeze_dims)
    self.out_tensor = out_tensor
    return out_tensor
```

The `Input` layer wraps placeholders for convenience (Example 8-8). Note that the `Layer.create_tensor` method must be invoked for each layer we use in order to construct a TensorFlow computational graph.

Example 8-8. The Input layer adds placeholders to the computation graph

```
class Input(Layer):

  def __init__(self, shape, dtype=tf.float32, **kwargs):
    self._shape = tuple(shape)
    self.dtype = dtype
    super(Input, self).__init__(**kwargs)

  def create_tensor(self, in_layers=None, **kwargs):
    if in_layers is None:
      in_layers = self.in_layers
    out_tensor = tf.placeholder(dtype=self.dtype, shape=self._shape)
```

```
    self.out_tensor = out_tensor
    return out_tensor
```

tf.keras and tf.estimator

TensorFlow has now integrated the popular Keras object-oriented frontend into the core TensorFlow library. Keras includes a `Layer` class definition that closely matches the `Layer` objects you've just learned about in this section. In fact, the `Layer` objects here were adapted from the DeepChem library, which in turn adapted them from an earlier version of Keras.

It's worth noting, though, that `tf.keras` has not yet become the standard higher-level interface to TensorFlow. The `tf.estimator` module provides an alternative (albeit less rich) high-level interface to raw TensorFlow.

Regardless of which frontend eventually becomes standard, we think that understanding the fundamental design principles for building your own frontend is instructive and worthwhile. You might need to build a new system for your organization that requires an alternative design, so a solid grasp of design principles will serve you well.

Defining a Graph of Layers

We mentioned briefly in the previous section that a deep architecture could be visualized as a directed graph of `Layer` objects. In this section, we transform this intuition into the `TensorGraph` object. These objects are responsible for constructing the underlying TensorFlow computation graph.

A `TensorGraph` object is responsible for maintaining a `tf.Graph`, a `tf.Session`, and a list of layers (`self.layers`) internally (Example 8-9). The directed graph is represented implicitly, by the `in_layers` belonging to each `Layer` object. `TensorGraph` also contains utilities for saving this `tf.Graph` instance to disk and consequently assigns itself a directory (using `tempfile.mkdtemp()` if none is specified) to store checkpoints of the weights associated with its underlying TensorFlow graph.

Example 8-9. The TensorGraph contains a graph of layers; TensorGraph objects can be thought of as the "model" object holding the deep architecture you want to train

```
class TensorGraph(object):

  def __init__(self,
               batch_size=100,
               random_seed=None,
               graph=None,
```

```
            learning_rate=0.001,
            model_dir=None,
            **kwargs):
"""

Parameters
----------
batch_size: int
  default batch size for training and evaluating
graph: tensorflow.Graph
  the Graph in which to create Tensorflow objects.  If None, a new Graph
  is created.
learning_rate: float or LearningRateSchedule
  the learning rate to use for optimization
kwargs
"""

# Layer Management
self.layers = dict()
self.features = list()
self.labels = list()
self.outputs = list()
self.task_weights = list()
self.loss = None
self.built = False
self.optimizer = None
self.learning_rate = learning_rate

# Singular place to hold Tensor objects which don't serialize
# See TensorGraph._get_tf() for more details on lazy construction
self.tensor_objects = {
    "Graph": graph,
    #"train_op": None,
}
self.global_step = 0
self.batch_size = batch_size
self.random_seed = random_seed
if model_dir is not None:
  if not os.path.exists(model_dir):
    os.makedirs(model_dir)
else:
  model_dir = tempfile.mkdtemp()
  self.model_dir_is_temp = True
self.model_dir = model_dir
self.save_file = "%s/%s" % (self.model_dir, "model")
self.model_class = None
```

The private method _add_layer does bookkeeping work to add a new Layer obect to the TensorGraph (Example 8-10).

Example 8-10. The _add_layer method adds a new Layer object

```python
def _add_layer(self, layer):
  if layer.name is None:
    layer.name = "%s_%s" % (layer.__class__.__name__, len(self.layers) + 1)
  if layer.name in self.layers:
    return
  if isinstance(layer, Input):
    self.features.append(layer)
  self.layers[layer.name] = layer
  for in_layer in layer.in_layers:
    self._add_layer(in_layer)
```

The layers in a TensorGraph must form a directed acyclic graph (there can be no loops in the graph). As a result, we can topologically sort these layers. Intuitively, a topological sort "orders" the layers in the graph so that each Layer object's in_layers precede it in the ordered list. This topological sort is necessary to make sure all input layers to a given layer are added to the graph before the layer itself (Example 8-11).

Example 8-11. The topsort method orders the layers in the TensorGraph

```python
def topsort(self):

  def add_layers_to_list(layer, sorted_layers):
    if layer in sorted_layers:
      return
    for in_layer in layer.in_layers:
      add_layers_to_list(in_layer, sorted_layers)
    sorted_layers.append(layer)

  sorted_layers = []
  for l in self.features + self.labels + self.task_weights + self.outputs:
    add_layers_to_list(l, sorted_layers)
  add_layers_to_list(self.loss, sorted_layers)
  return sorted_layers
```

The build() method takes the responsibility of populating the tf.Graph instance by calling layer.create_tensor for each layer in topological order (Example 8-12).

Example 8-12. The build method populates the underlying TensorFlow graph

```python
def build(self):
  if self.built:
    return
  with self._get_tf("Graph").as_default():
    self._training_placeholder = tf.placeholder(dtype=tf.float32, shape=())
    if self.random_seed is not None:
      tf.set_random_seed(self.random_seed)
    for layer in self.topsort():
```

```
    with tf.name_scope(layer.name):
      layer.create_tensor(training=self._training_placeholder)
    self.session = tf.Session()

    self.built = True
```

The method `set_loss()` adds a loss for training to the graph. `add_output()` specifies that the layer in question might be fetched from the graph. `set_optimizer()` specifies the optimizer used for training (Example 8-13).

Example 8-13. These methods add necessary losses, outputs, and optimizers to the computation graph

```
def set_loss(self, layer):
  self._add_layer(layer)
  self.loss = layer

def add_output(self, layer):
  self._add_layer(layer)
  self.outputs.append(layer)

def set_optimizer(self, optimizer):
  """Set the optimizer to use for fitting."""
  self.optimizer = optimizer
```

The method `get_layer_variables()` is used to fetch the learnable `tf.Variable` objects created by a layer. The private method `_get_tf` is used to fetch the `tf.Graph` and optimizer instances underpinning the `TensorGraph`. `get_global_step` is a convenience method for fetching the current step in the training process (starting from 0 at construction). See Example 8-14.

Example 8-14. Fetch the learnable variables associated with each layer

```
def get_layer_variables(self, layer):
  """Get the list of trainable variables in a layer of the graph."""
  if not self.built:
    self.build()
  with self._get_tf("Graph").as_default():
    if layer.variable_scope == "":
      return []
    return tf.get_collection(
        tf.GraphKeys.TRAINABLE_VARIABLES, scope=layer.variable_scope)

def get_global_step(self):
  return self._get_tf("GlobalStep")

def _get_tf(self, obj):
  """Fetches underlying TensorFlow primitives.
```

```
    Parameters
    ----------
    obj: str
      If "Graph", returns tf.Graph instance. If "Optimizer", returns the
      optimizer. If "train_op", returns the train operation. If "GlobalStep" returns
      the global step.
    Returns
    -------
    TensorFlow Object
    """

    if obj in self.tensor_objects and self.tensor_objects[obj] is not None:
      return self.tensor_objects[obj]
    if obj == "Graph":
      self.tensor_objects["Graph"] = tf.Graph()
    elif obj == "Optimizer":
      self.tensor_objects["Optimizer"] = tf.train.AdamOptimizer(
          learning_rate=self.learning_rate,
          beta1=0.9,
          beta2=0.999,
          epsilon=1e-7)
    elif obj == "GlobalStep":
      with self._get_tf("Graph").as_default():
        self.tensor_objects["GlobalStep"] = tf.Variable(0, trainable=False)
    return self._get_tf(obj)
```

Finally, the `restore()` method restores a saved `TensorGraph` from disk (Example 8-15). (As you will see later, the `TensorGraph` is saved automatically during training.)

Example 8-15. Restore a trained model from disk

```
def restore(self):
  """Reload the values of all variables from the most recent checkpoint file."""
  if not self.built:
    self.build()
  last_checkpoint = tf.train.latest_checkpoint(self.model_dir)
  if last_checkpoint is None:
    raise ValueError("No checkpoint found")
  with self._get_tf("Graph").as_default():
    saver = tf.train.Saver()
    saver.restore(self.session, last_checkpoint)
```

The A3C Algorithm

In this section you will learn how to implement A3C, the asynchronous reinforcement learning algorithm you saw earlier in the chapter. A3C is a significantly more complex training algorithm than those you have seen previously. The algorithm requires running gradient descent in multiple threads, interspersed with game rollout

---

code, and updating learned weights asynchronously. As a result of this extra complexity, we will define the A3C algorithm in an object-oriented fashion. Let's start by defining an A3C object.

The A3C class implements the A3C algorithm (Example 8-16). A few extra bells and whistles are added onto the basic algorithm to encourage learning, notably an entropy term and support for generalized advantage estimation. We won't cover all of these details, but encourage you to follow references into the research literature (listed in the documentation) to understand more.

Example 8-16. Define the A3C class encapsulating the asynchronous A3C training algorithm

```
class A3C(object):
  """
  Implements the Asynchronous Advantage Actor-Critic (A3C) algorithm.

  The algorithm is described in Mnih et al, "Asynchronous Methods for Deep
  Reinforcement Learning" (https://arxiv.org/abs/1602.01783).  This class
  requires the policy to output two quantities: a vector giving the probability
  of taking each action, and an estimate of the value function for the current
  state.  It optimizes both outputs at once using a loss that is the sum of three
  terms:

  1. The policy loss, which seeks to maximize the discounted reward for each action.
  2. The value loss, which tries to make the value estimate match the actual
     discounted reward that was attained at each step.
  3. An entropy term to encourage exploration.

  This class only supports environments with discrete action spaces, not
  continuous ones.  The "action" argument passed to the environment is an
  integer, giving the index of the action to perform.

  This class supports Generalized Advantage Estimation as described in Schulman
  et al., "High-Dimensional Continuous Control Using Generalized Advantage
  Estimation" (https://arxiv.org/abs/1506.02438).  This is a method of trading
  off bias and variance in the advantage estimate, which can sometimes improve
  the rate of convergence.  Use the advantage_lambda parameter to adjust the
  tradeoff.
  """
  self._env = env
  self.max_rollout_length = max_rollout_length
  self.discount_factor = discount_factor
  self.advantage_lambda = advantage_lambda
  self.value_weight = value_weight
  self.entropy_weight = entropy_weight
  self._optimizer = None
  (self._graph, self._features, self._rewards, self._actions,
   self._action_prob, self._value, self._advantages) = self.build_graph(
      None, "global", model_dir)
```

```
with self._graph._get_tf("Graph").as_default():
  self._session = tf.Session()
```

The heart of the A3C class lies in the `build_graph()` method (Example 8-17), which constructs a `TensorGraph` instance (underneath which lies a TensorFlow computation graph) encoding the policy learned by the model. Notice how succinct this definition is compared with others you have seen previously! There are many advantages to using object orientation.

Example 8-17. This method builds the computation graph for the A3C algorithm. Note that the policy network is defined here using the Layer abstractions you saw previously.

```
def build_graph(self, tf_graph, scope, model_dir):
  """Construct a TensorGraph containing the policy and loss calculations."""
  state_shape = self._env.state_shape
  features = []
  for s in state_shape:
    features.append(Input(shape=[None] + list(s), dtype=tf.float32))
  d1 = Flatten(in_layers=features)
  d2 = Dense(
      in_layers=[d1],
      activation_fn=tf.nn.relu,
      normalizer_fn=tf.nn.l2_normalize,
      normalizer_params={"dim": 1},
      out_channels=64)
  d3 = Dense(
      in_layers=[d2],
      activation_fn=tf.nn.relu,
      normalizer_fn=tf.nn.l2_normalize,
      normalizer_params={"dim": 1},
      out_channels=32)
  d4 = Dense(
      in_layers=[d3],
      activation_fn=tf.nn.relu,
      normalizer_fn=tf.nn.l2_normalize,
      normalizer_params={"dim": 1},
      out_channels=16)
  d4 = BatchNorm(in_layers=[d4])
  d5 = Dense(in_layers=[d4], activation_fn=None, out_channels=9)
  value = Dense(in_layers=[d4], activation_fn=None, out_channels=1)
  value = Squeeze(squeeze_dims=1, in_layers=[value])
  action_prob = SoftMax(in_layers=[d5])

  rewards = Input(shape=(None,))
  advantages = Input(shape=(None,))
  actions = Input(shape=(None, self._env.n_actions))
  loss = A3CLoss(
      self.value_weight,
      self.entropy_weight,
      in_layers=[rewards, actions, action_prob, value, advantages])
```

```
graph = TensorGraph(
    batch_size=self.max_rollout_length,
    graph=tf_graph,
    model_dir=model_dir)
for f in features:
  graph._add_layer(f)
graph.add_output(action_prob)
graph.add_output(value)
graph.set_loss(loss)
graph.set_optimizer(self._optimizer)
with graph._get_tf("Graph").as_default():
  with tf.variable_scope(scope):
    graph.build()
return graph, features, rewards, actions, action_prob, value, advantages
```

There's a lot of code in this example. Let's break it down into multiple examples and discuss more carefully. Example 8-18 takes the array encoding of the TicTacToeEnvir onment and feeds it into the Input instances for the graph directly.

Example 8-18. This snippet from the build_graph() method feeds in the array encoding of TicTacToeEnvironment

```
state_shape = self._env.state_shape
features = []
for s in state_shape:
  features.append(Input(shape=[None] + list(s), dtype=tf.float32))
```

Example 8-19 shows the code used to construct inputs for rewards from the environment, advantages observed, and actions taken.

Example 8-19. This snippet from the build_graph() method defines Input objects for rewards, advantages, and actions

```
rewards = Input(shape=(None,))
advantages = Input(shape=(None,))
actions = Input(shape=(None, self._env.n_actions))
```

The policy network is responsible for learning the policy. In Example 8-20, the input board state is first flattened into an input feature vector. A series of fully connected (or Dense) transformations are applied to the flattened board. At the very end, a Soft max layer is used to predict action probabilities from d5 (note that out_channels is set to 9, one for each possible move on the tic-tac-toe board).

Example 8-20. This snippet from the build_graph() method defines the policy network

```
d1 = Flatten(in_layers=features)
d2 = Dense(
    in_layers=[d1],
```

```
        activation_fn=tf.nn.relu,
        normalizer_fn=tf.nn.l2_normalize,
        normalizer_params={"dim": 1},
        out_channels=64)
d3 = Dense(
        in_layers=[d2],
        activation_fn=tf.nn.relu,
        normalizer_fn=tf.nn.l2_normalize,
        normalizer_params={"dim": 1},
        out_channels=32)
d4 = Dense(
        in_layers=[d3],
        activation_fn=tf.nn.relu,
        normalizer_fn=tf.nn.l2_normalize,
        normalizer_params={"dim": 1},
        out_channels=16)
d4 = BatchNorm(in_layers=[d4])
d5 = Dense(in_layers=[d4], activation_fn=None, out_channels=9)
value = Dense(in_layers=[d4], activation_fn=None, out_channels=1)
value = Squeeze(squeeze_dims=1, in_layers=[value])
action_prob = SoftMax(in_layers=[d5])
```

Is Feature Engineering Dead?

In this section, we feed the raw tic-tac-toe game board into Tensor-Flow for training the policy. However, it's important to note that for more complex games than tic-tac-toe, this may not yield satisfactory results. One of the lesser known facts about AlphaGo is that DeepMind performs sophisticated feature engineering to extract "interesting" patterns of Go pieces upon the board to make Alpha-Go's learning easier. (This fact is tucked away into the supplemental information of DeepMind's paper.)

The fact remains that reinforcement learning (and deep learning methods broadly) often still need human-guided feature engineering to extract meaningful information before learning algorithms can learn effective policies and models. It's likely that as more computational power becomes available through hardware advances, this need for feature engineering will be reduced, but for the near term, plan on manually extracting information about your systems as needed for performance.

The A3C Loss Function

We now have the object-oriented machinery set in place to define a loss for the A3C policy network. This loss function will itself be implemented as a Layer object (it's a convenient abstraction that all parts of the deep architecture are simply layers). The A3CLoss object implements a mathematical loss consisting of the sum of three terms:

a `policy_loss`, a `value_loss`, and an `entropy` term for exploration. See Example 8-21.

Example 8-21. This Layer implements the loss function for A3C

```
class A3CLoss(Layer):
  """This layer computes the loss function for A3C."""

  def __init__(self, value_weight, entropy_weight, **kwargs):
    super(A3CLoss, self).__init__(**kwargs)
    self.value_weight = value_weight
    self.entropy_weight = entropy_weight

  def create_tensor(self, **kwargs):
    reward, action, prob, value, advantage = [
        layer.out_tensor for layer in self.in_layers
    ]
    prob = prob + np.finfo(np.float32).eps
    log_prob = tf.log(prob)
    policy_loss = -tf.reduce_mean(
        advantage * tf.reduce_sum(action * log_prob, axis=1))
    value_loss = tf.reduce_mean(tf.square(reward - value))
    entropy = -tf.reduce_mean(tf.reduce_sum(prob * log_prob, axis=1))
    self.out_tensor = policy_loss + self.value_weight * value_loss
    - self.entropy_weight * entropy
    return self.out_tensor
```

There are a lot of pieces to this definition, so let's pull out bits of code and inspect. The `A3CLoss` layer takes in `reward`, `action`, `prob`, `value`, `advantage` layers as inputs. For mathematical stability, we convert probabilities to log probabilities (this is numerically much more stable). See Example 8-22.

Example 8-22. This snippet from A3CLoss takes reward, action, prob, value, advantage as input layers and computes a log probability

```
reward, action, prob, value, advantage = [
    layer.out_tensor for layer in self.in_layers
]
prob = prob + np.finfo(np.float32).eps
log_prob = tf.log(prob)
```

The policy loss computes the sum of all advantages observed, weighted by the log-probability of the action taken. (Recall that the advantage is the difference in reward resulting from taking the given action as opposed to the expected reward from the raw policy for that state). The intuition here is that the `policy_loss` provides a signal on which actions were fruitful and which were not (Example 8-23).

Example 8-23. This snippet from A3CLoss defines the policy loss

```
policy_loss = -tf.reduce_mean(
    advantage * tf.reduce_sum(action * log_prob, axis=1))
```

The value loss computes the difference between our estimate of V (reward) and the actual value of V observed (value). Note the use of the L^2 loss here (Example 8-24).

Example 8-24. This snippet from A3CLoss defines the value loss

```
value_loss = tf.reduce_mean(tf.square(reward - value))
```

The entropy term is an addition that encourages the policy to explore further by adding some noise. This term is effectively a form of regularization for A3C networks. The final loss computed by A3CLoss is a linear combination of these component losses. See Example 8-25.

Example 8-25. This snippet from A3CLoss defines an entropy term added to the loss

```
entropy = -tf.reduce_mean(tf.reduce_sum(prob * log_prob, axis=1))
```

Defining Workers

Thus far, you've seen how the policy network is constructed, but you haven't yet seen how the asynchronous training procedure is implemented. Conceptually, asynchronous training consists of individual workers running gradient descent on locally simulated game rollouts and contributing learned knowledge back to a global set of weights periodically. Continuing our object-oriented design, let's introduce the Worker class.

Each Worker instance holds a copy of the model that's trained asynchronously on a separate thread (Example 8-26). Note that a3c.build_graph() is used to construct a local copy of the TensorFlow computation graph for the thread in question. Take special note of local_vars and global_vars here. We need to make sure to train only the variables associated with this worker's copy of the policy and not with the global copy of the variables (which is used to share information across worker threads). As a result gradients uses tf.gradients to take gradients of the loss with respect to only local_vars.

Example 8-26. The Worker class implements the computation performed by each thread

```
class Worker(object):
  """A Worker object is created for each training thread."""

  def __init__(self, a3c, index):
    self.a3c = a3c
    self.index = index
    self.scope = "worker%d" % index
    self.env = copy.deepcopy(a3c._env)
    self.env.reset()
    (self.graph, self.features, self.rewards, self.actions, self.action_prob,
     self.value, self.advantages) = a3c.build_graph(
        a3c._graph._get_tf("Graph"), self.scope, None)
    with a3c._graph._get_tf("Graph").as_default():
      local_vars = tf.get_collection(tf.GraphKeys.TRAINABLE_VARIABLES,
                                     self.scope)
      global_vars = tf.get_collection(tf.GraphKeys.TRAINABLE_VARIABLES,
                                      "global")
      gradients = tf.gradients(self.graph.loss.out_tensor, local_vars)
      grads_and_vars = list(zip(gradients, global_vars))
      self.train_op = a3c._graph._get_tf("Optimizer").apply_gradients(
          grads_and_vars)
      self.update_local_variables = tf.group(
          * [tf.assign(v1, v2) for v1, v2 in zip(local_vars, global_vars)])
      self.global_step = self.graph.get_global_step()
```

Worker rollouts

Each `Worker` is responsible for simulating game rollouts locally. The `create_roll
out()` method uses `session.run` to fetch action probabilities from the TensorFlow
graph (Example 8-27). It then samples an action from this policy using `np.ran
dom.choice`, weighted by the per-class probabilities. The reward for the action taken
is computed from `TicTacToeEnvironment` via a call to `self.env.step(action)`.

Example 8-27. The create_rollout method simulates a game rollout locally

```
def create_rollout(self):
  """Generate a rollout."""
  n_actions = self.env.n_actions
  session = self.a3c._session
  states = []
  actions = []
  rewards = []
  values = []

  # Generate the rollout.
  for i in range(self.a3c.max_rollout_length):
    if self.env.terminated:
```

```
        break
    state = self.env.state
    states.append(state)
    feed_dict = self.create_feed_dict(state)
    results = session.run(
        [self.action_prob.out_tensor, self.value.out_tensor],
        feed_dict=feed_dict)
    probabilities, value = results[:2]
    action = np.random.choice(np.arange(n_actions), p=probabilities[0])
    actions.append(action)
    values.append(float(value))
    rewards.append(self.env.step(action))

  # Compute an estimate of the reward for the rest of the episode.
  if not self.env.terminated:
    feed_dict = self.create_feed_dict(self.env.state)
    final_value = self.a3c.discount_factor * float(
        session.run(self.value.out_tensor, feed_dict))
  else:
    final_value = 0.0
  values.append(final_value)
  if self.env.terminated:
    self.env.reset()
  return states, actions, np.array(rewards), np.array(values)
```

The `process_rollouts()` method does preprocessing needed to compute discounted rewards, values, actions, and advantages (Example 8-28).

Example 8-28. The process_rollout method computes rewards, values, actions, and advantages and then takes a gradient descent step against the loss

```
def process_rollout(self, states, actions, rewards, values, step_count):
  """Train the network based on a rollout."""

  # Compute the discounted rewards and advantages.
  if len(states) == 0:
    # Rollout creation sometimes fails in multithreaded environment.
    # Don't process if malformed
    print("Rollout creation failed. Skipping")
    return

  discounted_rewards = rewards.copy()
  discounted_rewards[-1] += values[-1]
  advantages = rewards - values[:-1] + self.a3c.discount_factor * np.array(
      values[1:])
  for j in range(len(rewards) - 1, 0, -1):
    discounted_rewards[j-1] += self.a3c.discount_factor * discounted_rewards[j]
    advantages[j-1] += (
        self.a3c.discount_factor * self.a3c.advantage_lambda * advantages[j])
   # Convert the actions to one-hot.
  n_actions = self.env.n_actions
```

```
actions_matrix = []
for action in actions:
  a = np.zeros(n_actions)
  a[action] = 1.0
  actions_matrix.append(a)

# Rearrange the states into the proper set of arrays.
state_arrays = [[] for i in range(len(self.features))]
for state in states:
  for j in range(len(state)):
    state_arrays[j].append(state[j])

# Build the feed dict and apply gradients.
feed_dict = {}
for f, s in zip(self.features, state_arrays):
  feed_dict[f.out_tensor] = s
feed_dict[self.rewards.out_tensor] = discounted_rewards
feed_dict[self.actions.out_tensor] = actions_matrix
feed_dict[self.advantages.out_tensor] = advantages
feed_dict[self.global_step] = step_count
self.a3c._session.run(self.train_op, feed_dict=feed_dict)
```

The Worker.run() method performs the training step for the Worker, relying on pro
cess_rollouts() to issue the actual call to self.a3c._session.run() under the
hood (Example 8-29).

Example 8-29. The run() method is the top level invocation for Worker

```
def run(self, step_count, total_steps):
  with self.graph._get_tf("Graph").as_default():
    while step_count[0] < total_steps:
      self.a3c._session.run(self.update_local_variables)
      states, actions, rewards, values = self.create_rollout()
      self.process_rollout(states, actions, rewards, values, step_count[0])
      step_count[0] += len(actions)
```

Training the Policy

The A3C.fit() method brings together all the disparate pieces introduced to train the
model. The fit() method takes the responsibility for spawning Worker threads using
the Python threading library. Since each Worker takes responsibility for training
itself, the fit() method simply is responsible for periodically checkpointing the
trained model to disk. See Example 8-30.

Example 8-30. The fit() method brings everything together and runs the A3C training algorithm

```python
def fit(self,
        total_steps,
        max_checkpoints_to_keep=5,
        checkpoint_interval=600,
        restore=False):
  """Train the policy.

  Parameters
  ----------
  total_steps: int
    the total number of time steps to perform on the environment, across all
    rollouts on all threads
  max_checkpoints_to_keep: int
    the maximum number of checkpoint files to keep.  When this number is
    reached, older files are deleted.
  checkpoint_interval: float
    the time interval at which to save checkpoints, measured in seconds
  restore: bool
    if True, restore the model from the most recent checkpoint and continue
    training from there.  If False, retrain the model from scratch.
  """
  with self._graph._get_tf("Graph").as_default():
    step_count = [0]
    workers = []
    threads = []
    for i in range(multiprocessing.cpu_count()):
      workers.append(Worker(self, i))
    self._session.run(tf.global_variables_initializer())
    if restore:
      self.restore()
    for worker in workers:
      thread = threading.Thread(
          name=worker.scope,
          target=lambda: worker.run(step_count, total_steps))
      threads.append(thread)
      thread.start()
    variables = tf.get_collection(
        tf.GraphKeys.GLOBAL_VARIABLES, scope="global")
    saver = tf.train.Saver(variables, max_to_keep=max_checkpoints_to_keep)
    checkpoint_index = 0
    while True:
      threads = [t for t in threads if t.isAlive()]
      if len(threads) > 0:
        threads[0].join(checkpoint_interval)
      checkpoint_index += 1
      saver.save(
          self._session, self._graph.save_file, global_step=checkpoint_index)
      if len(threads) == 0:
        break
```

Challenge for the Reader

We strongly encourage you to try training tic-tac-toe models for yourself! Note that this example is more involved than other examples in the book, and will require greater computational power. We recommend a machine with at least a few CPU cores. This requirement isn't too onerous; a good laptop should suffice. Try using a tool like htop to check that the code is indeed multithreaded. See how good a model you can train! You should be able to beat the random baseline most of the time, but this basic implementation won't give you a model that always wins. We recommend exploring the RL literature and expanding upon the base implementation to see how well you can do.

Review

In this chapter, we introduced you to the core concepts of reinforcement learning (RL). We walked you through some recent successes of RL methods on ATARI, upside-down helicopter flight, and computer Go. We then taught you about the mathematical framework of Markov decision processes. We brought it together with a detailed case study walking you through the construction of a tic-tac-toe agent. This algorithm uses a sophisticated training method, A3C, that makes use of multiple CPU cores to speed up training. In Chapter 9, you'll learn more about training models with multiple GPUs.

Training Large Deep Networks

Thus far, you have seen how to train small models that can be completely trained on a good laptop computer. All of these models can be run fruitfully on GPU-equipped hardware with notable speed boosts (with the notable exception of reinforcement learning models for reasons discussed in the previous chapter). However, training larger models still requires considerable sophistication. In this chapter, we will discuss various types of hardware that can be used to train deep networks, including graphics processing units (GPUs), tensor processing units (TPUs), and neuromorphic chips. We will also briefly cover the principles of distributed training for larger deep learning models. We end the chapter with an in-depth case study, adapted from one of the TensorFlow tutorials, demonstrating how to train a CIFAR-10 convolutional neural network on a server with multiple GPUs. We recommend that you attempt to try running this code yourself, but readily acknowledge that gaining access to a multi-GPU server is trickier than finding a good laptop. Luckily, access to multi-GPU servers on the cloud is becoming possible and is likely the best solution for industrial users of TensorFlow seeking to train large models.

Custom Hardware for Deep Networks

As you've seen throughout the book, deep network training requires chains of tensorial operations performed repeatedly on minibatches of data. Tensorial operations are commonly transformed into matrix multiplication operations by software, so rapid training of deep networks fundamentally depends on the ability to perform matrix multiplication operations rapidly. While CPUs are perfectly capable of implementing matrix multiplications, the generality of CPU hardware means much effort will be wasted on overhead unneeded for mathematical operations.

Hardware engineers have noted this fact for years, and there exist a variety of alternative hardware for working with deep networks. Such hardware can be broadly divided into *inference only* or *training and inference*. Inference-only hardware cannot be used to train new deep networks, but can be used to deploy trained models in production, allowing for potentially orders-of-magnitude increases in performance. Training and inference hardware allows for models to be trained natively. Currently, Nvidia's GPU hardware holds a dominant position in the training and inference market due to significant investment in software and outreach by Nvidia's teams, but a number of other competitors are snapping at the GPU's heels. In this section, we will briefly cover some of these newer hardware alternatives. With the exception of GPUs and CPUs, most of these alternative forms of hardware are not yet widely available, so much of this section is forward looking.

CPU Training

Although CPU training is by no means state of the art for training deep networks, it often does quite well for smaller models (as you've seen firsthand in this book). For reinforcement learning problems, a multicore CPU machine can even outperform GPU training.

CPUs also see wide usage for inference-only applications of deep networks. Most companies have invested heavily in developing cloud servers built primarily on Intel server boxes. It's very likely that the first generation of deep networks deployed widely (outside tech companies) will be primarily deployed into production on such Intel servers. While such CPU-based deployment isn't sufficient for heavy-duty deployment of learning models, it is often plenty for first customer needs. Figure 9-1 illustrates a standard Intel CPU.

Figure 9-1. A CPU from Intel. CPUs are still the dominant form of computer hardware and are present in all modern laptops, desktops, servers, and phones. Most software is written to execute on CPUs. Numerical computations (such as neural network training) can be executed on CPUs, but might be slower than on customized hardware optimized for numerical methods.

GPU Training

GPUs were first developed to perform computations needed by the graphics community. In a fortuitous coincidence, it turned out that the primitives used to define graphics shaders could be repurposed to perform deep learning. At their mathematical hearts, both graphics and machine learning rely critically on matrix multiplications. Empirically, GPU matrix multiplications offer speedups of an order of magnitude or two over CPU implementations. How do GPUs succeed at this feat? The trick is that GPUs make use of thousands of identical threads. Clever hackers have succeeded in decomposing matrix multiplications into massively parallel operations that can offer dramatic speedups. Figure 9-2 illustrates a GPU architecture.

Although there are a number of GPU vendors, Nvidia currently dominates the GPU market. Much of the power of Nvidia's GPUs stems from its custom library CUDA (compute unified device architecture), which offers primitives that make it easier to write GPU programs. Nvidia offers a CUDA extension, CUDNN, for speeding up deep networks (Figure 9-2). TensorFlow has built-in CUDNN support, so you can make use of CUDNN to speed up your networks as well through TensorFlow.

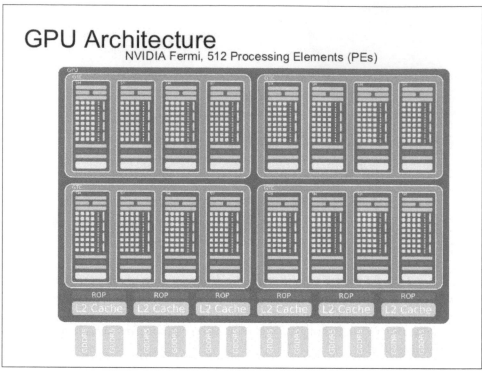

Figure 9-2. A GPU architecture from Nvidia. GPUs possess many more cores than CPUs and are well suited to performing numerical linear algebra, of the sort useful in both graphics and machine learning computations. GPUs have emerged as the dominant hardware platform for training deep networks.

How Important Are Transistor Sizes?

For years, the semiconductor industry has tracked progression of chip speeds by watching transistor sizes. As transistors got smaller, more of them could be packed onto a standard chip, and algorithms could run faster. At the time of writing of this book, Intel is currently operating on 10-nanometer transistors, and working on transitioning down to 7 nanometers. The rate of shrinkage of transistor sizes has slowed significantly in recent years, since formidable heat dissipation issues arise at these scales.

Nvidia's GPUs partially buck this trend. They tend to use transistor sizes a generation or two behind Intel's best, and focus on solving architectural and software bottlenecks instead of transistor engineering. So far, Nvidia's strategy has paid dividends and the company has achieved market domination in the machine learning chip space.

It's not yet clear how far architectural and software optimizations can go. Will GPU optimizations soon run into the same Moore's law roadblocks as CPUs? Or will clever architectural innovations enable years of faster GPUs? Only time can tell.

Tensor Processing Units

The tensor processing unit (TPU) is a custom ASIC (application specific integrated circuit) designed by Google to speed up deep learning workloads designed in Tensor-Flow. Unlike the GPU, the TPU is stripped down and implements only the bare minimum on-die needed to perform necessary matrix multiplications. Unlike the GPU, the TPU is dependent on an adjoining CPU to do much of its preprocessing work for it. This slimmed-down approach enables the TPU to achieve higher speeds than the GPU at lower energy costs.

The first version of the TPU only allowed for inference on trained models, but the most recent version (TPU2) allows for training of (certain) deep networks as well. However, Google has not released many details about the TPU, and access is limited to Google collaborators, with plans to enable TPU access via the Google cloud. Nvidia is taking notes from the TPU, and it's quite likely that future releases of Nvidia GPUs will come to resemble the TPU, so downstream users will likely benefit from Google's innovations regardless of whether Google or Nvidia wins the consumer deep learning market. Figure 9-3 illustrates the TPU architecture design.

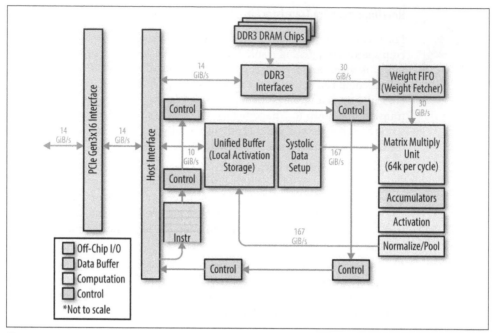

Figure 9-3. A tensor processing unit (TPU) architecture from Google. TPUs are specialized chips designed by Google to speed up deep learning workloads. The TPU is a coprocessor and not a standalone piece of hardware.

What Are ASICs?

Both CPUs and GPUs are general-purpose chips. CPUs generally support instruction sets in assembly and are designed to be universal. Care is taken to enable a wide range of applications. GPUs are less universal, but still allow for a wide range of algorithms to be implemented via languages such as CUDA.

Application specific integrated circuits (ASICs) attempt to do away with the generality in favor of focusing on the needs of a particular application. Historically, ASICs have only achieved limited market penetration. The drumbeat of Moore's law meant that general-purpose CPUs stayed only a breath or two behind custom ASICs, so the hardware design overhead was often not worth the effort.

This state of affairs has started shifting in the last few years. The slowdown of transistor shrinkage has expanded ASIC usage. For example, Bitcoin mining depends entirely on custom ASICs that implement specialized cryptography operations.

Field Programmable Gate Arrays

Field programmable gate arrays (FPGAs) are a type of "field programmable" ASIC. Standard FPGAs can often be reconfigured via hardware description languages such as Verilog to implement new ASIC designs dynamically. While FPGAs are generally less efficient than custom ASICs, they can offer significant speed improvements over CPU implementations. Microsoft in particular has used FPGAs to perform deep learning inference and claims to have achieved significant speedups with their deployment. However, the approach has not yet caught on widely outside Microsoft.

Neuromorphic Chips

The "neurons" in deep networks mathematically model the 1940s understanding of neuronal biology. Needless to say, biological understanding of neuronal behavior has progressed dramatically since then. For one, it's now known that the nonlinear activations used in deep networks aren't accurate models of neuronal nonlinearity. The "spike trains" is a better model (see Figure 9-4), where neurons activate in short-lived bursts (spikes) but fall to background most of the time.

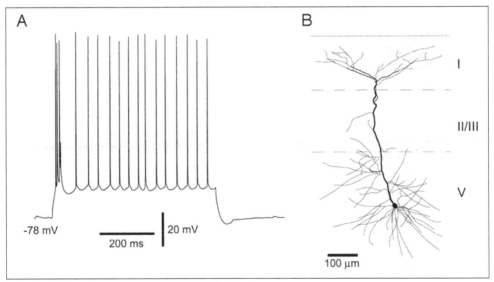

Figure 9-4. Neurons often activate in short-lived bursts called spike trains (A). Neuromorphic chips attempt to model spiking behavior in computing hardware. Biological neurons are complex entities (B), so these models are still only approximate.

Hardware engineers have spent significant effort exploring whether it's possible to create chip designs based on spike trains rather than on existing circuit technologies (CPUs, GPUs, ASICs). These designers argue that today's chip designs suffer from fundamental power limitations; the brain consumes many orders of magnitude less power than computer chips and smart designs should aim to learn from the brain's architecture.

A number of projects have built large spike train chips attempting to expand upon this core thesis. IBM's TrueNorth project has succeeded in building spike train processors with millions of "neurons" and demonstrated that this hardware can perform basic image recognition with significantly lower power requirements than existing chip designs. However, despite these successes, it is not clear how to translate modern deep architectures onto spike train chips. Without the ability to "compile" TensorFlow models onto spike train hardware, it's unlikely that such projects will see widespread adoption in the near future.

Distributed Deep Network Training

In the previous section, we surveyed a variety of hardware options for training deep networks. However, most organizations will likely only have access to CPUs and perhaps GPUs. Luckily, it's possible to perform *distributed training* of deep networks, where multiple CPUs or GPUs are used to train models faster and more effectively. Figure 9-5 illustrates the two major paradigms for training deep networks with multiple CPUs/GPUs, namely data parallel and model parallel training. You will learn about these methods in more detail in the next two sections.

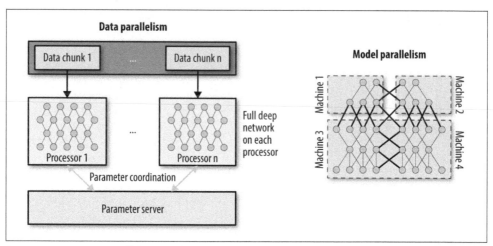

Figure 9-5. Data parallelism and model parallelism are the two main modes of distributed training of deep architectures. Data parallel training splits large datasets across multiple computing nodes, while model parallel training splits large models across multiple nodes. The next two sections will cover these two methods in greater depth.

Data Parallelism

Data parallelism is the most common type of multinode deep network training. Data parallel models split large datasets onto different machines. Most nodes are workers and have access to a fraction of the total data used to train the network. Each worker node has a complete copy of the model being trained. One node is designated as the supervisor that gathers updated weights from the workers at regular intervals and pushes averaged versions of the weights out to worker nodes. Note that you've already seen a data parallel example in this book; the A3C implementation presented in Chapter 8 is a simple example of data parallel deep network training.

As a historical note, Google's predecessor to TensorFlow, DistBelief, was based on data parallel training on CPU servers. This system was capable of achieving distributed CPU speeds (using 32–128 nodes) that matched or exceeded GPU training speeds. Figure 9-6 illustrates the data parallel training method implemented by DistBelief. However, the success of systems like DistBelief tends to depend on the presence of high throughput network interconnects that can allow for rapid model parameter sharing. Many organizations lack the network infrastructure that enables effective multinode data parallel CPU training. However, as the A3C example demonstrates, it is possible to perform data parallel training on a single node, using different CPU cores. For modern servers, it is also possible to perform data parallel training using multiple GPUs stocked within a single server, as we will show you later.

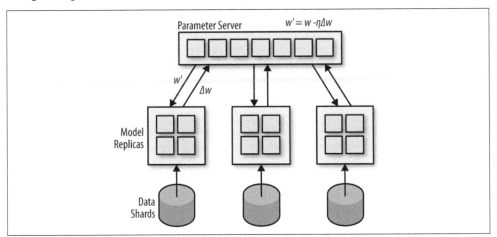

Figure 9-6. The Downpour stochastic gradient descent (SGD) method maintains multiple replicas of the model and trains them on different subsets of a dataset. The learned weights from these shards are periodically synced to global weights stored on a parameter server.

Model Parallelism

The human brain provides the only known example of a generally intelligent piece of hardware, so there have naturally been comparisons drawn between the complexity of deep networks and the complexity of the brain. Simple arguments state the brain has roughly 100 billion neurons; would constructing deep networks with that many "neurons" suffice to achieve general intelligence? Unfortunately, such arguments miss the point that biological neurons are significantly more complex than "mathematical neurons." As a result, simple comparisons yield little value. Nonetheless, building larger deep networks has been a major research focus over the last few years.

The major difficulty with training very large deep networks is that GPUs tend to have limited memory (dozens of gigabytes typically). Even with careful encodings, neural networks with more than a few hundred million parameters are not feasible to train on single GPUs due to memory requirements. Model parallel training algorithms attempt to sidestep this limitation by storing large deep networks on the memories of multiple GPUs. A few teams have successfully implemented these ideas on arrays of GPUs to train deep networks with billions of parameters. Unfortunately, these models have not thus far shown performance improvements justifying the extra difficulty. For now, it seems that the increase in experimental ease from using smaller models outweighs the gains from model parallelism.

Hardware Memory Interconnects

Enabling model parallelism requires having very high bandwidth connections between compute nodes since each gradient update by necessity requires internode communication. Note that while data parallelism requires strong interconnects, sync operations need only be performed sporadically after multiple local gradient updates.

A few groups have used InfiniBand interconnects (InfiniBand is a high-throughput, low-latency networking standard), or Nvidia's proprietary NVLINK interconnects to attempt to build such large models. However, the results from such experiments have been mixed thus far, and the hardware requirements for such systems tend to be expensive.

Data Parallel Training with Multiple GPUs on Cifar10

In this section, we will give you an in-depth walkthrough of how to train a data-parallel convolutional network on the Cifar10 benchmark set. Cifar10 consists of 60,000 images of size 32 × 32. The Cifar10 dataset is often used to benchmark convolutional architectures. Figure 9-7 displays sample images from the Cifar10 dataset.

Figure 9-7. The Cifar10 dataset consists of 60,000 images drawn from 10 classes. Some sample images from various classes are displayed here.

The architecture we will use in this section loads separate copies of the model architecture on different GPUs and periodically syncs learned weights across cores, as Figure 9-8 illustrates.

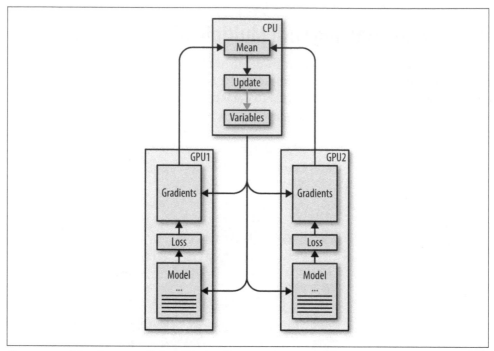

Figure 9-8. The data parallel architecture you will train in this chapter.

Downloading and Loading the DATA

The `read_cifar10()` method reads and parses the Cifar10 raw data files. Example 9-1 uses `tf.FixedLengthRecordReader` to read raw data from the Cifar10 files.

Example 9-1. This function reads and parses data from Cifar10 raw data files

```
def read_cifar10(filename_queue):
  """Reads and parses examples from CIFAR10 data files.

  Recommendation: if you want N-way read parallelism, call this function
  N times.  This will give you N independent Readers reading different
  files & positions within those files, which will give better mixing of
  examples.

  Args:
    filename_queue: A queue of strings with the filenames to read from.

  Returns:
    An object representing a single example, with the following fields:
      height: number of rows in the result (32)
      width: number of columns in the result (32)
      depth: number of color channels in the result (3)
```

```
    key: a scalar string Tensor describing the filename & record number
        for this example.
    label: an int32 Tensor with the label in the range 0..9.
    uint8image:: a [height, width, depth] uint8 Tensor with the image data
  """

class CIFAR10Record(object):
  pass
result = CIFAR10Record()

# Dimensions of the images in the CIFAR-10 dataset.
# See http://www.cs.toronto.edu/~kriz/cifar.html for a description of the
# input format.
label_bytes = 1  # 2 for CIFAR-100
result.height = 32
result.width = 32
result.depth = 3
image_bytes = result.height * result.width * result.depth
# Every record consists of a label followed by the image, with a
# fixed number of bytes for each.
record_bytes = label_bytes + image_bytes

# Read a record, getting filenames from the filename_queue.  No
# header or footer in the CIFAR-10 format, so we leave header_bytes
# and footer_bytes at their default of 0.
reader = tf.FixedLengthRecordReader(record_bytes=record_bytes)
result.key, value = reader.read(filename_queue)

# Convert from a string to a vector of uint8 that is record_bytes long.
record_bytes = tf.decode_raw(value, tf.uint8)

# Read a record, getting filenames from the filename_queue.  No
# header or footer in the CIFAR-10 format, so we leave header_bytes
# and footer_bytes at their default of 0.
reader = tf.FixedLengthRecordReader(record_bytes=record_bytes)
result.key, value = reader.read(filename_queue)

# Convert from a string to a vector of uint8 that is record_bytes long.
record_bytes = tf.decode_raw(value, tf.uint8)

# The first bytes represent the label, which we convert from uint8->int32.
result.label = tf.cast(
    tf.strided_slice(record_bytes, [0], [label_bytes]), tf.int32)

# The remaining bytes after the label represent the image, which we reshape
# from [depth * height * width] to [depth, height, width].
depth_major = tf.reshape(
    tf.strided_slice(record_bytes, [label_bytes],
                     [label_bytes + image_bytes]),
    [result.depth, result.height, result.width])
# Convert from [depth, height, width] to [height, width, depth].
result.uint8image = tf.transpose(depth_major, [1, 2, 0])
```

```
  return result
```

Deep Dive on the Architecture

The architecture for the network is a standard multilayer convnet, similar to a more complicated version of the LeNet5 architecture you saw in Chapter 6. The `infer ence()` method constructs the architecture (Example 9-2). This convolutional architecture follows a relatively standard architecture, with convolutional layers interspersed with local normalization layers.

Example 9-2. This function builds the Cifar10 architecture

```
def inference(images):
  """Build the CIFAR10 model.

  Args:
    images: Images returned from distorted_inputs() or inputs().

  Returns:
    Logits.
  """
  # We instantiate all variables using tf.get_variable() instead of
  # tf.Variable() in order to share variables across multiple GPU training runs.
  # If we only ran this model on a single GPU, we could simplify this function
  # by replacing all instances of tf.get_variable() with tf.Variable().
  #
  # conv1
  with tf.variable_scope('conv1') as scope:
    kernel = _variable_with_weight_decay('weights',
                                          shape=[5, 5, 3, 64],
                                          stddev=5e-2,
                                          wd=0.0)
    conv = tf.nn.conv2d(images, kernel, [1, 1, 1, 1], padding='SAME')
    biases = _variable_on_cpu('biases', [64], tf.constant_initializer(0.0))
    pre_activation = tf.nn.bias_add(conv, biases)
    conv1 = tf.nn.relu(pre_activation, name=scope.name)
    _activation_summary(conv1)

  # pool1
  pool1 = tf.nn.max_pool(conv1, ksize=[1, 3, 3, 1], strides=[1, 2, 2, 1],
                         padding='SAME', name='pool1')
  # norm1
  norm1 = tf.nn.lrn(pool1, 4, bias=1.0, alpha=0.001 / 9.0, beta=0.75,
                    name='norm1')

  # conv2
  with tf.variable_scope('conv2') as scope:
    kernel = _variable_with_weight_decay('weights',
                                          shape=[5, 5, 64, 64],
```

```
                                stddev=5e-2,
                                wd=0.0)
    conv = tf.nn.conv2d(norm1, kernel, [1, 1, 1, 1], padding='SAME')
    biases = _variable_on_cpu('biases', [64], tf.constant_initializer(0.1))
    pre_activation = tf.nn.bias_add(conv, biases)
    conv2 = tf.nn.relu(pre_activation, name=scope.name)
    _activation_summary(conv2)

  # norm2
  norm2 = tf.nn.lrn(conv2, 4, bias=1.0, alpha=0.001 / 9.0, beta=0.75,
                    name='norm2')
  # pool2
  pool2 = tf.nn.max_pool(norm2, ksize=[1, 3, 3, 1],
                         strides=[1, 2, 2, 1], padding='SAME', name='pool2')

  # local3
  with tf.variable_scope('local3') as scope:
    # Move everything into depth so we can perform a single matrix multiply.
    reshape = tf.reshape(pool2, [FLAGS.batch_size, -1])
    dim = reshape.get_shape()[1].value
    weights = _variable_with_weight_decay('weights', shape=[dim, 384],
                                          stddev=0.04, wd=0.004)
    biases = _variable_on_cpu('biases', [384], tf.constant_initializer(0.1))
    local3 = tf.nn.relu(tf.matmul(reshape, weights) + biases, name=scope.name)
    _activation_summary(local3)

  # local4
  with tf.variable_scope('local4') as scope:
    weights = _variable_with_weight_decay('weights', shape=[384, 192],
                                          stddev=0.04, wd=0.004)
    biases = _variable_on_cpu('biases', [192], tf.constant_initializer(0.1))
    local4 = tf.nn.relu(tf.matmul(local3, weights) + biases, name=scope.name)
    _activation_summary(local4)

  # linear layer(WX + b),
  # We don't apply softmax here because
  # tf.nn.sparse_softmax_cross_entropy_with_logits accepts the unscaled logits
  # and performs the softmax internally for efficiency.
  with tf.variable_scope('softmax_linear') as scope:
    weights = _variable_with_weight_decay('weights', [192, cifar10.NUM_CLASSES],
                                          stddev=1/192.0, wd=0.0)
    biases = _variable_on_cpu('biases', [cifar10.NUM_CLASSES],
                              tf.constant_initializer(0.0))
    softmax_linear = tf.add(tf.matmul(local4, weights), biases, name=scope.name)
    _activation_summary(softmax_linear)

  return softmax_linear
```

Missing Object Orientation?

Contrast the model code presented in this architecture with the policy code from the previous architecture. Note how the introduction of the Layer object allows for dramatically simplified code with concomitant improvements in readability. This sharp improvement in readability is part of the reason most developers prefer to use an object-oriented overlay on top of TensorFlow in practice.

That said, in this chapter, we use raw TensorFlow, since making classes like TensorGraph work with multiple GPUs would require significant additional overhead. In general, raw TensorFlow code offers maximum flexibility, but object orientation offers convenience. Pick the abstraction necessary for the problem at hand.

Training on Multiple GPUs

We instantiate a separate version of the model and architecture on each GPU. We then use the CPU to average the weights for the separate GPU nodes (Example 9-3).

Example 9-3. This function trains the Cifar10 model

```
def train():
  """Train CIFAR10 for a number of steps."""
  with tf.Graph().as_default(), tf.device('/cpu:0'):
    # Create a variable to count the number of train() calls. This equals the
    # number of batches processed * FLAGS.num_gpus.
    global_step = tf.get_variable(
        'global_step', [],
        initializer=tf.constant_initializer(0), trainable=False)

    # Calculate the learning rate schedule.
    num_batches_per_epoch = (cifar10.NUM_EXAMPLES_PER_EPOCH_FOR_TRAIN /
                             FLAGS.batch_size)
    decay_steps = int(num_batches_per_epoch * cifar10.NUM_EPOCHS_PER_DECAY)

    # Decay the learning rate exponentially based on the number of steps.
    lr = tf.train.exponential_decay(cifar10.INITIAL_LEARNING_RATE,
                                    global_step,
                                    decay_steps,
                                    cifar10.LEARNING_RATE_DECAY_FACTOR,
                                    staircase=True)

    # Create an optimizer that performs gradient descent.
    opt = tf.train.GradientDescentOptimizer(lr)

    # Get images and labels for CIFAR-10.
    images, labels = cifar10.distorted_inputs()
```

```
batch_queue = tf.contrib.slim.prefetch_queue.prefetch_queue(
    [images, labels], capacity=2 * FLAGS.num_gpus)
```

The code in Example 9-4 performs the essential multi-GPU training. Note how different batches are dequeued for each GPU, but weight sharing via tf.get_vari able_score().reuse_variables() enables training to happen correctly.

Example 9-4. This snippet implements multi-GPU training

```
# Calculate the gradients for each model tower.
tower_grads = []
with tf.variable_scope(tf.get_variable_scope()):
  for i in xrange(FLAGS.num_gpus):
    with tf.device('/gpu:%d' % i):
      with tf.name_scope('%s_%d' % (cifar10.TOWER_NAME, i)) as scope:
        # Dequeues one batch for the GPU
        image_batch, label_batch = batch_queue.dequeue()
        # Calculate the loss for one tower of the CIFAR model. This function
        # constructs the entire CIFAR model but shares the variables across
        # all towers.
        loss = tower_loss(scope, image_batch, label_batch)

        # Reuse variables for the next tower.
        tf.get_variable_scope().reuse_variables()

        # Retain the summaries from the final tower.
        summaries = tf.get_collection(tf.GraphKeys.SUMMARIES, scope)

        # Calculate the gradients for the batch of data on this CIFAR tower.
        grads = opt.compute_gradients(loss)

        # Keep track of the gradients across all towers.
        tower_grads.append(grads)

  # We must calculate the mean of each gradient. Note that this is the
  # synchronization point across all towers.
  grads = average_gradients(tower_grads)
```

We end by applying the joint training operation and writing summary checkpoints as needed in Example 9-5.

Example 9-5. This snippet groups updates from the various GPUs and writes summary checkpoints as needed

```
# Add a summary to track the learning rate.
summaries.append(tf.summary.scalar('learning_rate', lr))

# Add histograms for gradients.
for grad, var in grads:
  if grad is not None:
```

```
    summaries.append(tf.summary.histogram(var.op.name + '/gradients', grad))

# Apply the gradients to adjust the shared variables.
apply_gradient_op = opt.apply_gradients(grads, global_step=global_step)

# Add histograms for trainable variables.
for var in tf.trainable_variables():
  summaries.append(tf.summary.histogram(var.op.name, var))

# Track the moving averages of all trainable variables.
variable_averages = tf.train.ExponentialMovingAverage(
    cifar10.MOVING_AVERAGE_DECAY, global_step)
variables_averages_op = variable_averages.apply(tf.trainable_variables())

# Group all updates into a single train op.
train_op = tf.group(apply_gradient_op, variables_averages_op)

# Create a saver.
saver = tf.train.Saver(tf.global_variables())

# Build the summary operation from the last tower summaries.
summary_op = tf.summary.merge(summaries)

# Build an initialization operation to run below.
init = tf.global_variables_initializer()

# Start running operations on the Graph. allow_soft_placement must be set to
# True to build towers on GPU, as some of the ops do not have GPU
# implementations.
sess = tf.Session(config=tf.ConfigProto(
    allow_soft_placement=True,
    log_device_placement=FLAGS.log_device_placement))
sess.run(init)

# Start the queue runners.
tf.train.start_queue_runners(sess=sess)

summary_writer = tf.summary.FileWriter(FLAGS.train_dir, sess.graph)

for step in xrange(FLAGS.max_steps):
  start_time = time.time()
  _, loss_value = sess.run([train_op, loss])
  duration = time.time() - start_time

  assert not np.isnan(loss_value), 'Model diverged with loss = NaN'

  if step % 10 == 0:
    num_examples_per_step = FLAGS.batch_size * FLAGS.num_gpus
    examples_per_sec = num_examples_per_step / duration
    sec_per_batch = duration / FLAGS.num_gpus

    format_str = ('%s: step %d, loss = %.2f (%.1f examples/sec; %.3f '
```

```
                    'sec/batch)')
    print (format_str % (datetime.now(), step, loss_value,
                         examples_per_sec, sec_per_batch))

if step % 100 == 0:
  summary_str = sess.run(summary_op)
  summary_writer.add_summary(summary_str, step)
# Save the model checkpoint periodically.

if step % 1000 == 0 or (step + 1) == FLAGS.max_steps:
  checkpoint_path = os.path.join(FLAGS.train_dir, 'model.ckpt')
  saver.save(sess, checkpoint_path, global_step=step)
```

Challenge for the Reader

You now have all the pieces required to train this model in practice. Try running it on a suitable GPU server! You may want to use tools such as nvidia-smi to ensure that all GPUs are actually being used.

Review

In this chapter, you learned about various types of hardware commonly used to train deep architectures. You also learned about data parallel and model parallel designs for training deep architectures on multiple CPUs or GPUs. We ended the chapter by walking through a case study on how to implement data parallel training of convolutional networks in TensorFlow.

In Chapter 10, we will discuss the future of deep learning and how you can use the skills you've learned in this book effectively and ethically.

The Future of Deep Learning

In this book, we have covered the foundations of modern deep learning. We've discussed a wide variety of algorithms, and delved deeply into a number of sophisticated case studies. Readers who've been working through the examples covered in this book are now well prepared to use deep learning on the job, and to start reading the large research literature on deep learning methods.

It's worth emphasizing how unique this skill set is. Deep learning has had tremendous impact in the technology industry already, but deep learning is beginning to dramatically alter the state of essentially all nontech industries and to even shift the global geopolitical balance. Your understanding of this epochal technology will open many doors you may not have envisioned. In this final chapter, we will briefly survey some of the important applications of deep learning outside the software industry.

We will also use this chapter to help you answer the question of how to use your new knowledge effectively and ethically. Deep learning is a technology of such power that it's important for practitioners to think about how to use their skills properly. There have already been numerous misuses of deep learning, so it behooves new practitioners to pause before building sophisticated deep learning systems to ask whether the systems they are building are ethically sound. We will attempt to provide a brief discussion of ethical best practices, but caution the area of software ethics is complex enough that brief discussions are unlikely to do it full justice.

Finally, we will examine where deep learning is going. Is deep learning the first step toward building artificially general intelligences, computational entities that have the full range of abilities of humans? There exist a wide range of expert opinions, which we survey.

Deep Learning Outside the Tech Industry

Technological companies such as Google, Facebook, Microsoft, and others have made heavy investments in deep learning infrastructure. Most of these companies were already familiar with machine learning systems, likely from past experiences with machine learning such as with ad prediction systems or search engines. As a result, shifting to deep learning from older machine learning systems took only a small conceptual shift. Also, the success of past machine learning applications has made tech management quite open to the argument that deep learning could be more widely applied within companies. For these reasons, software companies are likely to remain the most prominent users of deep learning for the near future. If you intend to find a job using deep learning within the next couple years, it's likely that you will end up at a tech company.

However, at the same time, there is a broader shift brewing in which deep learning is beginning to infiltrate industries that historically have not used much machine learning. Unlike simpler machine learning methods, deep learning reduces the need for sophisticated feature preprocessing and allows for direct input of perceptual, textual, and molecular data. As a result, a number of industries are taking note, and large-scale efforts to overhaul these industries have already begun in many innovative startups. We will now briefly discuss some of the changes happening in nearby industries and note that many new job opportunities for deep learning experts may become available in the near future.

Applications Are Synergistic

You will soon learn about a number of deep learning applications in different industries. The striking fact about these applications is that all of them use the same fundamental deep learning algorithms. Techniques you've seen such as fully connected networks, convolutional networks, recurrent networks, and reinforcement learning are broadly applicable to any of these fields. In particular, that means core improvements in convolutional network design will yield fruit in pharmaceutical, agricultural, and robotics applications. In reverse, deep learning innovations discovered by roboticists will filter back and strengthen the foundations of deep learning. This virtuous cycle of fundamentals driving application driving fundamentals means that deep learning is a force that's here to stay.

Deep Learning in the Pharmaceutical Industry

Deep learning is showing signs of taking off in a big way in drug discovery. Drug discovery is broken down into multiple phases. There's the preclinical discovery phase, where the effects of potential drugs are tested indirectly in test tubes and in animals, followed by the clinical phase where therapeutics are tested directly in human volunteers. Medicine that passes both nonhuman and human testing is approved for sale to consumers.

Researchers have begun to construct models that optimize each part of the drug discovery process. For example, molecular deep learning has been applied to problems such as predicting the potential toxicity of putative medications and to chemical problems involved in the synthesis and design of drug-like molecules. Other researchers and companies are using deep convolutional networks to design new experiments that closely track cellular behavior on massive scales to obtain stronger understanding of novel biology. These applications have had some impact on the pharmaceutical world, but nothing dramatic yet since it isn't possible to build one drug discovery model that "designs" a novel drug. However, as more data gathering efforts continue and more biological and chemical deep learning models are designed, this state of affairs could change drastically in the next few years.

Deep Learning in Law

The legal industry relies heavily on precedent in the legal literature to make arguments about the legality or illegality of new cases. Traditionally, legions of paralegal researchers have been employed by large law firms to perform the needed lookups into the legal literature. In more recent years, legal search engines have become standard fare for most sophisticated firms.

Such search algorithms are still relatively immature, and it's likely that deep learning systems for neurolinguistic processing (NLP) can offer significant improvements. For example, a number of startups are working on building deep NLP systems that offer better querying of legal precedent. Other startups are working on predictive methods that use machine learning to predict the outcome of litigation, while a few are even experimenting with methods for automated generation of legal arguments.

In general, these sophisticated applications of deep models will take time to mature, but the groundswell of legal AI innovation likely heralds a dramatic shift in the legal profession.

Deep Learning for Robotics

The robotics industry has traditionally avoided deploying machine learning since it's not easy to prove that machine-learned systems are safe to deploy. This lack of safety guarantees can become a major liability when building systems that need to be safe for deployment around human operators.

In recent years, though, it's become clear that deep reinforcement learning systems, combined with low data learning techniques, can offer dramatic improvements in robotic manipulation tasks. Google has demonstrated that reinforcement learning can be deployed to learn robotic object control, using a factory of robotic arms to enable large-scale training on real robots (see Figure 10-1). It's likely that such enhanced learning techniques for robots will begin filtering into the larger robotics industry over the next few years.

Figure 10-1. Google maintains a number of robotic arms that it uses to test deep reinforcement learning methods for robotic control. This fundamental research will likely find its way to the factory floor in the next few years.

Deep Learning in Agriculture

Industrial farming is already heavily mechanized, with sophisticated tractors deployed to plant and even pick crops. Advances in robotics and in computer vision are accelerating this trend toward automation. Convolutional networks have already been employed to identify weeds for removal with less pesticide. Other companies have experimented with self-driving tractors, automated fruit picking, and algorithmic crop yield optimization. These are mainly research projects for the time being, but these efforts will likely blossom into major deployments over the next decade.

Using Deep Learning Ethically

Most of this book has focused on the effective use of deep learning. We've covered many techniques for building deep models that generalize well on different data types. However, it's also worth spending some time thinking about the societal effects of the systems we build as engineers. Deep learning systems unleash a host of potentially unsettling applications.

For one, convolutional networks will enable the widespread deployment of face detection technologies. China has taken a lead in real-world deployment of such systems (Figure 10-2).

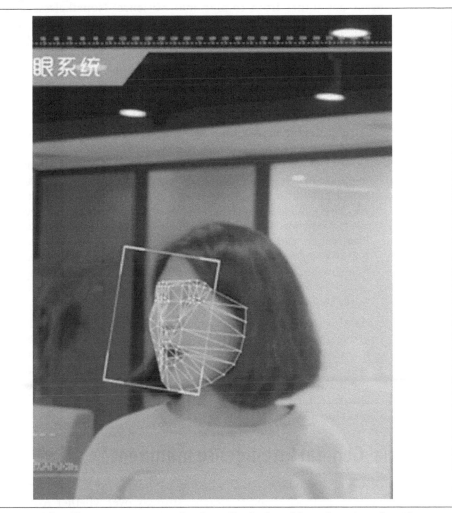

Figure 10-2. The Chinese government has broadly deployed face detection algorithms based on convolutional networks. The ability of these systems to track individuals will likely mean that anonymity in public settings will be a thing of the past in China.

Note that omnipresent facial detection will mean that public anonymity will belong to the past. Any actions taken in the public sphere will be logged and tracked by corporations and governments. This vision of the future should sound unsettling to anyone concerned with the ethical implications of deep learning.

The broader lesson here is that when algorithms can understand visual and perceptual information, nearly all aspects of human life will fall under algorithmic sway. This is a macroscopic trend, and it's not clear that any one engineer will have the power to prevent this future from coming into existence. Nonetheless, engineers retain the ability to vote with their feet. Your skills are valuable and in demand; don't work for companies following unethical practices and building potentially dangerous systems.

Bias in AI

Machine learning and deep learning provide the capabilities to learn interesting models from data without too much effort. This solidly mathematical process can provide the mirage of objectivity. However, it is strongly worth noting that all sorts of bias can creep into such analyses. Biases in the underlying data, drawn from historical, prejudiced records, can induce models to learn fundamentally unfair models. Google infamously once learned that a flawed visual prediction model had labeled black consumers as gorillas, likely due to biased training data that lacked adequate representation of people of color. While this system was rapidly corrected once brought to Google's notice, such failures are deeply troubling and are emblematic of more fundamental problems of exclusion in the technology industry.

As AI is increasingly used in applications such as prisoner parole granting and loan approval processes, it becomes increasingly important for us to ensure that our models aren't making racist assumptions or learning biases already present in historical data. If you are working on sensitive data, making predictions that may alter the course of human lives, check twice and check thrice to make sure that your systems aren't falling prey to biases.

Is Artificial General Intelligence Imminent?

There are widespread discussions about whether artificial general intelligence (AGI) will soon come into existence. Experts disagree strongly over whether AGI is worth seriously planning for. Our view is that while there's no harm in doing research on "AI value alignment" and "safe reward function" design, the artificial intelligence systems of today and the foreseeable future are unlikely to rapidly achieve sentience. As you will have learned first hand, most deep learning systems are simply sophisticated numerical engines, prone to many finicky numerical stability issues. It will likely take decades of fundamental advances before general intelligence becomes an issue. At the same time, as we've discussed in the previous section, artificial intelligence is already having dramatic impact on human societies and industries. It is absolutely worth worrying about the effects of AI without the need to conjure superintelligent bogeymen.

The Superintelligent Fallacy

The book *Superintelligence* by Nick Bostrom (Oxford University Press) has had a profound impact upon the discourse surrounding AI. The basic premise of the book is that an intelligence explosion could occur when models become capable of recursively improving themselves. In itself, the premise of the book isn't that radical. If AGI were to come into existence, there's no reason to suppose that it couldn't succeed in improving itself rapidly.

At the same time, deep learning expert Andrew Ng has gone on the record stating that worrying about superintelligence is like worrying about overpopulation on Mars. One day, humanity is likely to reach Mars. When enough people land on Mars, overcrowding will likely exist and may even be a very serious problem. None of this changes the fact that Mars today is an empty wasteland. So too is the state of the literature on creating generally intelligent AI!

Now, this last statement is hyperbolic. Solid progress in reinforcement learning and generative modeling holds much promise for creating more intelligent agents. But, stressing over the possibilities for superintelligent entities detracts from the very real challenges of automation coming our way. Of course, this doesn't even mention other serious challenges facing us, such as global warming.

Where to Go from Here?

If you've read along carefully in this book and have spent effort working with our code samples in the associated GitHub repo, congrats! You have now mastered the fundamentals of practical machine learning. You will be able to train effective machine learning systems in practice.

However, machine learning is a very rapidly evolving field. The explosive growth of the field has meant that dozens of worthwhile new models are discovered each year. Practicing machine learners should constantly remain on the lookout for new models. When looking at new models, a helpful trick for evaluating their usefulness is to try to think about how you can apply the model to problems you or your organization cares about. This test provides a good way to organize the large influx of models from the research community, and will give you a tool to prioritize your learning on the techniques that really matter to you.

As a responsible machine learner, make sure to think about what your data science models are being used for. Ask yourself whether your work on machine learning is being used to improve human welfare. If the answer is no, then realize that with your skills, you have the ability to find a job where you can use your machine learning superpowers for good, not evil.

Finally, we hope that you'll have lots of fun. Deep learning is an incredibly vibrant area of human inquiry filled with exciting new discoveries, brilliant people, and the possibility of profound impact. It's been our pleasure to share our excitement and passion for the field with you, and we hope you'll pay forward our efforts by sharing your knowledge of deep learning with the world around you.

Index

Symbols
2D convolutions, 138

A
a.eval(), 30
A3C algorithm
    A3C loss function, 196
    defining workers, 198
    overview of, 192
    training the policy, 201
A3C.fit() method, 201
accuracy, 107
accuracy_score(), 99
acknowledgments, xii
actions, 169
activations, 89
adding tensors, 32
add_output() method, 191
advantage functions, 178
adversarial models, 132
agents, 173
AI winters, 85
AlexNet, 6, 119
algorithms
    A3C algorithm, 192-196
    asynchronous training, 179
    black-box, 110
    catastrophic forgetting and, 177
    finding baselines, 111
    for reinforcement learning, 175-179
    graduate student descent, 113
    grid search, 114
    policy learning, 177
    Q-learning, 176

    random hyperparameter search, 115
AlphaGo, 12, 172, 174, 179, 196
Anaconda Python, 29, 94
architectural primitives, 3-5
architectures
    AlexNet, 6
    AlphaGo, 12
    generative adversarial networks (GANs), 13, 155
    Google's neural machine translation (Google-NMT), 9
    LeNet, 6
    neural captioning model, 8
    Neural Turing machine (NTM), 14
    one-shot models, 10
    ResNet, 7
argparse tool, 162
artificial general intelligences (AGIs), 179, 230
artificial intelligence
    cyclical development of, 85
    overhyped claims regarding, 84
ASIC (application specific integrated circuits), 209
Asynchronous Advantage Actor-Critic (see A3C algorithm)
asynchronous reinforcement, 192
asynchronous training, 179
ATARI arcade games, 169
atrous convolutions, 126
attributions, x
autoencoders, 131, 155
automated statistician project, 111
automatic differentiation, 86
    (see also backpropagation)

automatic differentiation systems, 53
automatic model tuning, 111

B

backpropagation, 85, 88
baselines, 111
binary classification
    balancing false positives/negatives, 107
    prediction categories, 106
black-box learning algorithms, 105, 110
blind optimization, 106
bounding boxes, 127
Breakout arcade game, 169
broadcasting, 37
build() method, 190
build_graph() method, 194

C

c.eval(), 38
casting functions, 35
catastrophic forgetting, 177
central processing unit (CPU) training
    benefits of, 206
    field programmable gate arrays, 211
    vs. GPU training, 207
    neuromorphic chips, 211
    TPU training, 209
character-level modeling, 159
chess match, 172
chip speeds, 209
Cifar10 benchmark set
    data loading, 216
    multilayer convnet architecture for, 218
    overview of, 215
    training on multiple GPUs, 220
classical regularization, 93
classification metrics, 144
classification problems
    defined, 46
    metrics for evaluation of, 78, 106
    toy classification datasets, 58
co-adaptation, 91
code examples, obtaining and using, x
coefficient of determination, 71
comments and questions, xi
computation graphs
    feed dictionaries, 60
    placeholders, 60
computational limitations, 87

computations in TensorFlow, 29-37
computer vs. human chess match, 172
confusion matrix, 109
contact information, xi
continuous functions, 44
continuous probability distributions, 56
contravariant indices, 29
control-flow operations, 153
convolutional kernels, 122
convolutional layer
    kernels in, 124
    overview of, 4
    transformations in, 122
Convolutional Neural Networks (CNNs)
    applications of, 127-134
    constructing, 125
    convolutional architectures, 120-126
    overview of, 119-120
    training in TensorFlow, 134-146
convolutional weights, 142
covariant indices, 29
CPU-based simulations, 179
cross-entropy loss, 49, 74
CUDA (compute unified device architecture), 207
CuDNN library, 153, 207
cutoffs, choosing, 108
Cybenko, George, 87
CycleGAN, 133

D

data parallelism, 213
debugging, visual vs. nonvisual styles, 70
decision trees, 113
declarative programming, 38
deep learning
    alternate applications of, 226
    architectures, 6-14
    defined, 84
    ethical use of, 228
    frameworks, 15-16
    history of, 1
    mathematical review, 43-55
    overhyped claims regarding, 84
    potential for artificial general intelligence, 230
    primitives, 3-5
deep networks
    benefits of, 88

defined, 82
training large deep networks, 205-223
DeepBlue system, 172
DeepChem
accepting minibatches of placeholders, 96
adding dropouts to hidden layers, 97
evaluating model accuracy, 98
hidden layers, 96
implementing minibatching, 98
installing, 94
MoleculeNet dataset collection, 95
reinforcement learning, 173
Tox21 dataset, 95
using TensorBoard to track model convergence, 99
DeepMind, 172, 196
derivative-driven optimization, 45
derivatives, 45
detection and localization, 127
diagonal matrices, 33
differentiability, 44, 53
dilated convolutions, 126
directed graphs, 186, 188
discounted rewards, 176
discrete probability distributions, 56
DistBelief, 213
distributed deep network training
data parallelism, 213
main modes of, 212
model parallelism, 214
Downpour stochastic gradient descent (SGD), 213
dropout, 91, 97
dtype notation, 35, 37

E
early stopping, 92
Eastman, Peter, 173
elementwise multiplication, 33
end-to-end training, 8
environments, 169, 173
epochs, 52
errata, xi
error metrics, 144
ethical considerations, 228
eval(), 38

F
face detection technologies, 229

false positives/negatives, reducing number of, 107
feature engineering, 196
featurization, 21
feed dictionaries, 60
fetches, 61
field programmable gate arrays (FPGAs), 211
filewriters (TensorBoard), 63
filters, 124
fit() method, 201
fixed nonlinear transformations, 125
for loops, 64, 114
Fourier series, 87
Fourier transforms, 89
frameworks, 15-16
fully connected deep networks
advantages of, 81
components of, 81
implementation in TensorFlow, 94-101
learning with backpropagation, 85
mathematical form of, 82
neurons (nodes) in, 83-85
training, 89-94
universal convergence theorem, 87
usefulness of deep networks, 88
fully connected layer, 3
function minimization, 45, 50
functional programming, 40
functions
differentiability and, 44
gradient of, 45
loss functions, 45-50
minima and derivative of, 45, 51
multivariate functions, 45
future rewards, 176

G
GAN (generative adversarial network), 13, 132, 155
gated recurrent units (GRU), 154
Gaussian probability distributions, 56
generalization, 104, 112
generalization of accuracy, 108
get_input_tensors(), 186
get_layer_variables() method, 191
Google neural machine translation (GNMT), 9, 155
gradient, 45, 51, 62
gradient descent, 50-53, 166

gradient instability, 152
graduate student descent, 113
graph convolutions, 129
graphics processing unit (GPU) Training, 207
graphs, 39
grid-search method, 114

H

handwritten digits, 134
hardware memory interconnects, 214
hidden layers, 96
hyperparameter optimization, 103-117
    algorithms for, 110-116
    automating, 111
    black-box learning algorithms, 105, 110
    defined, 103
    metrics selection, 105-110
    model evaluation and, 104
    overview of, 103
hyperparameters, defined, 52

I

IBM's TrueNorth project, 212
identity matrices, 33
image segmentation, 128
ImageNet Large Scale Visual Recognition Challenge (ILSVRC), 6, 108
images
    CNN networks for, 119
    generating with variational autoencoders, 131
    local receptive fields and, 121
    sampling, 131
imbalanced datasets, 95
imperative programming, 37
implicit type casting, 37
inference only hardware, 206
InfiniBand interconnects, 214
Intel, 209

J

JOIN command, 38

K

Kasparov, Gary, 172

L

L2 loss, 132

language modeling, 154
Laplace transforms, 89
large deep networks
    CPU training, 206-212
    custom hardware for, 205
    distributed training, 212-214
    overview of training, 205
    with multiple GPUs on Cifar10, 215-223
Layer object, 186
learnable parameters, 52
learnable representations, 89
learnable variables, 191
learnable weights, 50, 141
learned classes, 78
learning rates, 94
learning the prior, 52
Legendre transforms, 89
LeNet, 6
LeNet-5 convolutional architecture
    architecture for, 140-144
    MNIST dataset and, 134
    model evaluation, 144
    TensorFlow convolutional primitives, 138
    validation set selection, 138
Leswing, Karl, 173
limitations of TensorFlow, 16
linear regression
    model case study, 64-73
    toy regression datasets, 57
local receptive fields, 120, 129
localization, 127
logging statements, 63, 66
logistic regression, model case study, 73-78
long short-term memory (LSTM) cells, 5, 152, 164
loss functions, 45-50, 132, 196

M

machine learning
    chip speeds and, 209
    classification and regression, 46
    function minimization and, 45, 50
    mathematical tools, 43-55
    potential bias in, 230
    rapid evolution in, 231
    toy datasets, 55-59
Markov decision processes, 169, 173
master-level chess, 172
mathematical tools

automatic differentiation systems, 53
functions and differentiability, 44
gradient descent, 50-53
loss functions, 45-50
matrix mathematics, 24
matrix multiplication, 33-34
matrix operations, 33
max pooling, 125, 140
McCulloch, Warren S., 83
mean, 56
metrics
    classification metrics, 144
    defined, 105
    error metrics, 144
    for binary classification, 106
    for evaluating classification models, 78
    for evaluating regression models, 70
    for multiclass classification, 108
    regression metrics, 110
    role of common sense in, 106
minibatches, 52, 94-98
minima, 45, 51
Minsky, Marvin, 86
MNIST dataset, 134
model parallelism, 214
model-based algorithms, 175
model-free algorithms, 175
models
    adversarial models, 132
    deep models vs. good deep models, 103
    evaluating model accuracy, 98
    evaluating performance of, 104
    evaluating with error metrics, 144
    sequence-to-sequence (seq2seq), 155
    tracking convergence, 99
molecular machine learning, 138
multiclass classification, 108
multidimensional inputs, 124
multilayer perceptron networks, 86
    (see also fully connected deep networks)
multilinear functions, 28
multiplying tensors, 33
multivariate functions, 45

N

name scopes, 61
ndarray, 55
neural captioning model, 8
neural network layers

convolutional layer, 4
fully connected layer, 3
long short-term memory (LSTM) cells, 5
recurrent neural network (RNN) layers, 4
neural networks, 83
    (see also fully connected deep networks)
Neural Turing machine (NTM), 14
neuromorphic chips, 211
np.ndarray, 61
NumPy, 30, 55
Nvidia, 207, 209
NVLINK interconnects, 214

O

object detection and localization, 127
object orientation, 181
one-hot encoding, 159
one-shot models, 10
operator overloading, 32
optical character recognition (OCR), 6
optimization (see hyperparameter optimization)
optimization algorithms, 61
overfitting, 92, 104

P

Papert, Seymour, 86
parameterization, 50
Pearson correlation coefficient, 71, 110
Penn Treebank corpus
    basic recurrent architecture, 164
    limitations of, 160
    loading data into TensorFlow, 162
    overview of, 150, 159
    preprocessing, 160
perceptrons, 85
perplexity, 166
physics, tensors in, 27
Pitts, Walter, 83
placeholders, 60, 96, 143
policy learning, 177, 195
pooling layers, 125
precision, 107
prediction categories, 106
primitives
    deep learning, 3-5
    TensorFlow, 19-42
    TensorFlow convolutional primitives, 138
probability density functions, 56

probability distributions, 48
prospective prediction, 138
Python API, 29

Q

Q-learning, 176
questions and comments, xi

R

random forests method, 111
random values, 31
rank-3 tensors, 25, 36
read_cifar10() method, 216
recall, 107
receiver operator curve (ROC), 108
rectified linear activation (ReLU), 89
Recurrent Neural Networks (RNNs)
    layer abstraction, 4
recurrent neural networks (RNNs)
    applications of, 154-156
    Neural Turing machines, 157
    optimizing, 153
    overview of, 149
    recurrent architectures, 150
    recurrent cells, 152-154
    Turing completeness of, 159
    working with inpractice, 159-166
regression problems
    defined, 46
    linear and logistic regression with Tensor-
        Flow, 43-79
    metrics for evaluation of, 70, 110
    toy regression datasets, 57
regularization
    defined, 90
    dropout, 91
    in statistics vs. deep networks, 91
    weight regularization, 93
reinforcement learning (RL)
    A3C algorithm, 192-203
    algorithms for, 175-179
    history of, 169
    limitations of, 179
    Markov decision processes and, 173
    simulations and, 176, 179
    tic-tac-toe agent, 181-192
representation learning, 89
ResNet, 7
restore() method, 192

reuse_variables(), 165
rewards, 169, 174, 176
RGB images, 124
RMSE (root-mean-squared error), 71, 110
ROC-AUC (area under curve for the receiver
        operator curve), 108
rollout concept, 178
Rosenblatt, Frank, 85

S

sample_weight argument, 99
sampling, 131
sampling sequences, 155
scalars, 20
scaling, 32
scikit-learn library, 112
scopes, 61
SELECT command, 38
semiconductors, 209
sentience, 230
separating line, 78
sequence-to-sequence (seq2seq) models, 155
sess.run(), 64, 98
sess.run(var), 60
sessions, 39
set_loss() method, 191
set_optimizer() method, 191
shapes, manipulating, 35
sigmoid function, 73, 89
simulations, 176, 179
sklearn.metrics, 99
specificity, 107
speech spectrograms, 151
spike train, 211
spurious correlations, 90
squared Pearson correlation coefficient, 71, 110
standard deviation, 56
StarCraft, 180
stateful programming, 40
stationary evolution rule, 151
stochastic gradient descent (SGD), 213
Stone-Weierstrass theorem, 87
stride size, 123
structure agnostic networks, 81
structured spatial data, 119
summaries (TensorBoard), 63
superintelligence, 230
supervised problems, 46
supplemental material, x

About the Authors

Bharath Ramsundar received a BA and BS from UC Berkeley in EECS and Mathematics and was valedictorian of his graduating class in mathematics. He is currently a PhD student in computer science at Stanford University with the Pande group. His research focuses on the application of deep learning to drug discovery. In particular, Bharath is the lead developer and creator of DeepChem.io, an open source package founded on TensorFlow that aims to democratize the use of deep learning in drug discovery. He is supported by a Hertz Fellowship, the most selective graduate fellowship in the sciences.

Reza Bosagh Zadeh is Founder CEO at Matroid and Adjunct Professor at Stanford University. His work focuses on machine learning, distributed computing, and discrete applied mathematics. Reza received his PhD in Computational Mathematics from Stanford University under the supervision of Gunnar Carlsson. His awards include a KDD Best Paper Award and the Gene Golub Outstanding Thesis Award. He has served on the Technical Advisory Boards of Microsoft and Databricks.

As part of his research, Reza built the machine learning algorithms behind Twitter's who-to-follow system, the first product to use machine learning at Twitter. Reza is the initial creator of the Linear Algebra Package in Apache Spark and his work has been incorporated into industrial and academic cluster computing environments. In addition to research, Reza designed and teaches two PhD-level classes at Stanford: Distributed Algorithms and Optimization (CME 323), and Discrete Mathematics and Algorithms (CME 305).

Colophon

The animal on the cover of *TensorFlow for Deep Learning* is a thornback ray (*Raja clavata*). It lives in both open and shallow waters around the coasts of Europe, western Africa, and the Mediterranean Sea. The thornback is named for the backward-pointing spikes (formally known as "bucklers") on its back and tail.

As with other members of the ray and skate family, this animal has a flattened body with large wing-like pectoral fins. Thornback rays are often found in the mud or sand of the seabed, and so their color varies regionally for camouflage (from light brown to gray, with darker patches). Adults can grow to be about 3 feet long.

Thornback rays rest during the day on the ocean floor, and hunt at night—their diet is primarily made up of bottom-feeding animals like crabs and shrimp, but also small fish. Females can lay up to 150 egg cases each year (though the average is closer to 50–75), each containing one egg that will hatch after 4–5 months. These cases are stiff packages of collagen with horns at each corner, which are anchored to the seafloor with a sticky film. Empty cases often wash up on beaches and are nicknamed "mermaid's purses."

Many of the animals on O'Reilly covers are endangered; all of them are important to the world. To learn more about how you can help, go to *animals.oreilly.com*.

The cover image is from *Meyers Kleines Lexicon*. The cover fonts are URW Typewriter and Guardian Sans. The text font is Adobe Minion Pro; the heading font is Adobe Myriad Condensed; and the code font is Dalton Maag's Ubuntu Mono.

Learn from experts.
Find the answers you need.

Sign up for a **10-day free trial** to get **unlimited access** to all of the content on Safari, including Learning Paths, interactive tutorials, and curated playlists that draw from thousands of ebooks and training videos on a wide range of topics, including data, design, DevOps, management, business—and much more.

Start your free trial at:
oreilly.com/safari

(No credit card required.)